THE SOCIOLOGICAL REVOLUTION

'*The Sociological Revolution* is the long-awaited product of one of the best minds in British sociology. Brilliant in its argument and lucid in style, it will prove a milestone in the emancipation of sociology from the hegemony of philosophers and philosophoidal modes of thought.'

Stephen Mennell, *University College Dublin*

'This original and controversial book transcends currently fashionable debates and disputes in social theory. . . . The social sciences stand to benefit from the refreshed credentials the book establishes for the sociological imagination.'

Nico Stehr, *The University of British Columbia*

Did the advent of sociology in the eighteenth century, as the supreme science of 'society' constitute a revolution in knowledge?

Controversially turning away from the current debates which surround 'social theory', *The Sociological Revolution* provides a historical analysis of the 'profound burden' of sociology and its implications today. The author provides detailed studies of a number of contemporary theories, ranging from structuration theory, historical materialism, phenomenology, structuralism and world system theory and in doing so, contends that the rightful heir of the sociological tradition is the dynamic sociology of knowledge, in particular the figurational research programme of Norbert Elias.

Unique in its sociological analysis of philosophy, the book ranges from analyses of the Hegelian apogee to Marx's theory of knowledge, combined with an in-depth analysis of the current condition of sociology. *The Sociological Revolution* will be of interest to students across a number of disciplines, including philosophy, sociology, the history of ideas, political theory and cultural studies.

Richard Kilminster is lecturer in sociology at the University of Leeds.

THE SOCIOLOGICAL REVOLUTION

From the Enlightenment to the global age

Richard Kilminster

London and New York

First published 1998
by Routledge
11 New Fetter Lane, London EC4P 4EE

Simultaneously published in the USA and Canada
by Routledge
29 West 35th Street, New York, NY 10001

©1998 Richard Kilminster

Typeset in Baskerville by Routledge
Printed and bound in Great Britain by TJ International Ltd, Padstow, Cornwall

British Library Cataloguing in Publication Data
A catalogue record for this book is available from the British Library

Library of Congress Cataloging in Publication Data
Kilminster, Richard, 1942–
The sociological revolution: from the Enlightenment to the Global Age /
Richard Kilminster.
p.   cm.
Includes bibliographical references (p.   ) and index.
1. Sociology–History. 2. Sociology–Philosophy. 3. Knowledge, Sociology of.
I. Title
HM19.K48   1998
301'.09–dc21   98–23813
CIP

ISBN 0–415–02920–1

FOR MADELEINE AND LEWIS

One of the predicaments of the human sciences
 . . . is that they are widely dominated by people's attempts to run away
from themselves.

(Norbert Elias)

CONTENTS

PREFACE

I do not anticipate that this study will be *mis*understood; rather, I expect it will be *understood in different ways*. Readers will inevitably assimilate what I have to say through the spectacles of their own values, interests, ideological preferences and other presuppositions and preoccupations, so will find my presentation wanting in this or that respect, depending on the combination of assumptions they bring to bear. They will want me to answer the questions that they are prompted to ask and to include what – according to their scale of values – they regard me as having omitted. I am very conscious that these processes are out of my control. My aim in this preface is therefore to bring out some of the important motifs in this book and to recall some aspects of its genesis, so as to facilitate the understanding of the work as a whole.

This book takes a longer view of the vicissitudes of sociology and its current condition. In Part I, I establish sociology as emerging in the eighteenth century from the same developments of European societies that it was trying to understand and explain. The relatively autonomous sociological point of view derivable from this emergent tradition informs my subsequent argumentation. The pioneers, I argue, tried to accomplish the task of understanding the fate or destiny of society in a manner different from the older philosophies of history, which were absorbed into the emerging discipline of sociology and thereby transformed. As social diagnosis, sociology was thus from its inception 'evaluative' and 'philosophical', *as well as* 'scientific'. Both Marx and Comte, in their very different ways, can be seen with hindsight to have been grappling with these same mighty questions. I suggest that the range of social uniformities and regularities upon which sociology focused was an emergent reality *sui generis*, first theorized in its economic manifestation by the early political economists. It was this feature of the emerging area of inquiry which also distinguished sociology from psychology and biology as well as from the discipline of history. In short, I establish the autonomy of sociology developmentally and 'social-ontologically'.

Whilst this book is partly about contemporary sociological theory, in the sense that those developments have prompted my research and reflections, it is not intended to be a systematic introduction to the issues that are current in theory at the present time. There are plenty of other excellent books which provide that service. Many of the prominent current theories and controversies are nevertheless still discussed, but not in the form of an inventory of items, nor in their own terms. Rather, this study places the current sociological debates within a broader perspective deriving from the emergent sociological tradition. This entails coming up behind many of the current debates and going round them.

In establishing the discipline historically, I place considerable importance on the contribution of Marx, particularly in Chapter 3, but also in other places. He made a decisive, albeit partial, breakthrough towards a science of society. The subsequent codification and simplification of some of his ideas in forms of Marxism, and then its subsequent decline and fall in recent times, should not blind us to his towering individual status as a pioneer. Once we have corrected for meta-physical hangovers, teleology and economic and political overstatements in his work, which have systematically dogged the subsequent Marxian tradition, we can affirm the seminal advance that he made and upon which we can build.

The Marx–Hegel relation is now an unfashionable topic in sociology, for reasons that I try to explain in Chapter 8. However, as I maintain in Chapter 2, I think that it remains a crucial theoretical constellation for our understanding of the break with philosophy which constitutes one important dimension of the soci-ological revolution. It is important because in Hegel one can glimpse the furthest point that it is possible to reach within philosophy before the whole framework of concepts and argument founders on the rock of the social. There is a direct line of descent from Hegel and Marx through Weber to Mannheim and Elias and the dynamic sociology of knowledge, which enterprise I regard as the rightful heir of the sociological tradition. In this study, because of the stress I put on the impor-tance of a theory of knowledge, sociology and the sociology of knowledge are construed as effectively synonymous. Once one has looked beyond the red herring of relativism, the sociology of knowledge proves to be a highly effective means of epistemological control.

This book is, then, a robustly sociological piece of work, and one that puts the philosophers firmly, but politely, in their place, thus reversing the customary rela-tionship. This theme is discussed at length in Chapter 1, but pervades the entire work in different ways. I hope, however, that the spirit of good humour and respect which lies behind my critique comes across. Naturally, I do not gainsay the erudi-tion, intelligence and seriousness of philosophers and have no quarrel whatsoever with those who wish to pursue this kind of inquiry, whose integrity I am not impugning. Whether or not one accepts my interpretation of the long-term fate of philosophy, I think that the re-posing of the question of the relation between socio-logy and philosophy from the sociological point of view does open up a new range of issues and forces us to see older, taken-for-granted assumptions in a new light. My underlying concern is what kind of relationship with philosophy is in the best interests of the further development of sociology.

This book has grown out of the transformations of sociology and society over recent decades. It comprises interlinked essays written at different times around the same set of issues, but all rewritten to take account of later insights and experi-ences accruing from those developments. At one point in the early 1980s, as I delved deeper and deeper into philosophy, the history of sociology and the history of ideas, I began to toy with a seductive idea that was in the air at the time, i.e. that everything has been said before. It was suggested that we were condemned in sociology to continuous cycles of rediscovering the wheel and trumpeting rehashes of past conceptual or theoretical achievements as 'new'. At that time I planned to write a book which surveyed the then current plethora of theoretical schools and paradigms. It was to have been entitled *Wizards of Amnesia*, so as to capture that sense of forgetting.

However, I later came to see this view as a form of learned defeatism, embracing a tragic view of the sociological vocation, and one that often leads to cynicism. When ideas seem to 'come round again' they do so in a new situation, in a new form, as part of a higher level of social and scientific synthesis, something that, by the mid/late 1980s, I began to sense was occurring – although I could not have put it like that at that time. I abandoned the *Wizards* project as I sensed that social developments were beginning to render the plan redundant and the proposed book obsolete. The 'war of the schools' (Bryant), which had fuelled its focus, subsided: theoretical lions began to lie down with theoretical lambs and a new cognitive pattern was emerging. It was then that I began to think about sociology developing in phases and wondered what social forces might be driving their succession. The three-phase model presented in Chapter 8 grew out of these experiences and reflections.

The conception of phases, together with the longer view, led directly to the vexed question of cognitive progress in sociology. I thought all along that it was unlikely that the study of developments in sociology would reveal no progression *whatsoever*, a position that has increasingly in recent years become the prevailing wisdom. In Chapters 8 and 9 I try to open up in a provisional way the difficult problem of providing guidelines for sorting out what are the true advances and theoretical innovations from amongst the over-abundance of institutionalized sociological effort in the present period. There is, I believe, enough material mustered in this study as a whole to confirm that Baldamus was on the right track when he wrote that 'progress can materialize only as a disorderly imperceptible sequence of overstatement errors and their gradual elimination' (1976: 45). I am very aware, however, that much more comparative empirical research needs to be undertaken than I have been able to do, into the patterns of this movement in sociology and in other social science disciplines as well as in other national traditions of sociology.

In the present period, others (e.g. Mouzelis 1991 and 1995) have attempted diagnoses of the current situation of sociological theory, which is also partly what this book is trying to do. One significant difference between much of this important work of reassessment and the present study, is that I pay more attention to explaining how the present situation came about. It is my view that an understanding of genesis is an integral part of diagnosis. However, to have woven this now burgeoning literature into my argument would have cluttered this book too much and detracted from its central thrust. I will, therefore, simply mention in passing, in addition to the work of Mouzelis, the other excellent studies of Hekman (1986), Becker & Bryant (1989), Craib (1989), Bourdieu, Chamboredon & Passeron (1991) and Layder (1994) which complement my book and, taken together with it, constitute an interesting cluster of theoretical research monographs in the present period. We are all, to paraphrase Mannheim (1940: 32), trying to reach the same centre from different points on the periphery.

In summary, the study has two strands: first, establishing the far-reaching nature of the sociological revolution in such a way as to contribute to the process of breaking with older habits of thinking and acting in sociology, which still remain, on the whole, far too philosophical. Second, showing how, within that broad picture, all roads seem to lead towards the sociology of knowledge and, more specifically, towards the figurational or process sociology paradigm, which offers the most promising (and challenging) research programme at the present time. In this study I try to demonstrate its explanatory power not so much empirically as on the theoretical level, through studies of the work of a number of prominent authors and theories in various branches of contemporary sociology.

ACKNOWLEDGEMENTS

I am very grateful to the following people, either for commenting on parts of the manuscript and/or for many stimulating sociological conversations over many years: Gi Baldamus, Zygmunt Bauman, Godfried van Benthem van den Bergh, Artur Bogner, Roy Boyne, Eric Dunning, Norbert Elias, Aidan Foster-Carter, Johan Goudsblom, Anthea Kilminster, Stephen Mennell, Paul Nixon, Michael Schröter, Alan Scott, Ian Varcoe, Terry Wassall and Cas Wouters. In some places I draw on articles written jointly with both Ian Varcoe and Cas Wouters, which I gladly acknowledge. I must also thank the British Sociological Association for my co-convenorship of the Sociological Theory Group from 1983 to 1992, which put me in close touch with current trends. I am indebted to the Department of Sociology and Social Policy of the University of Leeds for granting me one semester's study leave in 1995, which was decisive in enabling me to bring the project to completion. My thanks are also due to the secretarial staff of the department, particularly Sarah Morrell and Marie Ross, who have been very helpful with software conversions and editing. At Routledge, Chris Rojek formerly and Mari Shullaw latterly, provided invaluable support and encouragement at crucial points.

Part I

FROM PHILOSOPHY TO THE SOCIOLOGY OF KNOWLEDGE

1

SOCIOLOGISTS AND PHILOSOPHY[1]

When reality is depicted, philosophy as an independent branch of knowledge loses its medium of existence.

(Marx & Engels 1845a: 38)

Philosophy has preserved essential traits of animistic modes of thought such as the over-estimation of the magic of words and the belief that real processes in the external world follow the lines laid down by our thoughts.

(Freud 1933: 212)

Preamble

Sociology emerged when European peoples became aware in the late eighteenth century that the patterns that their far-flung interdependent social relations made were increasingly exceeding the scope of individual actions on a large scale. In terminology developed by later sociologists for understanding the structure of these developments, these interdependencies constituted an emergent level of social organization *sui generis*. Groups of social scientific practitioners, propelled by various interests and purposes, began to investigate its autonomous patterns empirically – initially in the realm of economic regularities.

In this historical, emergent sense, sociology is its own justification. It does not need to be defended as a science any more than does physics or chemistry or biology, which simply investigate other levels of integration (Elias 1987a) within the overall socio-natural complex. Sociology only has to be defended as an enterprise because it is sometimes attacked for political, obscurantist or other extraneous reasons. Much of the fragmentation and lack of direction and consensus so characteristic of the discipline is mostly explicable by its relatively weak institutionalization of standards of scientific detachment and fact orientation, not anything inherently problematic about the nature of the discipline itself, as the science of society.

The advent of sociology also constituted, I will argue, a revolution in knowledge, whereby the epistemological, ontological and ethical concerns of European philosophy were gradually absorbed into the new discipline and *transformed*, thereby leaving philosophers historically defunctionalized. They have responded by creating (within various traditions) their own areas of competence and laying claim to expertise in them. This radical conclusion (stated baldly here) inevitably has implications for how we conceive of the proper and desirable involvement of sociologists with philosophy in the present period and in the future.

Probably quite a number of sociologists and philosophers would accept my interpretation of the origins, autonomy and social reception of sociology which I stated briefly in the first two paragraphs, or some variant of it. It is, however, my argument above, about the profound and radical character of the sociological revolution, that makes my subsequent reflections in this chapter and in the book generally, somewhat controversial. Let me make clear at the outset that I am not recommending, as Bryant (1992: 139) interprets me, that sociologists should ignore the writings of contemporary philosophers *altogether*. Obviously, if we did that then we would cut ourselves off from potential sources of illumination, empirical data or insights on various matters. Some books, nominally by philosophers, can contain analysis of a sociological kind, either theoretical or empirical. In these cases, the philosophers concerned are effectively doing sociology despite themselves. We would be foolish to disregard such work, although I still believe that it should be approached with caution, for reasons that will become clear in what follows.

The main prescriptions that beckon in this chapter and in the book generally, are that it would be better *for the development of sociology* if sociologists were (a) to concentrate more on developing their *own* epistemology, concepts and methods of investigation appropriate to exploring the emergent reality of society; and (b) to distance themselves from philosophers' instructions as to how those things should or should not be done. I regard these precepts as crucial, bearing in mind the prestige of philosophy, the relative power advantage of its establishment *vis-à-vis* sociologists and the tendency for higher ranking disciplines to impose their categories and patterns of thinking on to the lower ranking ones.

My route into this subject is to explore in the next sub-section the balance of power between sociologists and philosophers through a scrutiny of the culture of philosophers, as a professional group. I take culture to be an ordered pattern of symbols, knowledge, beliefs and ways of thinking and acting characteristic of a definite social group. This definition follows the long-established tradition of Tylor and Parsons,[2] but I provide the inquiry with a sociologist's stress on demonstrating the involvement of culture with group structure, inter-group relations and power. I thus treat the academic establishment of philosophers sociologically as a structured professional group with a characteristic culture of its own, and standing for the most part higher than sociologists in the hierarchy of status and prestige of groups of scientific and other specialists.

My examples draw mainly on the British experience, although my argument involves, as we will see, situating this case in the wider and longer-term development of sociology in European societies over the last two centuries. In my view the rise of sociology has had profound and irreversible repercussions on the subject-matter of philosophy and hence on the fate of its practitioners as a group. Readers will need to make their own corrections for differing patterns in the development of other national sociologies and philosophies, where the relationship between the two groups may have played itself out in different ways than in Britain.

By the nature of my inquiry I am compelled from time to time to make comparative judgements about the cognitive value of the statements of philosophers. The study of the culture of philosophers and the historical relationship between them and sociologists cannot be understood without taking into account the hypothesis mentioned before: that over a long period philosophers as a group have been deprived of their special area of competence. This has been the result of a number of interwoven social processes, one of which is the rise of the social sciences and sociology in particular. It is in the light of this finding (substantiated only in a preliminary way in this chapter) that I am able to evaluate the credibility and plausibility of philosophers' changing claims to disciplinary autonomy which I find embedded in their culture. As we will subsequently see, those justifications of the autonomy of the field called philosophy emerge as highly problematic, to say the least.

The culture of philosophers

The subject-matter of philosophy is notoriously difficult to pin down, partly because of its purely discursive character. It is much more straightforward to grasp the nature of the relationship between sociology and other human sciences such as economics, politics or psychology than it is to understand the relationship between sociology and philosophy. In the former cases, we can refer to the different, but related, levels or aspects of the total social process upon which each focuses, but sociology and philosophy cannot be related in this way because philosophy does not have an 'object' of inquiry in that sense. And the problem is compounded by the considerable vagueness and disagreement within philosophy itself about the nature of its tasks and aims. As the historian of science Ernan McMullin commented:

> In attempting to define what is meant by 'philosophy of science', the first problem one encounters is the notorious vagueness of the term 'philosophy' ... philosophy can in practice be anything from a cloudy speculative fancy to a piece of formal logic. The term has become almost hopelessly equivocal in modern usage.
>
> (McMullin 1970: 23)

Philosophers have indeed described the nature of their inquiries in a bewildering number of ways: as logic, as conceptual clarification, as method, as semantics, as thought-about-thought or even simply as an activity.[3] But most of its practitioners seem to agree that pure reasoning forms the basis of philosophy or, put another way, that their subject possesses a non-empirical or perhaps 'transcendental' subject-matter (Hartmann 1966). Philosophers' deliberations are, then, of a purely discursive nature, their culture placing a high premium on rigorous reasoning and logical argumentation.

Now, all specialists, scientific or otherwise, rely *partly* on their professional standing to provide the source of authority for their knowledge and expertise. But the non-empirical character of philosophy has an important consequence in this regard. It means that philosophical statements (they cannot accurately be described as findings) are not subject for their plausibility or justification to the direct control of evidence about the structure of social or natural processes in the same way as the scientific statements of sociologists or other scientists.[4] Without this external control from publicly checkable empirical data, however, the authority and credibility of philosophers' statements must therefore ultimately reside more or less *entirely* in their standing as philosophers, in the social weight of their status as a professional group.

The fashionable 'constructivist' tendency in the sociology of scientific knowledge in recent years (Knorr-Cetina 1983; Law 1986; Latour & Woolgar 1979) has swung the explanatory emphasis on to the artefactual or constructed nature of scientific objects as decisive in the development of scientific knowledge. This theoretical move virtually eliminates the controlling effect of the structure of the 'object' itself upon scientific concepts and theories, a commitment to which my argument about the historical autonomy of sociology relies. A few remarks on this approach are therefore necessary at this point.

The constructivist programme has been inspired by phenomenology, ethnomethodology, Kantianism and by the philosophical thesis of the underdetermination of theory by evidence derived from Willard Quine, Pièrre Duhem and Jules Poincaré. For the constructivist school, the objects of science are 'cultural objects' constantly created and recreated by scientists discursively in their ongoing activity, providing a means by which objects in the world can be recognized as such. Consistent with its latent Kantianism, this conception of science tacitly assumes that the structured levels of the real world are structure*less*. The conceptual constructions of science are regarded as simply part of discourses which are constitutive of social life and which enable us to orientate ourselves. Karin D. Knorr-Cetina (1983: 136) says that her constructivist epistemology 'conceives of *the order generated by science* as a material process of embodiment and incorporation of objects in our language and practices' (my emphasis).

In the short run, and particularly with regard to the institutional complexity of modern scientific specialisms and the highly technical character of many branches of physics and biology, the apparently entirely esoteric, self-referential and 'constructed' character of scientific objects in general can seem self-evident. This view will be reinforced if one restricts one's field of inquiry, as do many exponents of this approach, to the here-and-now situation of one laboratory or one short episode in the history of a particular science. As relatively autonomous human knowledge, scientific knowledge indeed has a cultural character in relation to its original producers, but its character is not arbitrary, being determined in the longer run to no inconsiderable degree by the structure of its object to which it *may* tend to become more adequate (Elias 1987a). It is this dimension that helps us to distinguish scientific from other forms of 'discourse'. Had scientific knowledge not become highly adequate to the nature of its object, in many fields, it would be difficult to explain how it has been possible to control natural events and processes for human purposes through its utilization.

To return to the philosophers' culture, there are, of course, other groups of specialists whose disciplines or subject areas also do not possess an 'object' of inquiry in the way that sciences do. But the important difference between, say, literary criticism or the history of ideas and philosophy is that, unlike philosophers, their practitioners do not set themselves up as the authoritative epistemological and conceptual judges of the sciences, including sociology. This alone is a good reason for subjecting the professional warrant for the pronouncements of philosophers to systematic scrutiny. It was probably both the vagueness of philosophy and the lack of consensus within it, as well as this latent arbitrariness, that Fustel de Coulanges had in mind when he said that 'To philosophize is to think what one wants' (quoted in Lukes 1975: 61). Later, in the 1930s, Paul Nizan said much the same thing in his epic polemic *Les chiens de garde*, which was a savage political attack on the philosophers of the Sorbonne at the time. But beneath the surface of Nizan's scathing hyperbole and *parti pris* is, however, an accurate perception of the dubieties and indefiniteness of the philosophy that we encounter in modern educational institutions. He wrote:

> Philosophy can say whatever it wants; it has no eternal vocation, it is not (and has never been) univocal; indeed, it may well be the ultimate form of equivocation. Philosophy-in-general is what is left of the different philosophies when these have been emptied of all substance and nothing remains but a kind of family atmosphere, an indefinable effluvium of traditions, private understandings and secret meanings. It is an entity composed solely of words.
>
> (Nizan 1971: 8)

It will be objected that whilst there may be equivocality and lack of consensus in philosophy, a similar lack of unity also exists within the fragmented discipline of sociology, which suggests that my comments in this regard are a paradigm case of the pot calling the kettle black. I am aware that sociology today is not in a unified phase of its development. Even though the 'war of the schools' of the 1970s is over, there is still a situation of paradigm pluralism, such that many sociologists would disagree with my whole approach and basic thesis in this chapter. But three points must be made immediately on this issue: (a) the extent of the disarray within sociology has been exaggerated, there being much more common ground among sociologists than appears to the outsider; (b) as we will see later in Chapter 8, the recent disarray was in any case a phase-specific phenomenon; and (c) there is a longer-term tradition of sociology stretching back more than 200 years in various national contexts which provides a core of theoretical and empirical findings and problems (Shils 1982), within which the current variegated state of sociology represents only a momentary phase, explicable partly by the cultural and structural dynamics I outline in the present chapter. In other words, *some* of the periodic disunity in sociology arises precisely from sociology's inability to emancipate itself sufficiently from philosophy, which engenders doubt, disorientation and failure of nerve on the part of sociologists. Many of the competing schools in sociology were or are philosophically inspired (for example, phenomenological sociology or ethnomethodology) or undergirded by philosophical abstractions of a Kantian kind (for example, structuralism or Althusserianism). This chapter is partly intended as a contribution towards correcting for the consequences of this tendency by re-posing the question of the relationship between sociology and philosophy from the less accustomed sociological point of view.

Two further features of the culture of philosophers stand out as important for understanding their relative advantage in the pecking order of academic establishments.

1. *Philosophy possesses enormous prestige.* This often has the effect of concealing its vagueness and equivocation: we tend to give philosophers the benefit of the doubt just *because* they are philosophers. The prestige of philosophy also partly accounts for why so many sociologists, representing the lower ranking discipline, have been attracted to philosophy and explains their general deference towards the tradition. The aura of philosophy must not be underestimated. Philosophy has developed, and actively cultivates, an image of profundity: it seems to offer involvement with the deeper truths of the human condition – basic questions about the nature of knowledge, reality and moral choice. The discipline is presented by philosophers as an ancient one, the repository for questions about the nature and meaning of existence itself. The appeal of being associated with, and conversant in, work of this level of grandeur and ambition is obvious.

2. *Philosophy is a highly verbal activity by its very nature.* Indeed, the standing and reputation of philosophers depends a great deal upon their ability to reason logically with rigour and skill, in order to be able verbally to convince others, apparently by force of argument alone. This skill is central to the *raison d'être* of philosophers and an important badge of rank of the profession. The philosopher Ben-Ami Scharfstein, in his unique psychological study of philosophers and philosophizing (Scharfstein 1980) has brought an insider's perspective to bear on this feature of the philosophers' habitus:

> When the philosopher demonstrates that he has learned how to use his professional code, he demonstrates a personal and social accomplishment that is its own reward .... His cleverness, intelligence, or professional mastery arouse others to emulate him, and, in this way, support a certain professional way of life. Professional philosophizing is less often a struggle with oneself than a struggle for status in the philosophical community.
>
> (Scharfstein 1980: 394)

Public disputation with philosophers of high intelligence and verbal dexterity – particularly those trained in the analytical school – can be an intimidating experience for people who are not trained to perform in this way. And this includes most sociologists. One consequence of this skill is further to augment the professional invulnerability of philosophers, because few outsiders are willing or able to challenge them on their own verbal terrain. This may be what Jonathan Rée (1997: 18) had in mind when he wittily commented that the obscure idea of an unconditional responsibility towards others found in the philosophy of Levinas 'makes a very tempting target for the roving logic-louts of analytic philosophy'.

When applied to sociological theory and research, the philosophical style of analysis (either verbally or in writing) often takes the form of making a number of fine conceptual distinctions, the evaluation of fetishized 'claims', 'theses' and 'positions' and the location of paradoxes or logical flaws in sociologists' works. The danger is that this activity can become an end in itself, blinding us to consideration of substantive matters. A disillusioned philosopher, J. M. Cohen, sardonically described some of these negative consequences. The professional philosopher is one who is

[A]lways on the scent of the slight mistake in what someone has said, abstracting from the idea or general conception it contains, who picks up the minute, carping put-down. . . . It is characteristic of this type that they come to think they can dismiss a complex theoretical system such as Marxism or psychoanalysis in a few deft 'moves' or with a few clever points, and to distrust whatever is not put in the professional patois of 'claims', unpacking, entailment, and which does not have the sleek professionalism and glibness that usually passes for brilliance and rigour.

(Cohen 1972: 8)

The extensive institutional expansion of the social sciences and of sociology in particular in the advanced societies in the 1960s and 1970s (Abrams *et al.* 1981 and Chapter 8 below) provided rich opportunities for the professional philosophers. They were able to bring their logical and conceptual skills to bear on the theory and research of the burgeoning discipline of sociology. And the sociologists looked to the prestigious philosophers for guidance and clarification, automatically deferring to their authority. But these reactions and attitudes were nothing new. In the French Third Republic at the turn of the century there was a comparable interest by philosophers in the activities of the then fashionable and budding science of sociology in France. They sought to circumscribe the field of the discipline and to curb the forays of its more ambitious practitioners into the fields of ethics and the solution of social problems. Unlike the situation today, however, at that time (at least in the French context) more sociologists were, it seems, sceptical about the attentions of philosophers. Gabriel Tarde, for example, shunned the philosophers with some sarcasm:

In the stories of our ancestors, when a child was born, all the fairies assembled around its cradle and each gave it a talisman with which it could perform miracles. At present when a science is born or even begins to announce its arrival, a certain number of philosophers encircle it, each bringing his own method for it to follow with the assurance of the greatest success if its rules are applied promptly and with perseverance, as if it were a method or program of discoveries of which nascent science is most in need!

(Tarde 1898: 73–4)

However much the nominalist Tarde disagreed with the realist Durkheim about the nature of the 'object' of sociology, they both shared the belief in the tactical need for sociology to distance itself from philosophy. As Durkheim declared in a debate with Tarde in 1904:

If sociology wants to live, then it will have to reject the philosophical character that it owes to its origin and approach the concrete realities via special research. It is desirable for the public to know that sociology is not purely philosophical and that it requires precision and objectivity.

(quoted in Clark 1969: 137)

The point is that the expansion of sociology in the contemporary period continues in a new phase a much longer-term sociological tradition going back to the classical *fin-de-siècle* age and earlier to the pioneers of the early nineteenth century, all of whom, as today, had to settle their accounts with philosophy in one way or another. In order to illuminate the current phase of this dialogue, it will be helpful to take a brief excursion into the origins of sociology in order to show how – right from the beginning – sociology took up and transformed into a different idiom questions about humankind and society which were previously the province of philosophers. Then, armed with this information, I will return to the role of philosophical culture today.

The sociological revolution

The emergence of the two first social sciences – political economy and sociology – in the late eighteenth and early nineteenth centuries was part of fundamental changes taking place in the structure of European societies.[5] Under the *ancien régime*, prior to what is usually regarded as the period of the onset of 'modernity', political economists such as the physiocrats and Adam Smith were showing, using evidence, that self-regulating laws operated in society independent of kings and ministers. They realized that there was a range of social phenomena such as the circulation of income between classes and its annual distribution, which had a measure of autonomy in relation to individual people's actions, no matter how powerful they were. Later, into the nineteenth century, the power of the industrial bourgeoisie and the working classes, with whom they were closely interdependent, increased considerably in relation to that of the aristocrats. This process made possible the extension of the science of political economy to embrace the autonomous social regularities of 'the economy' as such. This concept referred to the impersonal regularities of national and international markets and business cycles set in motion by free competition and independent of the actions of governments. It was the political economists who were first to establish, in Gabriel Tarde's words, the superiority of scientific observation in the social field over 'juridical, artistic, moral, theological and metaphysical points of view' (quoted in Clark 1969: 75).

The pioneers of sociology such as de Bonald, de Maistre, Saint-Simon, Comte, Marx and Spencer, were largely a product of post-revolutionary Europe, although only Comte and Spencer would, of course, have welcomed the label 'sociologist'. The others saw themselves as having very different political and scholarly aims. But they all shared a common belief that there was a broader field of self-regulating social forces wider than (though including) the autonomous regularities of the market located by the political economists. Marx is the most equivocal of the writers in this respect. Occasionally, as in the *Grundrisse*, he hints in an almost Durkheimian or Eliasian fashion at the 'general bond and all-round interdependence' (Marx 1857b: 161)[6] between people. But for the most part he only sees the spontaneous, objective bonds between interdependent people in their economic form, or as otherwise *derivative* of economic bonding, assumed to be ultimately determinative.[7]

All the writers whom we now regard as the early pioneers of sociology were all symptomatic of a growing realization in this period of the enigma of 'society'. People had become aware (and were often disorientated or afraid as a result) that in complicated ways individuals' planned actions had unplanned outcomes which they could not have foreseen and which could not be explained by the plans and intentions of people *who could be named*. These outcomes stemmed from the far-flung chains of interdependencies in which people, to a greater and greater extent, were becoming intertwined. The growing realization of the complex 'moral density' (Durkheim) of society in which people were living had important repercussions for the way in which the philosophers of the time and later tried to understand the questions of individual freedom and moral responsibility. Now there was a vortex of social changes which had an unplanned order which often, though not always, operated to thwart the wishes of individuals, for whom both the extent of their freedom of action and its limits were constrained by their interdependence with persons they did not even know.

Of the seventeenth and eighteenth centuries one could say that people did not experience their social interconnectedness as 'society', but rather the experience of society resulted from the actions of leading people such as kings and ministers. The upheaval of the French Revolution of 1789, the revolutionary wars, the Restoration in France, the reaction, the competing social movements and general unrest of the period, all contributed to this new realization. In order to try to capture the sum total of objective social relations which were self-regulating and unintended in these complex and ill-understood ways, the meaning of the word 'society' was spontaneously recast towards greater generality. It became from the late eighteenth century onwards also the general word used to describe these impersonal forces, adding another meaning to the more specific sixteenth- and seventeenth-century one of active companionship, as in friendly society or secret society (Williams 1976: 246).

The sociologists, and the increasingly professionalizing economists, though both focusing on the emergent social reality *sui generis*, had different emphases. The economists sought to elucidate the static regularities of markets, prices, income and profit, whilst the sociologists had in mind the broader and grander questions about the longer-term development of humankind and its fate. They were able to build on the ground and credibility already prepared and established by the political economists. Their stock-in-trade included the concepts of development, progress, tendency and other similar ones, with which they tried to grasp the driving forces of history which seemed to have torn apart the traditional society. All of them saw humankind as passing through a critical phase. They looked for the longer-run significance of the social processes, the momentous leading edge of which they felt they were living through, and tried to discern the shape of the future from the overall development. Though not a sociologist in the present sense of the term, François Chateaubriand nevertheless showed an eloquent awareness of the profundity of the changes through which a generation of European peoples, including many of the sociological pioneers, lived. Writing in 1834, he expressed his forebodings:

> What the new society will be I know not; I no more understand it than the ancients could understand the slaveless society born of Christianity. How

fortunes will be levelled, how wages will be equalized with labour, how
womanhood will attain complete emancipation, I do not know.
Presumably the *human species* will grow in stature, but it is to be feared that
the individual man may decline, certain eminent faculties of genius be
lost, and imagination, poetry and the arts perish in the cells of a hive-
society in which each individual will be nothing more than a bee, a cog in
the machine, an atom in organized matter. . . . Modern society has
taken ten centuries to establish, and now is in process of decomposition.
. . . This declining world will recover its energies only when that process
has reached its final stage, whereafter society will begin to ascend to a new
level of life.

(quoted in Evans 1951: 9)

From its inception, sociology took cognizance of the range of broader questions rhetorically expressed here by Chateaubriand, which we today would call
'moral', 'political', 'evaluative' or 'existential' matters. My contention is that these
issues – transformed to be sure – became *embedded in the conceptual structure* of the
emerging science of sociology. At the time they were regarded as the province of
philosophers and theologians or they were locked up and obscured within one or
other of the great nineteenth-century ideologies of liberalism, conservatism and
socialism, where they could only be addressed in highly one-sided ways. This
historically 'philosophical' character of sociology is not always obvious to us in the
present period when both sociology and philosophy have become very specialized,
fragmented and methodologically technical as part of their increasing professionalization.

To put the same point another way, in the nineteenth century the pioneering
sociologists directed their energies towards accumulating social scientific evidence
which would help them to make sense of the bewildering and far-reaching social
changes that were enveloping everyone, including themselves. But they did so
partly in order to contribute to an understanding of the feasibility of the plans and
goals offered by the various political doctrines and parties of the time to solve the
consequent social problems. The sometimes explicit, but often implicit, intention
was to delineate the social conditions for and limits of reform programmes and
revolutionary political manifestos which were phrased in the dominant philosoph-
ical-political language of the time: 'freedom', 'democracy', 'equality', 'tradition',
'socialism', 'emancipation', 'individualism' and so on. It gradually became evident
that a more comprehensive, inclusive and realistic assessment of these plans and
hopes was only possible via the more encompassing standpoint of sociology.

The case of Auguste Comte is instructive because here the serious, world-
changing, evaluative and, in a wider sense, 'political' intent of sociology is made
explicit. As is very well known, Comte believed that if sociology could be encouraged to achieve the positive stage of the development of human knowledge, then it
would embrace a form of non-theological, non-metaphysical knowledge more
appropriate to the emerging secular, industrial order, in which the power of the
Church was diminishing. He conceived of positivism (a term that did not then
possess the negative connotations it does now) as the fusion of two impulses, one
deriving from philosophy and the other from science. On the one hand, there was

Condorcet's emancipatory theory of progress which, however, blinded people to the achievements of the Middle Ages, which were dismissed out of hand as archaic. The writings of de Maistre, on the other hand, though inspired by a reactionary philosophy, provided the important and affirmative corrective about tradition which had been lost from view in people like Condorcet who were caught up in the revolutionary fervour of the post-1789 period. Comte ambitiously sees sociology as providing a reconciliation between these two antagonistic influences:

> The reconciliation could only be accomplished in a region of speculation lying above both revolutionists and reactionists. Here it is that the philosophic root of positivism joins its scientific root, which alone could furnish inspiration capable of becoming universal.
>
> (quoted in Thompson 1976: 11–12)

It would be easy to dismiss Comte's formulation as naive. But the point is that we can see him here struggling with an important issue, but still having to do so in the cumbersome philosophical language of 'speculation', 'reconciliation' and 'becoming universal'. With hindsight we can see his problem: it is how to render in sociological terms social processes, the effects of which exceed the scope and intentions of specific interest groups within the total social mesh. This sociological platform may then imply a human unity beyond those perspectives – perhaps the emerging unity of humankind in general across the globe. Comte thus represents an early phase in the development of a *non-partisan* (but not value-free) sociology which has as its heirs a whole tradition of inquiry cutting across national boundaries until the present day.

Many of the early pioneers as well as the sociologists of the 'classical' age of sociology at the turn of the century, encountered the problems connected with constructing a science of society in the works of influential and prestigious philosophers, or learned them within the culture of philosophers. This was bound up with the upgrading of philosophy in university reforms in the nineteenth century (Collins 1987: 66). Many of the pioneers were trained in philosophy and all of them were either inspired by, rebelled against or, at the very least, were influenced by their teachers. And then, as now, they felt compelled to engage with the works of a group who constituted a higher ranking group of inquirers than the one they aspired to join – the sociologists. This partly accounts for the energy and passion which they invested in settling their accounts with the philosophical tradition.

To take, briefly, three examples: it can be seen that Hegel, Rickert and Renouvier stood respectively behind Marx, Weber and Durkheim, providing the social scientists with certain problems – posed in a philosophical manner – which they then tried to solve in different ways and with varying degrees of success, *sociologically*. I will single out three such problems from a whole range of issues involved in the work of these pairs of writers, in order to make the point: (a) the relationship between 'being' and 'consciousness' (Hegel/Marx); (b) the prescriptive force of subjective values in science (Rickert/Weber); and (c) the moral significance of the individual's sense of dependence on others (Renouvier/Durkheim).[8] The sociologists' responses centred on (a) Marx's attempt to build a sociological theory of knowledge in his base and superstructure model;

(b) Weber's concept of rationalization and the 'ethic of responsibility' in political matters; and (c) Durkheim's analysis of individualism and individuation under conditions of mechanical and organic solidarity.

I cannot go into these questions in detail here. The point to emerge, however, is that in all three cases, and in different ways, each of the three sociologists concluded that the explanatory problems which they encountered were potentially more easily soluble if they made a *break* with philosophy. As Mannheim (1934: 214) put it: 'Sociology in all countries is born as the result of trespassing beyond the confines of pure philosophy.' It was, however, not a sharp, once-and-for-all break since they were all burdened in various ways with traces of the philosophy which they were trying to transcend (as we saw in the case of Comte and as I will show later in relation to Marx and Durkheim). Their work involved more of a *transposing* of the philosophically posed questions on to another level, consonant with the historical trend of sociology of which they were a part. The contemporary encounter between sociologists and philosophers in part recapitulates the substance and structure of the earlier interchanges, but does so in a new guise, on new questions, reflecting amongst other things the changing nature of philosophy over this period. This change has been a move towards technical problems, which reflects a shift in the 'power ratio' (Elias 1987a: 117) of professional philosophers *vis à vis* scientific specialists, including sociologists, slightly more in favour of the latter groups.

In the light of the interpretation of the historical development of sociology as the supersession of philosophy outlined above, I will return in the next two sections to the impact of philosophical culture upon sociologists in the present period. In the course of these remarks some of the points established here will be expanded further.

Sociology and philosophy today

Returning to contemporary sociology, however, we find that, with a few exceptions, sociologists are much less ambitious in defining the scope of sociology than their forbears and generally more deferential towards philosophy. During the expansion of sociology in the 1960s and 1970s, it was the sociologists, not the British philosophers, who mainly brought into intellectual debate in Britain the work of continental philosophers such as Hegel, Nietzsche, Heidegger, Husserl, Merleau-Ponty and Western Marxists, including the Frankfurt School. Many of the recognized authorities on the work of these philosophers are sociologists or teach on sociology courses. British sociological theory has become permeated in recent years with philosophical terminology and assumptions about the range of properly philosophical matters *vis-à-vis* sociological ones, derived from these traditions. These assumptions (see Figure 1) reinforced the already influential picture of the province of philosophy as 'second-order' analysis claimed by the indigenous Oxford analytic tradition.

The result of this philosophical influx has been that sociologists have come to accept as a matter of course a number of principles: (a) that sociology raises or presupposes a whole range of philosophical problems; (b) that sociology makes truth claims and hence needs philosophy to sort them out; (c) that sociological controversies (particularly conceptual ones) are partly philosophical and therefore cannot be settled in any other way than philosophically; and (d) that sociologists must separately settle the philosophical foundations of their research prior to empirical inquiries commencing or continuing.

Anthony Giddens goes so far as to create (or rather to resurrect from the 1930s) a distinction between sociological theory and 'social theory', partly in order to leave the door open to philosophical issues, tacitly assumed, without any argument, *to be autonomous*. He writes:

> I use the term 'social theory' to encompass issues that I hold to be the concern of all the social sciences. These issues are to do with the nature of human action and the acting self; with how interaction should be conceptualized and its relation to institutions; and with grasping the practical connotations of social analysis . . . 'social theory' involves the analysis of issues which spill over into philosophy, but it is not primarily a philosophical endeavour. The social sciences are lost if they are not directly related to philosophical problems by those who practise them.
>
> (Giddens 1984: xvii)

Many sociological works also contain the common disclaimer that there are irreducible philosophical questions which will perennially remain beyond the reach of sociology and apparently will remain unaffected by its findings. For example, Berger and Luckmann write:

> The philosopher, of course, will raise questions about the ultimate status of both this 'reality' and this 'knowledge'. *What is real? How is one to know?* These are among the most ancient questions not only of philosophical enquiry proper, but of human thought as such . . . we immediately disclaim any pretension to the effect that sociology has an answer to these ancient philosophical preoccupations.
>
> (Berger & Luckmann 1967: 13)

In modestly excluding those 'philosophical' questions from the purview of sociology, Berger and Luckmann are following a conventional division of labour between sociology and philosophy. This is one that, broadly speaking, allocates empirical inquiries to sociologists and a range of abstract reflections arising from that work to the philosophers. But notice that the respective responsibilities have been *defined by the philosophers*. Sociologists have acquiesced in this allocation in a taken-for-granted way, mostly out of deference towards the tradition of philosophy, when in fact the whole tenor of the sociological revolution in knowledge in the modern period points in the opposite direction – towards the supersession of philosophy as such and the reformulation of the problems once generated there on to another level by sociology.

Much contemporary discussion within sociology (and its para-sociological satellites such as social theory and social philosophy) implicitly embodies this conventional division of labour in the assumptions made and categories employed. Below I have set out as a table the dichotomies that have been created by philosophers (from various traditions found within the culture of philosophers) in order to delineate, and thus *to legitimate*, the areas of competence of the two disciplines.[9] As is characteristic of many philosophical distinctions, the oppositions are static and formalistic.

	Sociology		Philosophy	
	⌈ historical inquiry	⟺	systematic inquiry	⌉
1. Neo-Kantians[10]	⏐ empirical study	⟺	transcendental (non-empirical) reflection	⏐ ⏐
	⏐			
	⌊ facts	⟺	values	⌋
	⌈ context of discovery	⟺	context of justification	⌉
2. Logical Empiricists[11]	⏐ empirical matters	⟺	cognitive issues	⏐
	⌊ genesis	⟺	validity	⌋
	⌈ 'first-order' questions	⟺	'second-order' questions	⌉
3. Analytical philosophy[12]	⏐ descriptive (Is)	⟺	normative (Ought)	⏐
	⌊ factual	⟺	conceptual	⌋
	⌈ concrete historical expressions	⟺	universal subjective structures	⌉
4. Phenomenologists & existentialists[13]	⏐			⏐
	⏐ historical-causal hypotheses	⟺	*a priori* presuppositions	⏐ ⏐
	⏐ ontical inquiries (entities)	⟺	ontological inquiry (being)	⏐
	⌊			⌋
	⌈ finite	⟺	infinite	⌉
5. Hegelians[14]	⏐ particular	⟺	universal	⏐
	⏐ factual history	⟺	Universal History	⏐
	⌊ formalism	⟺	speculation	⌋

Figure 1 Philosophers' stipulations of disciplinary fields

For the most part the accuracy and legitimacy of these oppositions have not been questioned by sociologists and they remain generally unchallenged.[15] But a few remarks are in order in this direction, within the limited space of this chapter.

1. One can see how these pairings represent a typically philosophical viewpoint on the nature of sociology and human societies. Common to each grouping of oppositions is that the focus of philosophy is always to be on what is regarded as

timeless, static, unchanging, transcendental – perhaps eternal. This is true even in the apparently purely technical conception of philosophy. This idea is found in the analytical school and refers to reflection upon a range of mainly conceptual questions arising from the work of the sciences, including sociology. As Lawrence C. Becker points out, conceptual, i.e. non-empirical, questions exist in mathematics, but what distinguishes these from philosophical ones, he argues, is that the latter are essentially 'open', and thus not usually capable of resolution. In other words, on this view, this range of questions is bound to be continuously available for scrutiny, thus providing philosophers of this persuasion with a perennial rationale. Becker writes:

> The fact that a question is not finally resolvable does not mean that attempts to answer it are pointless. Progress on such questions amounts to increased sophistication rather than the achievement of solutions. Solutions are approached as limits.
>
> (Becker 1977: 250)

I think that this location of a unity of outlook within the segments of philosophical culture, as shown in the table, entitles us to conclude that philosophy constitutes a 'style of thought' in the sense developed by Karl Mannheim (1953: 76–7; 1929: 276).

2.   Within the terms of the oppositions, if it is possible to show that in the ongoing research practice of sciences there exists considerable interpenetration of the respective sides of these pairings, then some interesting consequences follow. Significant interplay or overlap between them would suggest that their mutually exclusive status *as definitive of autonomous areas of disciplinary competence* is not so much based in reality as in the analytical fiat of the profession of philosophers. This evidence could shed new light on the so-called autonomy of 'philosophical' questions in relation to sociology. What appears to have occurred is that philosophers have separated out the non-empirical aspects of ongoing scientific inquiry and inflated them to form the subject matter of a whole discipline, which they have then claimed as their own.

Much more research needs to be done on the applicability and usefulness of these oppositions as discipline defining and I cannot take the matter very far here. But two brief examples might illuminate how different the issue of 'philosophical' questions potentially looks from the sociological point of view. In both cases the empirically based procedures of sociology can be used to redefine the scope and limits of philosophers' statements.

Example 1   The centrality of the individual knowing subject in traditional epistemology can be shown to have arisen from the individual self-experience of people, particularly aristocratic and bourgeois intellectuals, during specific phases of the development of Western societies (Elias 1939). This self-experience has produced the *homo clausus* individual analysed by Elias (*ibid. passim*). This wider relocation of the matter affects the nature of the epistemological problem as originally posed by the philosophers. It suggests that the 'subject' of human knowledge is not the individual, but a long inter-generational process which has resulted from the inquiries of many people who were not known to each other. In this way we can demonstrate how 'genesis' affects 'validity', provided that we proceed with a wider and more differentiated picture of the nature of human knowledge to include a range of forms of knowing broader than the simpler, formal, logical types which made the 'genetic fallacy' argument plausible.

Example 2 I think it is also possible to transcribe what are usually called ethical issues or 'ought' questions into sociological terms. Here, too, one makes an empirical, sociological detour in order to redefine, for example, an assertion about the open possibilities of individual human 'freedom'. This might emerge as perhaps implying an untenable Romantic suggestion that people can live without any degree of external social constraint when all the evidence from a range of societies points to the contrary. Having located the partiality of the contention and its presuppositions, one is able to return to the problem as originally posed, but in a new form. This then has implications for the plausibility of the picture of omnipotent individuality painted by the various philosophies or political ideologies, say by existentialism or in anarchism and forms of radical, individualistic liberalism.

Whilst a new and more inclusive sociological framework of this kind is still in the course of development, one is inevitably constrained to some extent by the language of the older philosophical ways of posing the epistemological, ethical and existential questions (as were Marx, Comte and others of the nineteenth-century pioneers, to an even greater degree, as we have seen). So, *at this stage*, in attempting to move beyond the conventional division of labour between sociology and philosophy and its attendant assumptions and terminology, one is therefore operating at the edge of both intelligibility and credibility.

The sociological inquiry provokes the common accusation of failing to engage with the philosophical questions in the manner in which they have actually been posed. This objection, however, comes from the more dominant philosophers' standpoint and its cognitive power cannot be taken for granted. In fact, after a sociological reframing of the problem one returns to the issue better armed for seeing the partiality of the philosophical formulation as it is absorbed into a wider explanatory framework. The exclusively philosophical mode of elaboration then becomes simply untenable. However, this provokes anxiety in those for whom an important part of their identity is dependent upon the security of a philosophical way of thinking and acting which they sense is threatened by these sociological moves. The issue of the 'non-engagement of the question' is just as much an emotional as a logical one.

Philosophy as a culture of defence

Let us draw together the strands of the preceding sections. I have been arguing that the tendency of the sociological revolution in knowledge in the modern period has been towards the supersession (transcendence) of philosophy by sociology. With the rise of the social sciences, particularly sociology, philosophy was no longer the discipline competent to study and explain the social processes that

became known as 'society'. Step by step, over a long period of time, the epistemological and ethical deliberations of philosophy also became taken over on a new
level by sociology.[16] The epistemological issues became the province of the *sociology
of knowledge* and the questions raised by philosophy under the heading of wisdom,
i.e. matters concerning the 'good' life, human happiness and fulfilment, democracy, freedom, morality and so on, were transformed into the wider enterprise of
social diagnosis from a sociological point of view.

It is only our experience of the highly technicized disciplines of sociology and
philosophy in contemporary times that blinds us to the broader and more
profound character that sociology historically possesses. The trend of philosophy
has been that it has become more and more technical, concentrating on questions
of method increasingly, and less and less preoccupied with the grander questions
about human happiness and fulfilment. This is a symptom of philosophers having
become historically gradually more and more deprived of their area of competence, retreating into conceptual work, clarification, logic and such technicalities,
as the hallmark of the profession in the age of the social sciences. Instead of
viewing their relationship to philosophy from a historical and above all *sociological*
point of view, status-anxious sociologists in contemporary times, through deference to the profession of philosophers to whose prestige they aspire, have
acquiesced in the philosophers' stipulations as to the division of labour between
the two establishments.

It is only through acceptance of the philosophers' stipulations as to the respective areas of competence of the two disciplines, that sociologists have come to
accept as a matter of course that there are 'philosophical' problems in sociology at
all. However, the historical tendency of sociological inquiry points in the opposite
direction: it suggests – to invert the customary formulation – that there are sociological problems in philosophy. It also suggests that sociology constitutes a problem
for philosophy, because once the radical nature of the sociological revolution is
understood, the philosophers' claims to disciplinary autonomy emerge as questionable, if not perilous (more on this later).

One must not imagine that the sociological break with philosophy to which I
have referred was a sharp, clean or sudden one. I am rather talking about a long-
term process – still continuing, in forward and sometimes backward movements –
through which sociology has taken on board and transformed the concerns of
philosophy, which are preserved within it in a reformulated state, both on the levels
of epistemology and ethics. Underlying this synthetic trend are extra-theoretical
processes of group conflict through which sociological and philosophical specialists have struggled for the autonomy of interpretation and diagnosis of the
structure and tendency of the overall social process.

The work of sociologists – as we saw with Comte earlier – often bears the marks
of the philosophical forms of expression that they are struggling to transcend. This
is clear, for example, in the writings of Marx.[17] To anticipate one of the arguments
of Chapter 2, Marx tries to utilize the category of practice in order to transcend
the traditional dualistic epistemology of the rationalists and empiricists who
preceded him. For Marx, in the *Theses on Feuerbach*, there is no point in reducing
cognition to either of its material or ideal poles because both sides, are, and always
have been, in an active relation in human practical activity. But Marx is unable to

sustain this drive away from ontological reductionism, since the older dualisms of traditional metaphysics re-emerge in his attempt to build a sociological theory of knowledge. The theory of base and superstructure, or the determination of consciousness by 'social being', as he tellingly terms the economic base (Marx 1859: 181), falls back into the old static metaphysical dualism, implicitly assuming that the reified economic base and the superstructure of ideology are two separate entities.[18]

Comparable tensions and ambiguities can be detected in the work of Durkheim. As is well known, Durkheim attempted, in *The Elementary Forms of the Religious Life* (1915), amongst other things, to develop a sociological theory of knowledge which related collective representations to the structure of group life. His ambition (tellingly described as 'vaunting ambition' by the philosopher Steven Lukes (1975: 446)) was to resolve in a sociological manner the old philosophical debate between apriorism and empiricism. He was able to account sociologically for the origins of the collective and constraining universal Kantian categories which he felt the philosophers had left unexplained. At the same time, he satisfied the scientific aspirations of sociology by proceeding empirically, but without the individualistic implications of traditional empiricism (Durkheim 1915: 19).

But the new theory of Durkheim's is in effect a static sociological version of the two equally static philosophical doctrines which he was trying to transcend. Durkheim simply locates an abstract source for categoreal universality – society. He has begun to make the transition to a sociological epistemology, but his thinking still possesses a fundamentally philosophical cast from which he has been unable completely to free himself. He therefore laid himself wide open to the subsequent Kantian objection made by Gehlke (1915) and later Lukes (1975: 447–8) that he had confused the social causation of the specific categories with the *faculty or capacity* to think spatially, temporally, or whatever, which was already presupposed in his inquiry and therefore a priori. Durkheim could have immunized himself against this standard Kantian riposte with a more dynamic theory. This would have enabled him to have shown how specific concepts have *become* quasi-universal over many generations of social development. Or, more precisely, to show how they represent a higher level of conceptual synthesis (Elias 1992: 179ff).

If my general assessment of the historical supersession of philosophy by sociology has any cogency, then how are we to explain the continued existence of the discipline in educational institutions and the continued acceptance within sociology of the autonomy of philosophical questions? The answer to this question is *not* that there academic Departments of Eternal Verities in universities because there are eternal verities in the human condition perennially available to reflect upon (*philosophical* version). Rather, the answer lies in the dynamics of the status and power differentials between the sociological and philosophical academic establishments (*sociological* version). Viewed in the longer term, philosophy has been the higher ranking and relatively more powerful discipline (although the power ratio has been subject to fluctuations either way, relative to other scientific and political establishments across society as a whole). It has, therefore, tended to impose its categories and models of thinking on to the lower ranking disciplines, for example sociology.[19] As I showed earlier, sociologists have come to accept variants of what emerge under scrutiny as dubious oppositions created by philosophers to demarcate the subject-matter of the two disciplines, but which merge and blur on examination. (For reasons of space I was only briefly able to mention two – genesis/validity and descriptive/normative – and point out the similar structure of thinking underlying them all. But a more detailed case could be made out for inter-play between each of the other discipline-defining dualisms.)

These dichotomies legitimize a division of labour between the two disciplines and form part of a culture of professional closure to protect the peculiarity and specificity of the area of expertise claimed by the philosophical establishment, which has been increasingly under threat by the rise of the social sciences and by sociology in particular. Philosophy is, however, by no means a monolithic disci-pline and there is little consensus within it as to its aims and scope. Its purely verbal character makes it vulnerable to the charge that its statements in general are uncheckable and arbitrary, depending for their plausibility only on the social pres-tige, and hence credibility, of philosophers as a profession. As outsiders, we are also reliant solely upon that status for accepting the proposition that there are autonomous philosophical questions at all. I do not think that this can be taken for granted, although I have no doubt at all of the integrity and sincerity of philoso-phers in pursuing their inquiries, which for them have the highest value and most profound import.

Philosophers' self-definitions

In addition to the table of disciplinary responsibilities which I assembled earlier (Figure 1), the philosophers' culture has also generated a range of specific self-defi-nitions of the scope of philosophy which are closely related to the right-hand (philosophy) side of the table and which to some extent overlap with it. In briefly discussing some of these self-definitions, my strategy will be the same as before: to undermine the plausibility of these justifications of the philosophical enterprise in such a way as to reveal the anatomy of the academic philosophical establishment underlying them, for which I think they provide a culture of defence.

1. There is a cluster of conceptions of the subject-matter of philosophy which broadly centre on the hallmark of *technique*. These regard the central subject-matter of philosophy to be either logic, method (sometimes referred to merely as an activity) or conceptual clarification. These ideas derive from the influ-ential analytic and linguistic schools of philosophy associated with Russell, G.E. Moore, Wittgenstein and their later followers. The conception of philosophy as 'second-order' theorizing is also associated with this tendency though not its exclu-sive property.[20] Logic is the study of inference and its rules and is a discipline dealing with pure relations between symbols. It is closely related to mathematics and some of its component parts are widely regarded as being part of mathe-matics (e.g. set theory). It is not, therefore, a very strong argument to equate philosophy with logic since it is already an independent discipline. Such a move simply cedes the autonomy of philosophy rather than establishing it.

Nor is regarding philosophy as a method or an activity likely to provide the discipline with an indubitably irreducible subject-matter, except in a trivial or circular sense. Philosophers sometimes say, following this view, that philosophy is a way of looking at things or perhaps a 'puzzle-solving' activity. The problem here is, though, that puzzles come in many guises and occur in many fields and human activities and are solved, concretely, in given cases. Astronomical puzzles are solved by astronomers, chemical ones by chemists, sociological ones by sociologists, and so on. In many cases, philosophers would be unqualified to solve some puzzles, although they might be able to solve others. It is not a strong claim to disciplinary autonomy to say that philosophy is a generalized sense of puzzlement about anything puzzling within the competence of the philosopher. This view is perilously close to the empty circularity that philosophy is what philosophers do, in this case solving puzzles, so when they are doing it, it must exemplify philosophy.

The self-definition of philosophy as conceptual analysis presents an image of philosophers as conceptual trouble-shooters, arriving on the doorstep of the sciences, including sociology, with a conceptual toolkit ready to tune up their theories. Parasitic upon sociology, philosophers provide a rigorous, conceptual expertise in the interest of clarification. As one sociologist sympathetic with this conception expressed it:

> Philosophy of science can help us here. It cannot do the job for us; it isn't the philosopher's stone so long sought by sociologists. But it can help us to clarify quite what is involved in empirical inquiry, and what limits must be imposed upon the claims that we make. In offering us a kind of map, a framework within which to conceptualize our activities, it can guide us, though no more than that, to the places at which we must forge new connections.
>
> (Tudor 1982: 182)

The burden of this chapter is to argue against the viewpoint expressed here. Sociology is an empirical discipline and as such has both a theoretical and an empirical level which are interrelated. The theoretical side is comprised of concepts and of course in this area sociologists should be rigorous, systematic, concise and clear in their formulations. But there is no reason that sociologists cannot learn these skills and, indeed, many already possess them. The philosophers might also be so skilled and, indeed, this is the *raison d'être* of most of them. But as far as sociology is concerned, conceptual clarity is part of sociological theory. A separate profession of conceptual clarifiers is redundant.[21]

Moreover, one deleterious consequence of the kind of philosophers' advice mentioned in the quotation from Tudor above, is that it could lead to the surreptitious imposition on to sociological research of rigid, static philosophical categories and modes of thinking which, far from enabling us 'to forge new connections', could block the development of new insights. Furthermore, the schools of philosophy I have been discussing here have been famous, in opposition to all forms of metaphysics, for advocating that philosophy should tackle small, modest and manageable topics in a piecemeal fashion. This circumspect attitude has probably already percolated into sociology, producing a constraining effect on the ambitions of sociologists, deflecting them into a cautious choice of narrower questions and problem areas. It has reinforced other pressures on sociologists in recent years to narrow the scope of their research programmes (Kilminster 1992b).

2. Many philosophers have described their field as inquiries of a *transcendental*

(non-empirical) kind, which have always stood in an ambiguous relationship to scientific knowledge (see Bieri, Horstmann & Krüger 1979). This programme derives mainly from influential Kantian tradition, although variations of the same idea are found in phenomenology and in inquiries into 'fundamental ontology'. As Hartmann (1966: 224) points out, on the European continent a large number of philosophers and schools from Fichte, Hegel and Husserl, to Heidegger, Sartre and hermeneutic philosophy, come under the scope of 'transcendental' philosophy, broadly conceived. The oppositions listed under group 4 in Figure 1 above, exemplify the distinction between empirical and transcendental inquiry applied to cognition and ontology. Philosophers have attached considerable importance to this kind of inquiry as the hallmark of the profession. As Rorty has put it:

> [T]ranscendental arguments seem the only hope for philosophy as an autonomous critical discipline, the only way to say something about human knowledge which is clearly distinguishable from psychophysics on the one hand and from history and sociology of knowledge on the other.
>
> (Rorty 1979: 77)

In Kant, what was transcendental was the logical apparatus of a priori concepts and principles common to all rational minds (the Categories of the Understanding). In the 'new apriorism' of recent philosophers such as Karl-Otto Apel and Jürgen Habermas, the scope of transcendental inquiry has shifted away from 'consciousness as such' towards the transcendental importance of language and language communities.[22] But the structure of this mode of thinking remains the same: transcendental inquiry is said to be an autonomous level of reflection which seeks out the 'conditions of existence' (variously also referred to as 'presuppositions', 'preconditions' or 'that which makes possible ... X or Y') of society, the sciences, particularly the human sciences, and human speech acts as part of communication. It is in this area of investigation into *presuppositions* that many philosophers have staked their claim to autonomy.

The most well-known contemporary product of transcendental inquiry which has been taken up by sociologists is the notion of the 'ideal speech situation' postulated by Habermas (1970a). Built into all individual speech acts, he says, is the assumption that one can be understood by potential interlocutors who are equal partners in the discourse. This is a transcendental presupposition for all communication. Karl-Otto Apel (1980) argues similarly that the *real* communication community which has developed socially and historically presupposes an *ideal* communication community in which people are capable of adequately understanding each other's arguments and judging their truth. For Apel, an ideal 'unlimited community of interpretation' (1980: 123) is a transcendental presupposition of all discussion. Apel then makes dependent upon the plausibility of 'regulative principles' derived from these assertions a whole range of moral and political principles and commitments.

But my feeling is that if one sows these intellectual seeds, one has planted a very low-yield crop. What does the inquiry produce, when boiled down to its essentials? It produces highly abstract transcendental generalizations which are, I would suggest, of little cognitive value. It would be tempting to dismiss, as some people have, Habermas's and Apel's work on the ideal speech community as a high-flown way of expressing the banality that when people speak to each other they expect that they will be understood. But, taking transcendental inquiry of this type seriously as the pursuit of non-empirical constants, it is surely legitimate to ask: what is the significance and cognitive pay-off of the abstract propositions about the conditions of existence of speech acts? Does not this kind of inquiry produce only empty abstractions? The elevation of the presuppositions to the status of a priori universal limits of knowledge, cognition, communication, or whatever, only serves to conceal the essential vacuity of transcendental reflection and the emptiness of its products (see Kilminster 1982b).

3.   Philosophers often absolutize their activity by claiming that what they are doing – philosophy – is just the contemporary continuation of what is a *permanent feature* of the relationship between humankind and the world. This ontological condition continually reproduces human wonderment and hence the characteristic philosophical problems of the ages: to do with knowledge, reality and the good life (see Rotenstreich 1972: 115 and 183–5 for a typical account of this conception). The insistence in the modern period on the ontological permanence of philosophical problems and hence the perennial renewal of the subject is, I would suggest, partly a defensive posture on the part of philosophers, a reaction to the rise of sociology and the challenges of historicism and relativism. As Karl Jaspers tellingly affirmed:

> Philosophy seeks its enlightenment in thoughts which are themselves always still relative. The one truth is the truth of *Existenz* which moves in the ideas and finds its ground in Transcendence . . .
>
> (quoted by Hoffman 1957: 113)

Accepting a phenomenological version of this conception of philosophy, Maurice Merleau-Ponty, for example, was able to make sociology and philosophy compatible by regarding them simply as different modes of knowing. Both are held to be fundamentally based in intersubjective lived experience.

> Philosophy is thus not defined by a particular domain of its own: all it speaks of, just like sociology, is the world, men and the mind. What distinguishes it rather is a certain *mode* of the awareness that we have of others, nature or ourselves: . . . we not only have to say that philosophy is compatible with sociology, we have also to say that it is necessary for it, as a constant recall to its tasks, and that each time that the sociologist comes back to the living sources of his science, to what it is that operates in him as the means of understanding even the most distant culture formations, then he is spontaneously already engaged in philosophy. . . . Philosophy is not a particular science, it is the vigilance that does not let us forget the source of all science.
>
> (Merleau-Ponty 1960: 157)

It follows for Merleau-Ponty that 'The sociologist begins to do philosophy to the extent that he takes it on himself not simply to note down facts, but rather to understand them' (*ibid.*: 146). This is because in 'understanding' he or she must automatically exemplify the fundamental, intersubjective commonality of all human beings: and this is a universal, ontological presupposition of all inquiry, which philosophy as a discipline merely expresses.

The self-definitions grouped in point 3 above (including Merleau-Ponty's) are variants on the theme that philosophy is autonomous because it expresses an ineliminable and timeless human level of experience of nature and other people. This justification implies the peculiar circularity that when people are wondering or understanding they are doing philosophy and doing philosophy is to wonder and understand. But it is a viewpoint that enables the philosophers to take their place alongside the sciences, which also investigate different aspects of that which exists, even though the philosophers' claimed area of inquiry – Being and its modes – is entirely of their own creation and not amenable to empirical confirmation.

The 'end of philosophy' thesis

I have tried to demonstrate in this chapter that there is compelling evidence that the issues traditionally addressed by philosophers have *already* been transposed on to another level and reframed as the result of the ongoing sociological revolution in knowledge of modern times. Philosophy in its present guise still tries to preserve those issues and concerns mostly, though not always, still expressed in their archaic, pre-revolutionary form and terminology. The philosophers have protected their dwindling area of expertise with dubious claims to an autonomous subject-matter. It is only their relatively high place in the prestige ranking order of academic establishments that ensures that their authority to make these and other claims is rarely challenged. These findings throw into question the conventional (philosophically defined) division of labour between the two disciplines, in which most sociologists have hitherto acquiesced, to their great cost.

Having said that, however, because of the pervasiveness of philosophical modes of thinking and acting, I suspect that the structure and *sociological* specificity of my position will be widely misrecognized. This chapter will inevitably be subsumed in some quarters into the genre of *philosophical* proclamations announcing 'the end of philosophy'[23] which appear in every generation (for discussions of this phenomenon see Manser 1973; Cumming 1979: 19–20; and Crook 1991: 79). Thus pigeonholed, it will probably provoke the common, but erroneous, rejoinder that I have produced here a philosophical refutation of philosophy; that, in the very act of trying to eliminate or otherwise explain away philosophy, I have exemplified precisely what I am attempting to move beyond. Thus, even the refutation has inadvertently contributed to the perennial renewal of the subject (see Rotenstreich 1972; Mueller 1983).

The circular principle underlying this response has nowhere been more succinctly expressed than in the publisher's flyer describing the book by Mueller (1983): 'This volume is based on the premise that nothing can be said for or against philosophy which is not already revealing a philosophical consciousness.' So long as one remains within philosophy and its constitutive assumptions, there is no way out of this conundrum. This stock philosophical rejoinder is easily recognizable as deploying a combination of a 'transcendental' argument and one from 'immanence', to use the terminology of the old code.

The rejoinder depends for its rhetorical effect on a cleverly expressed paradox, to which it is difficult to respond without appearing foolish. You cannot challenge it without exemplifying what you are trying to eliminate. This is a philosophers' gambit which depends ultimately upon an irrefutable assertion of the immanence of philosophizing in the human condition, an argument that has its roots in the theological origins of philosophy (Rotenstreich 1972: 83–5, ch. XI). The function that the argument performs for philosophers is, however, clear. It is always available as a last resort to protect them against any conceivable intellectual or scientific challenge to their claim to disciplinary autonomy. Even though it is nothing more than an insignificant artifice of logic, it is an arresting rhetorical device which will continue to be unquestioningly regarded as decisive and credible as long as the philosophers' establishment retains its intellectual authority.

2

THE HEGELIAN APOGEE[1]

It is the fashion of youth to dash about in abstractions: but the man who
has learnt to know life steers clear of the abstract 'either–or' and keeps to
the concrete.

(Hegel 1830a: 146)

Kant and Hegel

The development and character of European sociology cannot be fully understood without taking into account the ways in which its practitioners have tried –
though not always fully successfully – to transform into social scientific research
programmes various problems and issues they encountered in the writings of
philosophers. The sociological revolution in knowledge, I am arguing, constituted
a *break* with philosophy which has had profound consequences for the practice of
both philosophy and sociology.

In settling their accounts with the prestigious European philosophical tradition,
the most important specific philosophers whom the pioneering sociologists of the
nineteenth century as well as the sociologists of the *fin-de-siècle* age of sociology
confronted, were Kant and Hegel and their later followers. True, other philosophers in what Hartmann (1966) has referred to as the great 'transcendental'
European tradition, such as Nietzsche, Husserl and Heidegger, have also, for
better or for worse, played a role at various times, and continue to do so. And one
could add the names of Scheler, Husserl, Schutz, Merleau-Ponty, Wittgenstein and
many others. But it is neo-Kantianism that looms largest in the shaping of the
sociological tradition as a whole, including American developments from Parsons
and certain figures in the Chicago School onwards (Münch 1987; Alexander
1987a). And it is Hegel who stands behind Marx and the influential Marxian
paradigm of social science generally (with the exception of the work of Louis
Althusser, whose structuralist leanings give his reflections a Kantian cast – see
Chapter 5).

In rooting theology and the traditional philosophies of knowledge and morality
concretely and non-individualistically in society, politics and history, Hegel had
propelled himself to the threshold of social science. From the point of view of my
argument in this book, Hegel represents a crucial watershed. The sophisticated
dialectics of Hegel's philosophy, whereby the dualisms of Western thought are
contained in a metaphysical synthesis of considerable artifice and theoretical

tension, constitutes the furthest point that it is possible to reach within the old code of European philosophy. My contention is that progression beyond this point necessitates – as the politicized Marx perceived clearly, albeit partially – abandoning philosophy altogether and moving into a different, social scientific idiom. The drive towards synthesis then takes on a new form, whereby the metaphysical overtones, including all traces of teleology, are discarded. In other words, the horizon of Hegel's inquiries – and those of his subsequent followers – is philosophy itself, the autonomy of which is taken for granted.

The philosophical task after Kant was how to overcome the problems associated with (a) the a priori categoreal limitation he placed on empirical knowledge; (b) the contradictory idea of the 'thing-in-itself'; and (c) his separation of theoretical and practical (moral) Reason.[2] For a period in the 1820s it had become fashionable in Germany for philosophers to disavow the label 'Kantian', but Hegel noticed how Kantian many of them ultimately remained. Hegel also detected that many of the critiques offered by various philosophers of the time were inevitably drawn towards subjectivism, irrationalism or mysticism or else conceived of the Absolute as a purely abstract and empty 'beyond' (Hegel 1822: 235–6). This was because they implicitly accepted as a starting point the Kantian doctrine that only finite appearances were scientifically knowable, not the Infinite; whereas, for Hegel (following various Renaissance neo-Platonists such as Pico della Mirandola and Nicholas Cusanus) the Infinite was universality embodied here and now in a determinate way, *in and through* the particularities of the finite, concrete human historical world. Hence, in principle, the Infinite, in all its dimensions, was eminently knowable. This was the burden of the Hegelian notion of the 'concrete universal'.

That most of the classical sociology of the early twentieth century (Weber, Simmel, Durkheim) was founded on a neo-Kantian philosophical paradigm is well known. What the Hegelian philosopher Gillian Rose controversially argued, however, in her highly original book *Hegel Contra Sociology* (1981) was that the domination of Kantian thinking in modern sociology and philosophy is virtually total. Where writers such as Mannheim, Dilthey, Gadamer and Heidegger made efforts to move beyond Kantianism, their 'metacritiques' remained in its thrall, still exhibiting transcendental features. And the same goes for much of the German strand of Western Marxism, the work of whose main founders, including Lukács and Adorno, was also burdened by the same dominant neo-Kantian paradigm which they were seeking to transcend. It was not strictly speaking 'Hegelian' at all, as we have been led to believe. As regards the neo-Kantian sociologies, they have focused on the transcendental conditions of possibility for human society and have separated facts from values. This has resulted in these sociologies tending uncritically to take for granted the existence of society and to become caught up in abstract oppositions such as action/structure, holism/individualism and *Verstehen/Erklären*.

Rose maintains, however, that in his critique of Kant's philosophy Hegel had anticipated and criticized the antinomies thrown up by the whole later neo-Kantian endeavour. Hegel also developed a form of analysis that did not take the present social order as an immediate, fixed datum, but which contained dialectically self-moving concepts as well as a phenomenology designed to point beyond it, though in a determinant way. Rose's book is partly an appeal for a renewal of sociology, symptomatic of the tangled political and theoretical disputes associated with the latter part of sociology's conflict phase in the late 1970s. It is a philosophical synthesis which implicitly (and sometimes explicitly) attempts to resolve the epistemological and sociological antinomies and moral and political dilemmas thrown up by the contestations through which its author lived. This is to be achieved by simply lifting Hegelian philosophy in its purest form, lock, stock and barrel, out of the early nineteenth century and planting it in the present day, so as to take advantage of its synthesizing and reconciliatory force.

In technical terms, the renewal of sociology is to be achieved by encouraging people to undergo a philosophical re-education of a 'speculative' kind. Following Hegel, speculative experience is characterized as 'the experience of difference or negation, of relative identity of a contradiction between consciousness's definition of itself and its real existence which is misrecognised and recognised at the same time' (*ibid.*: 103). This comprehensive way of looking at social existence has to be 'retrieved' because it has become lost or blurred through bourgeois property relations continually reproducing experiences which determine thinking into non-speculative patterns, including neo-Kantian philosophy and its sociological offshoots. Hence, Kantianism emerges as the highest point reached by philosophical thinking under bourgeois social conditions and expresses the abandonment by this class of its revolutionary ambitions. The dominance of neo-Kantianism has induced even many Marxists to read Marx and Hegel through Kantian, Fichtean, or otherwise non-'speculative' spectacles, thus further justifying the very society they are seeking to change.

The Kantian hegemony

In the writings of Rudolph Lotze in the 1870s occurs a transformation of the Kantian problem of what constitutes the objective validity of knowledge (for Kant the synthesis of appearances by the mind) which provided a framework for all subsequent neo-Kantian schools. Lotze posited two separate spheres of life, the reality of validity (*Geltung*) which was independent of empirical reality, and the reality of values (*Werte*) which people hold with the conviction of their conscience and with which they attribute meaning to what they do. These values were accorded an ultimate and undeniable validity on a par with the propositions occupying the realm of validity. Subsequent neo-Kantianism became caught up in problems associated with this distinction. Values could be seen either as primarily determinant in human life (both of logical validity and of moral law) or both realms could be regarded as equally ultimate and underivable. Another consequence was that the autonomy of *Geltungslogik* became methodologism, a general form of the logic of validity, separated from cognition of the facts of reality. This development led to a tendency in subsequent Kantianism to debase reality itself (which partly inspired the existentialist reaction) and to regard the rules of validity as *creating* the object domains of the rules, in this case in particular the object domains of the sciences.

Sometimes the various neo-Kantians accorded primacy to validity over values and sometimes the reverse. One could, for example, claim that autonomous value was the determinant of moral action but not of theoretical validity; or perhaps that empirical reality itself is completely subordinated to a transcendent realm of value. The *Geltungslogik* increasingly gave extraordinary autonomy to judgements of validity. Some writers accorded such judgements an independent ontological status, others regarded logical thought as autonomously productive and generative of reality, independent of perception and the processes of consciousness. Coupling this tendency with a notion of the primacy of values, Rickert, for example, propagated the doctrine that it is the prescriptive force (which has its origins in values) of a judgement that confers validity and authority on truth, with no reference to reality at all. The reality of validity judgements, though based in value, was a different mode of reality from the existence of things and was underivable, not dependent on the judging subject and *sui generis*.

In Weber's and Durkheim's attempts to found scientific sociologies, they sought to bring the question of validity to bear on, respectively, the realms of values and moral facts, both wanting to avoid psychologism by bringing in society or culture as conferring objective validity on either values or moral facts. Thus, in a 'quasi-transcendental' way, society becomes a cultural apriori, a precondition for actual social values. This strategy was always precarious because in the case of Durkheim, in a circular manner society was both the transcendental, i.e. non-empirical, condition for morality and at the same time was held to have the status of object or cause of the morality. And the same contradiction existed in relation to Durkheim's social derivation of the Kantian categories in the *Elementary Forms of the Religious Life*.[3]

. Weber, on the other hand, followed Rickert to give priority to values over validity. For Weber, we only pick up on segments of reality because of the values we bring to bear on them, which are ineliminable and not rational. The investigator compares and measures value-related ideal-type constructs against reality, mindful that science itself must scrupulously admit its relation to values in order to claim some form of validity. Ideal types were constructs, which were related to reality by the principle of 'objective possibility', via a method that was itself a value. The ideal types were purely constructs, heuristic and *regulative* postulates only, to be used for the purpose of seeking to connect the objects of experience. Quite consistently with his philosophical assumptions, for Weber, a legitimate, i.e. 'valid', social order is defined by the subjective meaning (values) of its participants, the kinds of legitimate validity (order) that people acknowledge. Hence, Weber's sociology could only locate social reality 'within the realms of consciousness and its oppositions' (Rose 1981: 21). The priority of values also informed Simmel's forms of sociation and resurfaces in Parsons' general theory of action, which saw society as a system of values and theoretical constructs as regulative, heuristic principles or 'fictions'.

Granting priority to validity informed a further wave of sociology and social philosophizing which, following Habermas and others, Rose calls 'metacritique'. Dilthey, Heidegger, Mannheim, Benjamin and Gadamer transformed the question of validity into a historical critique of the whole endeavour of methodologism and brought back existence, reality, life or being, debased by the neo-Kantians, into the centre of the stage. In this sense they adopted a strategy already developed by Durkheim, i.e. deriving the Kantian categories from social presuppositions or preconditions, in this case 'social situation', history, culture or *Dasein*. But, like Durkheim, and despite their radical intentions, they remained trapped in the Kantian transcendental circle, because 'the condition of the possibility of experience ... is likewise the condition of the object of experience' (Rose 1981: 23). The argument remains endlessly circular, trying to resolve the problems of the paradigm of *Geltung*, but still from within its assumptions.

Here the analysis reaches the same point that I did in the previous chapter when I drew attention to the empty circularity of transcendental arguments. That is, recognizing the paradox of being unable to examine the limits of reason or explain its origins without exemplifying (presupposing) it, which Kantians and others seem to regard as the clinching argument in favour of the existence of the apriori. For Rose, the way out of the paradox must avoid recourse to an arbitrary starting point or to further empty circularity or regression. The solution is to '*make the transition to a speculative position*' (Rose 1981: 24, my emphasis), i.e. to embrace Hegel. This is where I part company from Rose and the Hegelian programme generally. For me, the way forward is to transpose the issues into *sociology*. Not via another version of 'metacritique', but through socio-genesis, thus reframing the whole matter. This truly takes us beyond Hegel. In my scheme of things, the exponents of metacritique have indeed ultimately failed to break with Kantianism, but equally the exponents of Hegel have failed to break with philosophy itself.

The Hegelian temptation

The limitations of the Kantian method, notably its purely formal, abstract unification of theoretical and practical reason, places limitations on the type of social and political theory produced. Kant could only entertain knowing the Absolute (the unconditioned) within the framework of practical (moral) Reason, and even then only formally, in relation to moral objects in general, not specific contents. This Kantian conception was thus unable to conceive of *concrete* freedom, in a positive way, in relation to real social objects, but only in the negative, abstract form as a freedom *from* the realm of necessity. Specific, historical aspects of social life are therefore removed from the equation and morality falls back into the abstracted moral individual, who is in reality, according to Hegel, the real, specific, legal individual of bourgeois property relations, presupposed in the Kantian analysis. Moreover, Kant's conception unrealistically excluded desire and inclination from a positive definition of freedom because these were to be subjugated to pure, abstract reverence for the law of the time. This formalism also produced the paradox that a subjective maxim which is formally moral may be immoral in its *contents*. It is therefore important to move away from the abstract Kantian moralism towards Hegel because the categoreal limit placed on valid theoretical and practical knowledge means that we can only know all natural and moral objects through finite forms, so we never properly know them, even *qua* finite objects.

For Hegel, this limitation forces us into irrationally yearning for an inaccessible and unknowable Infinite. Through such generalized longings we have not rationally grasped, fully, the 'infinite' dimension of human life which *also* constitutes those finite conditions and social relations. (There is a theological assumption present here.) So, in the Kantian framework, our knowledge is doubly impoverished. Its individualizing and formal character blinds us to the concrete embodiment of ethics objectively in social life, which results in 'the unknowability of ourselves, both as subjects of experience ... and as moral agents capable of freedom' (Rose 1981: 44). As Hegel argued, if we have no conception of an ineliminable *unconditioned* infinite dimension to social life, then we might be deceived by a spurious universalizing of something *conditioned*, say private property and the abstract legal rights associated with it, as the authentic Absolute.

The analysis suggests, at any rate, a sociology of a different kind from the amoral sociology of the scientific, transcendental, Kantian-inspired kind. For Hegel, matters of knowledge and morality are both to be concretely rooted in human society and history as it would be contradictory to root them anywhere else. In his Jena writings in particular, Hegel replaced the Kantian abstract justification of moral judgements by the idea of the 'absolute ethical life', regarded as embedded in social reality (Hegel 1796, 1798). For him, the attempt to justify theoretical and moral judgements apart from their use in social life is contradictory, as are the Kantian distinctions between knowable appearances and unknowable things-in-themselves and Finite and Infinite, in particular. The move towards Hegel is a move away from individualism, moral formalism, abstraction and dualism, towards concrete reality. Many sociologists could readily identify with Hegel's injunction quoted as the epigraph to this chapter, to the effect that we should steer clear of the abstract 'either–or' of dualisms in favour of concrete analysis. But the move towards Hegel is also towards a mode of analysis that does not divide consciousness or reality into Finite and Infinite in an abstract and diremptured way. It is here, however, that the metaphysical warning bells begin to ring. I will return to this point in the next section. Meanwhile, consider Rose's succinct summary of the Hegelian fusion:

> *Sittlichkeit*, 'ethical life', refers to the unity of the realms of morality and legality, and 'the absolute' to the unity of the finite and the infinite. What *Sittlichkeit* is cannot be pre-judged, but the morality of an action cannot be 'judged' apart from the whole context of its possibility. It cannot be judged by separating its morality from its legality, by separating its meaning from the social whole.
>
> (Rose 1981: 46–7)

How does Hegel defend, justify or otherwise 'prove' the precarious veracity of these unities, which bespeak the presence of an absolute *Sittlichkeit* (the true freedom of humankind) which is as yet not known, not lived, yet not merely an abstract yearning? For Hegel, the unity of the Finite and Infinite should not be justified transcendentally, declared methodologically unknowable or simply assumed: rather its presence in the socio-historical whole can only *become* known. It has to be *achieved* as 'a result of the process of the contradictory experiences of consciousness which gradually comes to realise it' (Rose 1981: 46), i.e. phenomenologically. The idea of the 'absolute ethical life' is not to be justified abstractly, as an ideal, but dealt with only by presenting in works of dialectical analysis, the contradictory human experiences that imply it, or indicate its presence, *concretely* in society.

Hegel demonstrates that certain social experiences induce people to mistake the 'relative ethical life' (lack of identity) of bourgeois property relations for the 'absolute ethical life' (a different kind of unity or human identity being implied). Hegel seeks to re-present these experiences (particularly in his *Phenomenology*) in such a way that people's moral and political consciousness can gradually come to comprehend them as determinations of the absolute ethical life, held to be built into the real private property relations of his time. The absolute ethical life cannot be regarded as the sum total of social relations at any one time but the unity of those relations with an identity they *lack*. For Hegelians, it is this feature that makes his philosophy truly *critical*. Rose declares: 'It is only by acknowledging the lack of identity as the historical fate (*Bestimmung*) of a different property structure that the absolute ethical life can be conceived' (*ibid*.: 58).

Hegel developed the important idea (subsequently taken up by Marxian socialists) that people can misread the nature of bourgeois society and its property relations and erroneously come to believe that their merely formal equality as individual legal persons was true universality, the ultimate unity of a free humanity. The 'absolute ethical life' was, however, held to be concretely present, contradictorily entwined with the 'relative ethical life', i.e. bourgeois property relations. The actual realization of this concrete potentiality would of course imply the transcendence of the bourgeois property relations and law which sustained the illusion that they embodied true universal freedom. Far from justifying the inequalities and unfreedom of bourgeois society, Hegel's philosophy, with its standpoint of the absolute ethical life, was critical of bourgeois property relations. His dictum 'What is rational is actual and what is actual is rational' has been misread as a vindication of the present social order.

Phenomenology in Hegel's philosophy is not a method on Kantian lines. Rather, it is a speculative way of representing the deformations and illusions of 'natural' (subjective) consciousness in order to provide a gradually more comprehensive grasp of the universal substance of which they are misapprehensions. It is a way of educating people's 'natural' consciousness to grasp the ever-present Absolute by traversing the contradictions inherent in various one-sided modes of consciousness by which that universal substance is misrecognized, but without prejudging that Absolute in advance of its achievement. For Hegel, so long as it is impossible for the absolute ethical life to be fully realized under prevailing conditions of bourgeois property and law, then it can only be stated as an abstract *Sollen* (Ought) in the manner of Kant or Fichte. In these circumstances, even Hegelians (the enemies of abstraction) can only think the Absolute to some extent abstractly, acknowledging an element of *Sollen* in such thinking (*ibid*.: 204 and 208). But this limit must be acknowledged, lest we produce a conception of the Absolute which lends itself to imposition in practice by political élites.

By conventional standards of defence and proof, this position is inherently precarious. For Rose, the absolute ethical life cannot be rationally justified: it is, she says at one point, 'invisible' (*ibid*.: 62 and 202) and more or less unstatable, because it is only known through the progressive comprehension of the ways in which it is persistently misrecognized. And the prospect of it being realized, of being truly ours, is dependent upon the transcendence of the bourgeois property relations which sustain its misrecognition. In other words, we are talking here about a revolutionary change to bring about the true recognition of ourselves.

Following Hegel, Rose concludes that the vocation of philosophy in our time has been determined by the experience of the lack of freedom of the bourgeois 'relative ethical life'. It has become abstract, re-presenting that ethical life as the illusory, spurious and negative Absolute of abstract bourgeois rights. The fate of philosophy has therefore been to be continually understood non-speculatively (and this includes Marx's reading of Hegel) because the 'reality of unfreedom has determined its reading' (*ibid*.: 184). This has produced two tendencies:

1   That of the imposed *Sollen* of Right Hegelianism, which has been used to reinforce prevailing law, thus proclaiming the 'end of philosophy' because it was declared as already realized as that law.

2   The *Sollen* has been abstractly and undiscriminatingly imposed as a critique of the existing bourgeois law. Politically this formed Left Hegelianism, which also declared the 'end of philosophy' by seeking to realize it in practice. This tendency developed into the new culture of Marxism, although it was basically of an abstract Fichtean character, which thus lent itself to further imposition and political and social perversion, as we saw in the former Soviet Union.

The same social conditions accordingly produce and reproduce the antinomic neo-Kantian sociology based in the paradigm of validity/values, sometimes with the Fichtean characteristics. For example, the action/structure dualism reproduces the Fichtean antinomy for the positing ego and the posited non-ego, i.e. the individual posited over and against an abstract, collective force (society). Because of this abstract separation, this model has no conception of the relation between ego and 'non-ego' as 'transformative activity' (*ibid*.: 204 and 213) or 'productive activity' (*ibid*.: 204), nor of the property relations which produce the subjective illusion of free and unconstrained action that underpins it. Hence, the solipsistic phenomenology of Schutz simply treats people's misrecognition of reified social institutions, though their own products, as facts of consciousness (*ibid*.: 24).

In the tradition of Left Hegelianism, Marx's work was largely of a pre-speculative, Fichtean nature, and he misread Hegel accordingly. Although he oscillates in his writings here and there, between Hegelian and Fichtean positions, for the most part Marx's work reinforced abstract oppositions such as being/consciousness, theory/practice and materialism/idealism. (See Chapter 3 where I deal with these dualisms from a sociological perspective.) More importantly, Marx's theory lacked in any developed degree an incorporation of the Hegelian idea according to which 'theory recognises the intuition or object which practice suppresses' (Rose 1981: 215). Hence, Marx's abstract base/superstructure model of society did not contain any notion of representing the misrepresentations of social relations. The nearest Marx came to a phenomenology in this sense was in his theory of commodity fetishism. So, Marx lacked the politics implied by the Hegelian phenomenology, whereby people's consciousness can be educated into reforming itself. Rose believes that Lukács' *History and Class Consciousness* was a neo-Kantian inspired attempt to give Marx this dimension. But its latent Fichteanism could only laud an abstract change in consciousness, not its successive reformation.[4] Right from the start Marx's work lacked a concept of *Bildung*. Hence, in its abstract and structural way, it simplified the prospects for, and the inhibitions to, the development of revolutionary class consciousness.

Sociological observations

1.   At first glance, the return to Hegel seems to promise much, both for the politically minded and sociologically. *Politically*, it potentially provides a way of seeing through spurious Absolutes and formal freedoms without imposing a rival abstract Absolute in their place, as well as a conception of positive freedom. In periods of social conflict and polarization, in particular, though not only at such times, Hegel's synthesis also offers to some people a principled political refuge whereby political extremes and overstatements can be avoided and, indeed, reconciled. As the Hegelian political philosopher R.N. Berki put it:

> The transcendence of politics in the form of philosophical awareness liberates from (or rather it is in itself the liberation from) concrete ideological commitment; at the same time, however, it is itself the deepest form of commitment, but this commitment is to the whole of the epoch.
>
> (Berki 1981: 104)

2.   *Sociologically*, Hegel seems to offer much: a method for exposing the all-pervasive static formalism of Kantianism undergirding the sociological tradition; a way out of the circularity of transcendental argumentation; a dynamic orientation moving away from individualism, dualism and abstraction; the rooting of moral questions in concrete social relations; a conception of action as transformative; a historical approach to the succession of philosophical systems; the recognition of the centrality of human desire; and an orientation towards a synthesis of perspectives!

3.   But before we all reach for the *Science of Logic* or the *Phenomenology*, hoping to find the sociologist's stone, we need to pause for a moment. All those progressive motifs above, which can arguably be read out of Hegel's philosophy, carry with them, however, a number of sociologically dubious and unacceptable assumptions. The unity of theoretical and practical contraries in Hegel's work, which undergirds his dialectically self-moving concepts, is fundamentally a *metaphysical* one. The posited finite (particular) and infinite (universal) dimensions of existence are regarded as held in a dynamic historical, social and cosmic tension-field, sustained in human consciousness. For the Hegelian, to grasp this reality it is necessary to abandon conventional logic, particularly the law of contradiction, and to regard all things, social or natural, described through oppositions such as subject/object, general/particular, freedom/necessity and other paired interpenetrating oppositions, as simultaneously constitutive of both seemingly mutually contradictory sides. And it is, moreover, held to be possible to come to 'know' the contradictory Absolute in which these opposites inhere, through a process of phenomenological recapitulation of the successive ways in which in various fields it is both recognized and misrecognized at the same time.

4.   Completely consistently with those assumptions, Rose's extraordinary claim is that 'Hegel's philosophy has *no* social import if the absolute is banished or suppressed, if the absolute cannot be thought' (*ibid.*: 42). It seems that this statement is meant to be taken literally, not as simply a generalized injunction always to bear in mind universal principles when evaluating societies. It is something to which anyone going over to Hegelian philosophy in its entirety must be committed. A heavy theoretical and political load is placed on the importance for sociology and for social criticism of something that most sociologists and many philosophers would regard as a form of mysticism, i.e. the possibility of someone actually *coming to know* the Absolute. 'The limitation of "justified" knowledge of the finite [in Kant's philosophy] prevents us from recognising, criticising, and hence from changing the social and political relations which determine us. If the infinite is unknowable, we are powerless' (Rose 1981: 45).

5.   The last point alone is sufficient to signal that the advocacy at the present time of a purist Hegelianism, lifted straight out of the early nineteenth century, inevitably commits us to a paradigm suffused with religious and mystical thinking. This (pre-modern) dimension of Hegel's orientation is played down by writers such as Marcuse, Kojève and Rose and the Hegelian Left generally, who interpret him in a more 'secular' fashion as a critical, progressive social philosopher seeking the realization of Reason in human affairs. However, as Adorno (1973: 405) said: 'If Hegel's absolute was a secularization of the deity, it was still the deity's secularization.' Expressed in Hegel's works in a baroque and forbiddingly complex and plastic manner, are, nevertheless, important insights. To recover the spirit (no pun intended) rather than the letter of Hegel, one needs to break with his archaic metaphysics and appropriate the dynamic, relational and synthesizing force of his work in a sociological fashion and go forward. This truly constitutes the 'end of philosophy'. Marx made the first significant move in this direction, although, as we have seen in Chapter 1, his effort was partial and one-sided and burdened with debilitating traces of what he was seeking to transcend. (I will return to this theme in Chapter 3.)

6.   The Hegelian diagnosis of the modern social condition reveals clearly its theological roots and the tragic consciousness that it embodies at its core. Like Marxists, followers of Hegel attempt to locate orthodox social science or philosophies (e.g. vulgar political economy, positivism, instrumental Reason, Kantian formalism, etc.) as continuously reproduced and determined by the unfree, or partially free, alienated *status quo*. Those paradigms are said to take that social order for granted, or perhaps universalize it as the best of all possible worlds or otherwise reinforce its inequalities, so long as the realm of freedom remains partially recognized and unrealized. For a Hegelian, neo-Kantianism is an expression of 'unfreedom' because it denies the possibility of people truly knowing what is universal, so has no conception of positive, concrete freedom. This diagnosis essentially says that humankind is tragically suspended between the realm of necessity and the realm of freedom. Humans are always on the verge of creating a just society where real social relations will be supposedly transparent and individual and universal consciousness coincide, but always knowing that new conflicts will arise because a total reconciliation of subjectivity and objectivity is never

possible, as Hegel taught. Until the realm of freedom truly arrives its possibility can only be stated abstractly.

> Absolute ethical life is a critique of bourgeois property relations. It may be elusive, but it is never dominant or pre-judged. Minerva cannot impose herself. Her owl can only spread its wings at dusk, and herald the return of Athena, freedom without domination.
>
> (Rose 1981: 91)

7.   The vindication of the whole Hegelian programme ultimately rests on the efficacy and legitimacy of 'speculation'. This cognitive model is, however, by no means unproblematic. Hegelians imply that the thinking of people who do not embrace this aspect of Hegel's philosophy has been determined by the 'reality of unfreedom' into non-speculative, i.e. non-dialectical, forms of thought, such as Kantianism. But one must ask: why has there been wave after wave of neo-Kantians? The answer to this question is mainly a sociological one, in which one would need to take into account the pecularities of German social development and the way in which philosophy was institutionalized in German universities (Collins 1987). But there are two internal, theoretical reasons which suggest themselves. First, these writers may have found Kant rather than Hegel more amenable to the task of delineating the parameters of scientific knowledge at a time of growing scientific specialization in a number of fields. It is not clear how sciences and the specificity of scientific knowledge can be explained and justified from a Hegelian point of view. Second, many people may not have wanted to 'make the transition to the speculative position' and embrace Hegel because they did not believe that Hegel's thought in this respect was respectable. Rightly or wrongly, the move towards speculation and Hegelian phenomenology would have been regarded, if not as a move towards mystical or religious thinking, then certainly towards an unacceptable form of objective idealism, the arguments for which did not convince them.

8.   Put at its baldest, Hegelian 'speculation' is said to articulate the consciousness of the objective context of the alienation of the absolute ethical life under bourgeois socio-economic conditions. But it is surely legitimate to ask: what is the relationship beween the religious or supposed spiritual dimension and the whole cluster of related concepts which Hegel employs, 'absolute/relative ethical life', 'Finite/Infinite', 'Absolute', 'Spirit'? How far does the theological dimension impinge on our acceptance of 'speculation' and the whole grouping of philosophical concepts with which it rises or falls? Is not the whole Hegelian programme only conceivable if one makes a prior theological assumption about the omnipresence of God in the universe and within humankind? As Löwith (1941: 16) observed: 'it is characteristic of Hegelian philosophy, which includes everything in its dualities, that it is a philosophy of the spirit based on the Christian logos, a philosophical theology'. The only way in which Hegel could escape from the straitjacket of the Kantian antinomies was to move towards theology. He wanted to move beyond what he regarded as a dead contrast, deriving from the Enlightenment, between faith and knowledge, which he found built into Kant's philosophy of categoreal limits. Hegel believed that unless we have genuine knowl-

edge of God or the Infinite, then 'neither genuine faith nor true knowledge can exist' (*ibid.*: 330).

9.   A brief look at the Hegelian viewpoint on the basic sociological problem of the relationship between individual and society reveals the nature of the problems we encounter once we go down the Hegelian road, however inviting it may seem in offering solutions to key sociological problems. Hegel's idea of Spirit (the German word is *Geist*, which is etymologically linked with the word 'ghost') is the contradictory entity in which human subjects can identify with each other and still at the same time remain their individual selves, i.e. as non-identical (Rose 1981: 41 and 69). This is the only way, remaining within Hegelianism, that it is possible to conceptualize the social interconnectedness of isolated individual monads, who are invariably placed abstractly over and against a hypostatized 'society' in many versions of orthodox dualistic sociology, as Hegelians rightly point out. But because they have acknowledged a crucial sociological problem does not mean that we should accept their solution. The problem is only 'solved' by the simple assertion, using essentially philosophical–theological categories, of an obscure metaphysical (speculative) unity of finite humans with the Infinite, a unity that is somehow continually recognized and misrecognized at the same time. The task then is to build up more and more illustrations from economics, religion, politics and philosophy (as Hegel did) to show that this recognition/misrecognition structure is continually being reproduced in human societies and shows a historical movement towards progressive reconciliation.

10.   The sociological tradition, on the other hand, would encourage us to look towards the structured character of human interdependencies (Durkheim, Elias) for a more comprehensive, differentiated and empirically founded understanding of this issue. Hegel, and his later followers such as Marcuse, Kojève and Rose, compound the mythology of *Geist* by claiming that (a) people can at some point in history potentially come to know the unity of the two domains (the Finite and the Infinite) in practice as the realm of freedom is concretely ushered in; and (b) prior to that putative state of affairs it is possible for individuals actually to come to know this unity (the Absolute) through a process of the phenomenological recapitulation of modes of experience.

11.   In my view, the alternative to this quasi-theological programme is to break with this tradition and develop a sociological model of the emergent and developing reality of society as a level of integration *sui generis*, amongst others (Elias 1987a). Such a model of integrative levels, which is amenable to empirical testing and confirmation, will replace Hegel's metaphysical unity of the Finite and the Infinite. And empirical research programmes, producing publicly available reliable knowledge, will render the quasi-mystical Hegelian model of phenomenological recapitulation redundant. At the same time, sociology can tell us how philosophers like Kant and Hegel came to see the world as they did and how this kind of philosophizing has been perpetuated within academic establishments. Already we are reframing the issues here. Philosophical argumentation within the Hegelian tradition, on the other hand, unintendedly gives credence to the individualism found, for example, in utilitarianism and neo-liberalism, which it was otherwise designed to counter. It does so by simply asserting that modern economic individuals (taken as given) are both social *and* divine. Philosophical

treatments of these matters contain no theoretical device to explain how the modern experience of self-enclosed individuality, which undergirds so much of the ego-centred European philosophical tradition, as well as political and economic theory, arose in the first place. It is taken for granted, or at best regarded as not a philosophical matter.

11.   The wider issue here is that the whole social science enterprise (particularly sociology) historically emerged in dialogue not only with philosophical but also with theological views of the world, which included speculations about the 'universal' or eternal significance of humans. Sociologically speaking, we can see that in the case of Hegel, his work has its origins in the mainstream of Protestant theology. Arising out of the conflicts between Church and State in his time, he was trying theologically to reconcile the Catholic idea of a divine *Logos* existing in nature with a Protestant notion of God alienated from nature and in whom belief was a personal, individual matter. Hegel explicitly described himself as the culmination of both traditions and was known in his time as the philosopher *par excellence* who had reconciled philosophy and theology (Löwith 1941: 14 ff.). He had also translated the works of Renaissance neo-Platonic mystics, from whom he had derived his central speculative notion of the 'union of contraries'[5] and the monistic coincidence of the Finite and the Infinite in all things (Wind 1967: 192–196 and 220–31). In their time Hegel and Schelling were extolled as the foremost interpreters of neo-Platonic texts (*ibid.*: 193).

12.   From a sociological point of view, it is significant that Hegel says that God cannot be extrinsic to human affairs or nature and at the same time he (Hegel) never allows finite temporal concerns vainly to place themselves above the Godhead. Nor does he envisage a complete reconciliation of the gulf which the sin of man has introduced between himself and God's benevolence (what Rose calls 'unfreedom'). The point is that some of the character and paradoxes of Hegel's thought are traceable to the incredible balancing act he was trying to perform between theological traditions, in the context of the emerging abstract bourgeois property rights of his time, which had the effect of reinforcing the feeling of isolation of individuals. It was imperative for Hegel to find some way of regarding the emergent economic and political individuals of his time as *simultaneously* united with God, thus reconciling Romantic-conservative and bourgeois tendencies (Mannheim 1927: 162–3). The Hegelian paradox that we are condemned to think the Absolute to some extent abstractly, acknowledging an element of *Sollen* (Ought) in such thinking, has its origins in the *historically specific* set of antinomies which Hegel's dynamic thinking was attempting, with great ingenuity to be sure, to reconcile. Our evaluation of this paradox and the relevance of Hegel's synthesis to contemporary sociology have to be seen in this light.

13.   Hegelian 'speculation' creates a self-confirming philosophy. Hegelians claim to be arguing from a phenomenologically achieved, speculative, absolute standpoint and they further assume, like most philosophers, that sociological paradigms must possess philosophical underpinnings or make philosophical assumptions. These paradigms will include examples of 'metacritique' such as the work of Durkheim, Mannheim or Habermas, whereby culture, society, social situation or *Dasein* become the 'quasi-transcendental' presuppositions behind the universal a priori categories. From the Hegelian point of view, all other

philosophies must fall short of the achieved speculative level of absolute knowledge. In other words, the range of penetration of Kantian (and other non-'speculative') philosophy cannot on this view be an empirical question, because its extent has been philosophically assumed in advance. Indeed, that has been, and will remain, the historical fate of philosophy so long as the realm of 'unfreedom' associated with bourgeois property relations exists. This tragic Hegelian projection is shot through with mythology, although I do not doubt the integrity and serious-ness of its exponents. It runs entirely counter to the argument I am advancing, which is that Hegelian dialectics is the furthest point it is possible to reach within the philosophical tradition and that its advances have already been incorporated and reformulated on to another level as part of the sociological revolution in knowledge. To return to it in the twentieth century in its pure form is to fall back in a singularly mystifying fashion some way behind the sociological ground that has already been gained.

Metacritique or socio-genesis?

The influence of Kantianism has been extensive in sociology and Hegelians have made a useful contribution in pointing this out, but they can only explain its tenacity and persistence through a resort to the myth of the fate of human unfreedom which is held to determine the entire character of our perception. Moreover, Kantian assumptions do not pervade all of sociology and social psychology. What of G.H. Mead? Pareto? Garfinkel? Spencer? Norbert Elias? The latter's figurational approach presents difficulties for the Hegelian critique which, in relation to some other mainstream sociological approaches, does, however, on some issues, make some valid points and suggestions, as we saw in the second para-graph of the previous section.

Elias makes central to his inquiries an explicit attempt to transcend exactly the sociological individualism and the antinomies that Rose accurately locates in much orthodox sociology (Elias 1978a, 1987a). Elias offers an alternative theory of society to Hegel's political economy and Rose's Marxian sociology of economic contradictions to explain the development of experienced individuality in European societies (Elias 1978a, 1982). Elias also makes the historical transforma-tion of the whole personality the centrepiece of his analysis of Western 'rationality', through the notion of the social regulation of affect. Hence, he has *already* made central the dimension of desire, said to be neglected in Kantian soci-ology. Moreover, Elias's sociology also forswears philosophical justification of, or inspiration for, its programme, whether or not from within the frameworks of validity and/or values.

The question then becomes: is Elias's sociogenetic paradigm yet another example of 'metacritique'? I think not. In fact, for Elias, neo-Kantian metacritique constituted a *point of departure* for the development of his sociological outlook (see Kilminster & Wouters 1995; and Chapter 4). This suggests the possibility not of a Hegelian sociology to replace the dominant Kantian sociologies, but a sociological framework which goes beyond *both* of them. Indeed, it is my argument that this constitutes the profound burden of the sociological tradition. The programmatic implications of this realization will be explored in the subsequent chapters.

3

MARX'S THEORY OF KNOWLEDGE AS A PARTIAL BREAKTHROUGH[1]

Zeal without knowledge is a runaway horse.

(Old English proverb)

The theory and practice dualism

In everyday usage, the opposition between theory and practice is used in constructions such as: in theory everyone should have a television licence, but in practice not everyone has. Or: in theory there is equality of opportunity, but in practice there is inequality of condition. The terms are also commonly used to refer to the body of principles of proper procedure in a profession, trade or craft, as opposed to their practical application. A preliminary glance at these meanings in English reveals two important features which will be relevant to the later discussion.

1. Implied in virtually all uses of the dualism is a distinction between practical, lived social life as opposed to abstract ideas, or perhaps action (practice) versus reflection or thinking (theory). This feature points to the opposition of theory and practice and its derivatives, being a product of the same stage of social development (the seventeenth century) to which also corresponded the dualistic metaphysics of rationalistic European philosophy after Descartes. A look at the *Shorter Oxford Dictionary* confirms this.[2] That tradition of philosophy also operates with distinctions of a fundamentally similar kind to theory and practice: mind and matter, consciousness and being, thought and reality, and ideality and materiality, around which polarities epistemological and ontological debate revolves. (The antithesis theory and practice is also used specifically in philosophy.)

Its level of generality means that a number of theoretical problems, social activities and social phenomena can be accommodated under the dualism. It is very flexible in its application. For example, Marxist philosophers often lump together under the term 'theory' both sides of the sociological enterprise, i.e. theory and empirical observations; and 'practice' for them refers loosely to any social activity, directly political or not. For the Greek philosophers, by contrast, *theoria* and *praxis* were not separate spheres of thought and action but different walks of life, called by Aristotle the contemplative and the political or practical (Lobkowicz 1967: 3–5).

2. Modern usages sometimes, though not always, also carry a connotation of ideality on the side of theory, which may bespeak the same origin. We find this

idealization in formulations of theory such as Max Weber's ideal types or Boyle's law of gases, both of which refer to ideal states of affairs in society or experimental conditions which may not appear in empirical reality (practice). Another kind of idealization occurs when, for example, the opposition of theory to practice refers to principles or rules of proper procedure and their application, where there is often a strong implication present that practice *should be* congruent with theory. Here a state of play between theory and practice is implied which *ought* to exist.

In contemporary sociological and political theory the opposition of theory and practice refers to a number of aspects of the relationship between theories of various kinds and social life. It can refer, for example, to the relationships between the various sciences (particularly the social sciences) and their 'objects', between scientific knowledge and its necessary practical applications and broadly between social science and politics (Fay 1975: ch. 1; Bryant 1995: ch. 5).

Many Marxist writings since Lenin have attempted to unite those three levels in a theory of the total society with a practical intent. This theory is intended to inform practical political activity to change the complex of social institutions which make the theory itself possible, in this way abolishing the theory in practice. That theory and practice in this sense can inseparably inform each other in this way within the politics of the labour movement, was one meaning in the former Soviet Marxism of the phrase 'the unity of theory and practice' (Lachs 1967: 90–2; Meyer 1954: 104–7; Wetter 1958: 256–7), although Marx himself does not use this phrase.

Following one interpretation of Marx's *Theses on Feuerbach*, Marxists have assumed that if a theory relating to society is accurate, it will be transcended (abolished) in the mass practical political activity undertaken informed by it. In order to try to conceptualize such putative moments of transition when a theory apparently becomes real, some writers in this field have adopted the Greek word *praxis* in order to refer to revolutionary *praxis*, although it is clear that this concept cannot be a category of empirical, sociological enquiry (Kilminster 1992d). Conversely, if the theory is untrue, or otherwise flawed, then the activity undertaken will demonstrate its inadequacies, necessitating the elaboration of further theory, which will suggest further action, and so on. Karl Mannheim said that this Marxist-Leninist view of the relationship between theory and practice 'bears the imprint of an advanced discussion of the problem'. By this he meant that a great deal of past experience and discussion were embedded in it. He summarized the process as follows:

> (1) Theory is a function of reality; (2) This theory leads to a certain kind of action; (3) Action changes the reality, or in the case of failure, forces us to a revision of the previous theory. The change in the actual situation brought about by the act gives rise to a new theory.
>
> (Mannheim 1929: 112–13)

Because of that practical (political) intent, exponents of Marxist theory have spent a good deal of time trying to demonstrate the implicit practical intent embodied in other theories which do not explicitly have the same practical orientation as their own, e.g. those informed by positivism or hermeneutics. These implicit practical applications are then related to the function that such theories perform in society. Habermas, for example, has described his own aim as to develop a theory of society with a practical intention and 'to delimit its status with respect to theories of different origins' (Habermas 1974: 1). For all these reasons, it is more accurate to refer to Marx's theory, and many of the later Marxist versions, as a practical–theoretical framework. As Habermas explains:

> Historical materialism aims at achieving an explanation of social evolution which is so comprehensive that it embraces the interrelationships of the theory's own origins and application. The theory specifies the conditions under which reflection on the history of our species by members of this species themselves has become objectively possible; and at the same time it names those to whom this theory is addressed, who then with its aid can gain enlightenment about their emancipatory role in the process of history. The theory occupies itself with reflection on the interrelationships of its origin and with anticipation of those of its application, and thus sees itself as the necessary catalytic moment within the social complex of life which it analyses; and this complex it analyses as integral interconnections of compulsions, from the viewpoint of the possible sublation – resolution and abolition – of all this.
>
> (Habermas 1974: 1–2)

In the subsequent sections I will go back to Marx himself to bring out, from the point of view of a sociological theory of knowledge, the positive and negative consequences of the role of politics in the formation of his theory of society as well as the more remote and deeper presuppositions embedded in his work.

The primacy of the practical

That there is a significant relationship between practical social life and the theories of various kinds which people develop within it, was legacy of the Enlightenment which was first given a systematic social scientific formulation by Marx. He enshrined it in his theory of 'social being' and consciousness or base and superstructure. It is epitomized by his frequent inversions whereby he would talk of explaining the theory by the practice and not the practice by the theory or urge his readers not to look everywhere in history for the category but to explain the category from real history (Marx & Engels 1845a: 50 and *passim*). It was an insight developed in secular opposition to idealist philosophers and theologians who seemed to be suggesting that infinite, spiritual consciousness was, if not the motor of social and natural reality, then certainly its ultimate level. In his time, particularly in the German context, Marx had to fight for the contrary view against those who thought of practical affairs as secondary or vulgar.

The conception of the primacy of practical, social conditions in society and its entire determinacy in explaining human thinking and action, was therefore for Marx what Paul Tillich (1933: 114) called a *Kampfbegriff*, a polemical concept born in argument, debate and controversy. It had, obviously, important political resonances. But from the point of view of today, Marx's declaration in the *German*

Ideology (Marx & Engels 1845a: 31) that 'The premises from which we begin are not arbitrary ones . . . . but real premises . . . the real individuals, their activity and the material conditions under which they live' is a sociological truism. But this characterization does not denigrate Marx. By a process of historical transmission and sedimentation (not solely from Marx, although he is an important exemplar) this fundamental, secular starting point for a social science is today built into sociology and historiography as an assumption, hardly even in need of being made explicit. Indeed, it may even be said to have become part of the modern mentality (Remmling 1967).

Hence, no secular school of social science would deny the general principle of the primacy of the structure of practical, human social relations as the sole locus for the adequate explanation of the ways in which people come to develop ideas about those relations, human relations in general and about the natural world. Today we do not have to ask the question 'Is human thought determined by the structure of social relations?', but rather the key question is exactly *how* it is, as an empirical question. The trajectory of what Mannheim (1932–3) called a 'sociology of the mind' since Marx, has been that that basic insight has been systematically differentiated and empirical enquiries undertaken into *kinds* of correspondences between consciousness and practical social life.

The young Marx's remarks on knowledge and action in the *Economic and Philosophic Manuscripts*, on the other hand, were pervaded by a utopian vision of a self-determining humankind, creating in practice a more or less total reconciliation of subjectivity and objectivity and of philosophy and social life.

> Subjectivism and objectivism, spiritualism and materialism, activity and suffering, only lose their antithetical character, and thus their existence, as such antitheses in the social condition; . . . the resolution of the *theoretical* antitheses is *only* possible *in a practical way*, by virtue of the practical energy of men. Their resolution is therefore by no means merely a problem of knowledge, but a *real* problem of life, which *philosophy* could not solve precisely because it conceived this problem as *merely* a theoretical one.
>
> (Marx 1844: 102 (italics in original))

Not surprisingly, Marx was not interested in which relations between 'thought' and 'reality' might remain the same whilst others might change as the result of specific forms of social action, nor in which were more readily subject to being altered by specified forms of practical activity on various levels (see Kilminster 1979: ch. 2; and 1992d). Because of the domination of his thinking and acting by politics, Marx only touches on the epistemological issues incidentally, often in brilliant, undeveloped asides about the sociological character of natural science knowledge (e.g. Marx & Engels 1845a: 28, 57ff.). Generally, though, Marx's formulation of the sociological problem of knowledge is rather undiscriminating and he either subsumes the issues into politics or is deflected from their discussion by his preoccupation with political matters (legitimate and principled though that commitment was). I am simply making a longer-term sociological judgement with the benefit of hindsight.

'Explaining the theory by practice', as another way of referring to one aspect of the sociology of knowledge, entails sometimes demonstrating empirically that groups of people have been concealing, dissimulating, justifying or in various other ways legitimating their activity, especially to their own advantage. These are the kinds of connnections that most interested Marx. But the connection between consciousness and social activity is not necessarily always of this kind. As Elias (1971) has shown, once one makes the necessary differentiations, then the socio-logical approach to explaining the genesis of thought forms need not entail that one asserts relativistically the ideological character of all knowledge, in the sense of all knowledge being reducible to its justifying or rationalizing function in given cases.

This method has an important advantage. Traditionally Marxists have assumed that if a theory is true then it will be transcended (abolished) by the practice under-taken on its basis; and if it is not true, then the extent of its error will be revealed by the practice it initiates. This notion lends itself, however, to powerful political groups legislating by fiat on the status of the state of affairs that has ensued from a phase of action of one kind or another. Or, conversely, consistent with this concep-tion, powerful groups can easily claim, as a way of legitimating their power advantage, to have special access to a 'correct' theory of social dynamics prior to its supposed realization in various kinds of practical activity (see Kilminster 1979: part 2). In other words, the doctrine of successively testing theories in action can have an ideological function. A sociological analysis, however, can potentially better enable us to understand whether either of those two kinds of legitimation is occurring in given cases, something that relying on the (Marxian) self-descriptions of the groups concerned would not.

Marx's synthesis: the practical core

My contention is that there are fundamental, but historically produced, patterns of thinking and assumptions present in Marx's theory which shape in advance for later adherents the ways in which society is grasped and, consequently, the way in which the theory is held to relate to practical social life. At the same time, he made some decisive moves in the historical overcoming of philosophy. As a preliminary characterization, I find helpful the time-honoured formulation that Marx's social science was a synthesis of English political economy, French utopian socialism and German philosophy (Lenin 1913). Political economy provided the social scientific concepts from the most developed social science at Marx's disposal, and socialism the vision of a classless society of human association and the planful cooperation of labour. A 'secularized' version of the Hegelian dialectic united the first two traditions in the notion of the historical necessity of socialism, social scientifically shown to be built into the structure of history.

From the point of view of epistemology, I think the significance of Marx's use of the category of practice is as follows. At the historical stage at which he stood, Marx inherited the philosophical vocabulary of traditional European episte-mology, mediated to him via the legacy of Kant and Hegel. Following in the wake of Newtonian science, traditional epistemology had a particular cast in which, polarized into rationalists and empiricists, philosophers from Descartes onwards debated the foundations of knowledge in terms of the two sides of cognition: the individual thinking mind and what it experiences. Debates thus circulated around the issues of how the human mind comes to know what it does and what part it and the 'external', mechanical, world, known to humans through the senses, respectively play in the creation of ideas. Some of the characteristic epistemological dualisms of the tradition included subject/object, thought/reality, reason/experience, the intellect versus the senses, the ideal and the real, and consciousness and being.

For Marx, the various positions taken in these debates are epitomized by the polar doctrines of idealism and materialism. Kant and Hegel had both insisted in their different ways that consciousness was active in shaping its perception of the world. In the *Theses on Feuerbach* (Marx 1845) Marx mentions that idealists had stressed this side but says that idealism played down sensuous reality. Materialism, on the other hand, stressed that experience was the final arbiter in assessing the validity of knowledge and materiality the fundamental stratum of reality, but the doctrine lacked an active element. This meant that materialists tended to regard the mind as passive in the process of cognition.

Utilizing the category of practice, meaning mundane human social activity, Marx argues (to use the formulation of Schmidt 1971: 114) against materialism in an idealist fashion and against idealism in a materialist fashion.[3] He sees their unity as continuously constituted in practical activity. For Marx, there is no point in reducing cognition to either of its material or ideal poles because both sides are, and always have been, in an active relation in human practical activity. Objective reality is ineradicably subjectively constituted through practice since conscious, labouring humankind is part of nature. Hence, nature inevitably has a socially imprinted character and an autonomous role in human affairs at the same time. Human beings only encounter, and hence know, the world through their active contact with it. As Kolakowski (1971: 75) has put it, for Marx, 'Active contact with the resistance of nature creates knowing man and nature as his object at one and the same time.' In the secondary literature this world-constituting active sense contact takes one meaning of the term *praxis*. Interestingly, though, Marx is unable to carry through this Hegelian drive away from ontological reductionism and his mature social scientific theory remains burdened with the dualistic ontology of traditional metaphysics. The sociological theory of base and superstructure, or the determination of social consciousness by 'social being', falls back into the old static dualism, implicitly assuming that the reified economic base and the superstructure of ideology are two separate entities.

As has been pointed out by many philosophers (Kolakowski 1971; Bloch 1971; Rotenstreich 1965), Marx's practical theory of truth, even if he himself never made it explicit, effectively meant that the classical definition of truth (agreement of concept with reality) was thrown into question. Marx said that if the correspondence of thought and reality, or knowledge and the world, was ongoingly maintained by human practical activity in ordinary life, then the relationship between them was, therefore, subject to being changed by practical activity. In other words, the question of truth as the correspondence between thought and reality could not be settled entirely in theory – it was partly a practical question.[4] Since Marx was talking about human practical activity here in a social sense, then the practical aspect of the problem of knowledge as he saw it inevitably began to shade over into politics. Indeed, it was partly Marx's overwhelming political commitments that gave him the impetus to achieve these pathbreaking, though partial, insights.

Hence, Marx's (often unpublished, and mostly unsystematic and polemical) ruminations about epistemology in the traditional categories of idealism and materialism were not intended as contributions to that field. The whole point of his discussions of materialism and idealism was that for him various positions defined within that polarity carried with them (once one has switched to regarding socio-natural reality as actively constituted in practice) by their very nature, practical *political* implications. The idea that consciousness was cognitively active in real, practical, productive activity, suggested that people could actively move to change the world that their active, practical cognition constituted. This was something that a passive materialist theory could not theorize. Indeed, adherence to such a one-sided theory actually justified a kind of political practice by its epistemological exclusions. For example, the kind of materialist theory that stated that ideas were simply a reflection of the circumstances and environment surrounding people, implied politically that if one changed people's circumstances then they as people would correspondingly be changed as well. Such a view lent itself to élitist forms of utopian socialism. Similarly, Marx links materialism with the individualism of bourgeois liberalism: 'the highest point attained by that materialism which only observes the world . . . is the observation of particular individuals and of civil society' (Marx 1845: 84). It had been long known that materialism was an individualistic doctrine. But Marx ingeniously connects this assumption with the individualism associated with the emerging economic and political liberalism of his time.

In the 1840s, when Marx was most concerned to develop a unified theory of society and history which would inform politics, Left Hegelians like Bruno Bauer were rabidly anti-liberal through what they all called 'critique' (see Stepelevich 1983). This Hegelian exercise entailed the critical comparison of some aspect of society with its ideal, or perfect potentiality, which was embedded within it. They would critically compare, for example, a given particular set of judicial institutions with the pure, universal category of Justice, of which the institutions were only an imperfect embodiment; or, say, a particular constitution with the universal idea of Democracy. Naturally, against a criterion of such absolute critical power, in all cases these institutions would be found wanting. At the height of his own commitment to this kind of criticism, Marx called for 'The reckless critique of all that is' (from a letter to Feuerbach, 1843, in McLellan 1971: 80).

Later, however, Marx is scathing about the pretentiousness and political impotence of the Left Hegelian critics. This is reflected in the full title of the book which he wrote jointly with Engels in 1845: *The Holy Family, or Critique of Critical Criticism: Against Bruno Bauer and Company* (Marx & Engels 1845b).[5] Marx sees this critical procedure as ineffective verbal radicalism only, and enjoins 'practical-critical activity' (Marx 1845: 82).[6] This compound phrase, which he puts in inverted commas, suggests a fusion of the mundane and the practical with the more lofty reflections of a specifically Hegelian critical kind. It suggests that what he has in mind (although he does not develop the point very far and we have to infer this from the stage of development of the discussions of the issues which is presupposed in his reflections), is not just comparing – on the theoretical plane of ethics – social reality with what it ideally ought to be, but actually trying in practice to *make* reality accord with what it ought to be.

Such a conception implies a considerable knowledge of society to determine areas where action to bring about changes could be strategically targeted, and a degree of systematic and rational appraisal of possibilities. In various phases of action, although this is not spelled out by Marx, presumably the 'ought' postulates of philosophical ethics would be transcended (abolished) in practice. This is, I think, the force of Marx's dictum 'You cannot transcend philosophy without realising it and you cannot realise it without transcending it' (Marx 1843: 121–2). He is, in effect, talking about creating a society which no longer requires ethics because Is and Ought would have become one. Here Marx is probably stating in a different way an idea common amongst many of the Left Hegelians. As August von Cieszkowski declared: 'Only the act can prevail fully over the ought' (cited in Stepelevich 1983: 84).

In a word, Marx tries to unite epistemology and ethics by yoking together the traditional epistemological doctrines of idealism and materialism with the great ideologies of the nineteenth century – liberalism, conservatism and socialism. The result is, he hoped, a more comprehensive synthesis, epistemologically and ethically, the practical *political* implications of which refer not to the individualistic bourgeois society but to the whole of humankind: 'the standpoint of the new materialism is human society or social humanity' (Marx 1845: 85). So, for Marx, humankind makes its own social world, which it constitutes by its practical activity, which therefore means that it can potentially consciously change it in various ways. Under conditions of social class-fettered historical alienation, however, this constituting process has become lost to consciousness, exacerbated by social life under advanced stages of the division, and alienation, of labour.

The point is that for Marx questions of knowledge and questions of ethics are to be fed into a scientifically informed politics on behalf of the current major underprivileged class. The task of politics is to hasten the historical process towards the idealized state of socialism, which is held to be immanent in its tendency. What others think merely *ought* to be (a just society) is actually embodied in what *is* as its *telos*, as Hegel taught. It reaches real, historical maturity whether people have ideals about it or not.[7] 'Communism is for us not a state of affairs which is to be established, an ideal to which reality will have to adjust itself. We call communism the real movement which abolishes the present state of things' (Marx & Engels 1845a: 48).

Another way of putting these matters which will bring out the issues from a different angle, is to see Marx's programme, following Rotenstreich (1977: 58–82), as seeking in practical politics the unity of the philosophical realms of theoretical and practical reason. These remarks develop further the analysis of Hegel in the previous chapter. In attempting famously to reconcile the 'starry heavens above me and the moral law within me', Kant had separated nature and practical reason (ethics) or, more broadly, science and morality. Both theoretical and practical reason were spontaneous aspects of Reason, the latter being the domain of ethical imperatives, a practical sphere separate and alongside the reality of nature. Hegel, however, claimed, against Kant, as we saw in the last chapter, that the world (both finite and infinite) is knowable because it is inherently rational. Reason has complete spontaneity on the intellectual plane as Kant had said, but this only made reality knowable because the object was the objective embodiment of Reason anyway.

The Hegelian embodiment of Reason in the world meant that it could be demonstrated that history was its gradual teleological unfolding in various spheres as determinations of the Idea. But it also meant that practical reason (ethics) could not be maintained as a separate sphere on the Kantian model, because, like Reason in general, it must also be embodied in the world as well. So, for Hegel, there was no need to assure the actualization of Reason in practical life by the creation of a separate Kantian ethical sphere because the level of speculation in his system assured their unity in the world. As Gramsci (1971: 219) later put it: 'Reality is ethical.' This position constituted the standard post-Hegelian wisdom on these issues, and was part of the philosophical culture which Marx took for granted. All of the stages in the complex elaborations of these issues prior to Marx are presupposed in his starting point, even if he was unaware of some of them and could never have put the matter in this way.

For Marx, however, the Young Hegelians could only put to real people in real societies the 'moral postulate of exchanging their present consciousness for human, critical . . . consciousness' (Marx & Engels 1845a: 30; see also 276, 282 and 290). In other words, there was no passage from the level of knowledge achieved through Hegelian speculation to the *practical* realization of the unity of Reason in the world. The Young Hegelians were the '*staunchest conservatives*' (*ibid.*: 30, my emphasis), declares the politically conscious Marx. For him, implicitly, society is the arena for the practical actualization of Reason on the two dimensions. This translates into the proposition (expressed as the development of the forces of production outstripping their necessary relations of production) that in practice people must realize the inherent rational potentiality for social organization, development and progress spontaneously bequeathed by history to the bourgeois epoch. It is this potential that is fettered by archaic social class relations, necessitating revolutionary change.

Marx's theory of history as a series of progressive socio-economic formations is predicated on the assumption that they have been mediated by their necessary *telos* of socialism as the end to the alienated 'pre-history' of humankind. Indeed, the Hegelian philosophy of history is seen by Marx as a 'metaphysically travestied' (Marx & Engels 1845b: 164) version of what is a real, scientifically describable, historical process. The forces and relations of production dialectic in Marx parallels Hegel's categoreal unity of content and form, whereby it is the developing *content* (forces of production) that determines changes of *form* (relations of production) towards the self-development of the Idea (socialism). (All this is working in Marx's thought at a very deep level of presuppositions.) Once Marx has translated the Hegelian conception of history as the embodiment and realization of Reason (both theoretical and practical) into the terms of a socio-economic theory of development, then the theory articulating the process and a moral indictment of society were for him necessarily the same thing. On this arguably authentic Marxian view, communism did not and does not require a separate ethical system or other moral justification.

The theoretical inertia of the Marxian tradition

1.   I have been arguing that the use of the category of practice in Marx's synthesis enabled him to effect a social scientific advance of a profound kind over the philosophical paradigm he inherited. However, his political animus, though paradoxically providing the driving force behind his break with philosophy, combined with metaphysical hangovers in his thinking to limit his breakthrough to a partial one. The framework of practical–theoretical social science handed down to us by Marx was thus permeated with the traditional philosophy in a dialogue with which it had been forged, both epistemologically and ethically. Marx reconciles idealism and materialism on the plane of social practice but still refers to his new position by the metaphysical term 'materialism'. The dualistic social theory of base and superstructure also lapses into the being/consciousness polarity of traditional metaphysics; and the notion of active subjective cognition indissolubly constituting its objects in practice is still a resolution of the subject–object problem that remains within the dualism itself.

2.   Marx's attempt to bring together the traditional antithetical philosophical doctrines of idealism and materialism with socialism, conservatism and liberalism in a theory that would link epistemology and ethics in practical politics, represented a specific attempt at synthesis. It clearly bears the marks of the stage of social and scientific development at which it was elaborated and has a very marked political undertone, which leads to epistemological overstatements and the exclusion of key scientific issues. It has also established for later generations who draw on the Marxist tradition the spurious correlation that the espousal of various philosophical doctrines about the character of ideas defined in terms of sense perception (such as materialism and idealism), derived from the superseded European epistemological tradition, automatically ensures specific political outcomes for their advocates.

3.   Like Comte and Saint-Simon, amongst others, Marx was grappling with the important problems of how a theory of society was related to human social development, its subject-matter, and what the practical implications of types of sociological theory were. He shared with them the Enlightenment view that an adequate theory of society can facilitate the practical steering of social processes for the benefit of humankind. Without good theory, action is blind. Because of the stage at which he stood, however, he could only articulate the problem employing the traditional epistemological vocabulary available to him, synthesized with political economy and the great nineteenth-century ideologies. The epistemology had been a product of individualistic philosophers ruminating upon the implications of Newtonian science for human knowledge and the political economy and the ideologies related to the stage of economic development and corresponding political integration that Marx was living through. Today, however, we have to ask ourselves whether we can any longer relevantly pose the problem of the relation between theories of various kinds and practical social life (traditionally identified as issues of theory and practice) in those terms. If not, then the problem has to be thought out in a different way.

4.   Marx was only able to incorporate ethics into his practical–theoretical framework by paying the price of teleology. He effectively translated the Hegelian

conception of the historical realization of Reason embodied in the world into a historical, dialectical progression of socio-economic epochs preparing humankind for the ideal state of socialism. To repeat: he wrote the utopian ideal of socialist equality, freedom and human cooperative association, which others merely thought desirable, or for the lack of which they indicted bourgeois society in moral terms, into the real movement of history and claimed this process to be scientifically demonstrable. Later on, in the 1920s, it was the removal from Marx's theory (indeed from any theory) of this supposition that social reality was inherently meaningful and rational in its tendency towards what society ought to be, which gave rise to the problem for Marxists of how to re-incorporate this ethical level into a social science that had been denuded of the principle of historical necessity. Max Weber's work was influential here.

5.   In many forms of social scientific enquiry today it is common to find a pre-Hegelian separation of matters of fact from questions of value, of Is and Ought, science and morality and factual and normative questions, enshrined in the different disciplines of sociology and social philosophy. The same separation is embodied in the positivists' exclusion of value judgements from valid knowledge. These separations are not only regarded as logically or methodologically sound, but also as providing a bulwark against the abuse of the supposed Marxian fusion of Is and Ought by bureaucratic socialist élites. They have sometimes justified directive and totalitarian political practices by claiming that their policies are not only based on a correct scientific analysis of socio-economic development, but are also, in virtue of that fact, *morally* right.

6.   It is significant that in eastern Europe prior to 1989, philosophy often performed the function of social criticism under conditions of generalized censorship, central control and repression. The writings of authors such as Heller, Féher, Markovic, Bauman and Kolakowski are haunted by the ghosts of these experiences. Intellectuals and dissidents developed philosophies of value, philosophical anthropology and 'critical' sociologies, all ultimately designed to develop criteria for indicting the societies controlled by the all-pervasive state bureaucratic élites (see Kilminster & Varcoe 1996b). Under these conditions Hegelian philosophy, for example, is a potentially powerful political tool because the central idea of the unity of the relative and absolute ethical life enables one to expose the spurious ideological claims of the bureaucratic rulers about the alleged existence of true socialism in those countries.

7.   Returning to Marx's theory itself: it defines methodologically the relevant theoretical problems, shapes the way in which theories are seen as related to social life, moulds in advance the parameters of sociological enquiry and delimits in a characteristic way the questions that can be put to society. The inherently dualistic character of the theory has inevitably led to the insoluble problem of how to resolve the reciprocal effectivity of 'ideal' and 'material' factors in the social process, 'material' having been linked by Marx with economic activity. This characteristic has thus *structured* later inquiries into scholastic adaptations and sophistications of the base and superstructure model. But these elaborations still reproduce the fundamentally metaphysical structure of the theory and thus remain trapped within its basic antinomy, trying to correlate two entities which do not exist.

8.   Even though the practical questions asked by the later Marxist practitioners related closely to the political and economic circumstances they lived through, the ways in which they interpreted their society and its problems were determined by the framework's basic assumptions. It induced its adherents into asking questions such as: what is preventing 'the revolution' from taking place, given that the level of socio-economic development seems or has seemed apposite? What are the cultural mechanisms whereby working-class consciousness is systematically dismantled? Is there a substitute proletariat to be seen? Arguably, a factor in the genesis of the contemporary 'postmodern' sensibility (particularly in France) was the disillusionment felt by many Marxists that their revolutionary hopes had been dashed after the 1968 events. My point is that that radical disillusionment – and the theoretical overreactions that went along with it – did not occur so profoundly in those who had not viewed those events through Marxian spectacles in the first place.

9.   Against the proposition that political activity should be geared towards the total goal of the revolutionary victory of the proletariat which will usher in socialism, all other activity towards, for example, minimizing social inequality or social constraints can only be described as reformism. Revolution *versus* reform is a politicized antinomy which flows directly from a theory that assumes that practical activity can hasten the arrival of an idealized state of communal equality said to be embodied in the historical process. On this view, the vital issue of *what can and cannot* realistically be changed in society is systematically suppressed.[8]

10.   The two examples of Adorno and Habermas will concretize my general point about the inertia of the theory. In both cases we see the fascinating interplay between the social developments they are responding to and the presuppositions of the theory they are bringing to bear on them. Adorno justified his philosophical quietism after the late 1930s because the historical opportunity of the emancipation of humankind by the revolutions of the proletariat (the realization of philosophy) had, he claimed, been 'missed' (Adorno 1973: 3). As a result, he was condemned to maintain an abstract, 'negative' critique of society which shows the existing order as perennially capable of becoming something other than it is. This philosophizing keeps alive the generalized possibility of human emancipation. This strategy still assumed, however, that 'the revolution' *should have* occurred and that *if it had done* so it would have liberated humankind. It therefore took seriously, as a real possibility, social consequences predicted by the mythological strand embedded in Marx's thought, i.e. the practical fusion of Is and Ought in a future world of human association for which history had been preparing humankind. Once one has made that assumption, then its non-arrival leads to the conviction that the idealized sequence is 'more real' than the empirical reality and something to which reality must ultimately adjust itself. But if it is held that the moment to realize human emancipation has been lost, then we have in this position a kind of theological picture that in the present conditions humankind is living, if not in a fallen state, then certainly in purgatory. The result is tragic pessimism.

11.   In the early work of Habermas, which was still recognizably 'critical' in this sense, we can see how he operates within the structure of the Marxist tradition and takes up from his mentor Adorno the redefinition of the problems of theory and practice after Stalinism, fascism and the thesis of the disenchantment of the

world elaborated by philosophers in modern times (Heinemann 1953; Steiner 1978: chs II and III). The notion of the ideal speech situation can serve again to illustrate the transcendental structure of much sociology and social criticism. Built into all individual speech acts, Habermas argues, is the assumption that one can be understood by potential interlocutors who are equal partners in discourse. This is a transcendental presupposition for all communication. This idealized state of affairs (the ideal speech situation) is no mere abstract utopia, for it is partly present now, in society, in every individual speech act. It is, therefore, not an arbitrary postulate of a total community of equality, for it is already, as it were, partly realized. The postulate thus provides a critical yardstick for objectively evaluating given societies as only providing conditions of 'distorted communication' compared with those of the ideal speech situation, which those instances of distorted communication also *are*. Habermas's work represents a hybrid of Kantian transcendentalism and Left Hegelian critique in a modern guise. The ideal speech situation corresponds to Hegel's *telos* of self-knowing Reason embodied as universality in all particularity, which was reworked by Marx as the utopian tendency of history. Habermas has tried to ground more systematically Adorno's Hegelian idea of the 'utopian moment of the object' and his crusade against 'identity thinking' as the means of negatively criticizing what *is* in terms of what it could ideally *become* (Adorno 1973).

12.   The point is that the Marxist tradition itself, as adapted to twentieth-century conditions, provides the framework that has posed the problems and the parameters of their solutions. Critical theory and critical sociology reproduce the Marxist social and economic theory of history but without the original agent, the proletariat, and without the original catalyst, the party. The result is that the 'critical' theory remaining after those excisions must necessarily have to replace the old *telos* of history with an idealized state of affairs which *cannot be realized*.[9] Two main reasons for this can be distinguished.

(i)   *The socialist utopia cannot any longer credibly be justified as the outcome of historical necessity*. The critical theorists of contemporary times are effectively post-Weberians who, like many of the existentialists, believe that since the Middle Ages European societies have become increasingly depleted of inherent religious meaning. After the 'death of God', the Marxist concept of historical necessity only reproduces Christian theology in a secular form, with socialism taking the place of heaven. Marx had in effect said that history has an empirically discoverable sense or meaning, which is that it has been preparing humankind for their final liberation. In any case, for many writers, the moment to realize this outcome was deemed to have been missed, which threw the idea itself into question. Moreover, historical necessity was also associated with orthodox, bureaucratic Marxism, which was at least a necessary condition for Stalinism.

(ii)   *It is politically dangerous to suggest that there is a real possibility of the realization of any idealized, utopian society.* This suggestion would lend itself to abuse by bureaucratic socialist and other élites in practice because it would give them the theoretical means by which to claim that the society in which they had specific power advantages *was* its embodiment. This would thus preclude further social critique since the standard had been proclaimed as realized. (One can see how the 'secular' interpretation of Hegel as a radical social critic committed to the realization of Reason and freedom arose as Soviet Marxism became increasingly apologetic.) The ideal speech situation, however, though present in all individual speech acts, is never totally realizable. Habermas has implicitly developed the later Marx's acknowledgement of the perennial 'realm of necessity' in human affairs, which the early Frankfurt School enshrined as the notion of the necessity of some form of alienation in society; and there is a distant echo in this aspect of his work of the existentialists' insistence that both authenticity and inauthenticity are distinctive, necessary and irreducible modes of existence. Consequently, Habermas's theory entails that conditions maintaining *some* distorted communication must, dialectically speaking, *always* be present for the ideal speech situation to have any putative existence and critical purchase.

13.   The result of this combination of two factors is that the socialist utopia in these later developments of Marx's ideas in the 'critical theory' school, had to become a *postulate*, a possibility. It had to be grounded in some way that was more amenable to empirical reference and more academically credible than the Hegelian dialectics of Adorno, but which still provided a non-arbitrary, objective criterion of social critique which had more power than mere moralizing. One answer lay in the ideal speech situation, knowable in theory but by definition unrealizable in its entirety in practice.

14.   The search continues within this tradition for a credible *universal* principle to provide a justified basis for social criticism to replace the discredited Marxian *telos* of history and 'standpoint of the proletariat'. (I cannot go into all these alternatives here, except to say in passing that some of them are highly complex and abstract and make some dubious metaphysical assumptions.)[10] My point has simply been to draw attention to the character of the style of thinking, which *structures* the parameters of the inquiry and makes that search seem so imperative for its practitioners. But the 'critical theory' school does not possess the monopoly of social critique. One result of the pervasiveness of this kind of inquiry is that it has diverted the energies of sociologists away from developing the sociological tradition itself which, I am arguing, is *already* 'evaluative' or 'critical' in a much more inclusive sense.

Part II

FIGURATIONAL
EXPLORATIONS

4

THE LIMITS OF
TRANSCENDENTAL
SOCIOLOGY[1]

Why put 'actions' in the center of a theory of society and not the people who act? If anything, societies are networks of human beings in the round, not a medley of disembodied actions.

(Norbert Elias 1970: 277)

The ubiquity of transcendentalism

The basic message conveyed by the recent revival of interest in Parsons (Alexander 1983, 1987a; Münch 1987, 1988; Holton & Turner 1986; Mouzelis 1995; Holmwood 1996) is that, cleansed of its more crass misrepresentations and distortions, Parsons' conceptual scheme offers a still unsurpassed theoretical synthesis of significant insights from the classical sociological legacy – notably from the work of Durkheim and Weber – which is highly appropriate for understanding differentiated, specifically 'modern' societies. As Alexander (1987a) has pointed out, the whole of sociological theory since 1945 has effectively developed in a dialogue with Parsons, who provided the point of departure for so many subsequent efforts. His work cannot be avoided and has to be reckoned with. There are enough neo-Parsonians in the present period to constitute a tendency. In Chapter 8 I will address their significance as part of a trend towards theoretical synthesis in contemporary sociology, as well as try to explain sociologically why the criticisms of his work took the form that they did.

Here, however, I want to address some more fundamental matters concerning the nature and shortcomings of sociological theories, such as that of Parsons, which take as their inspiration transcendental philosophy of one kind or another, be it neo-Kantianism, phenomenology, Hegelianism, social phenomenology or fundamental ontology. Transcendental philosophies in the widest sense, as inspiration or as embedded in the conceptual apparatus, are very pervasive in sociology, both in its mainstream and in some of the currents and eddies. The work of Durkheim, Simmel, Weber, ethnomethodology, Schutzian social phenomenology, theorizing, critical theory and Althusserian Marxism could all be cited in this respect, as well as the work even of Giddens. He ostensibly tries to go beyond the structural functionalism of Parsons, but his work is arguably still burdened with it. Not only in the obvious sense of the places where he reproduces a contemporary version of Parsons' pattern variables (Giddens 1991: 189–209) but also Giddens' metatheoretical investigations still possess the same transcendental structure as

that of the master he was so strenuously seeking to overcome. His work on structuration theory, for example, though embracing a more nuanced model of the
knowledgeable actor than that found in Parsons, is ultimately still trying to map the
preconditions of action (see Chapter 7).

My discussion here continues the theme of sociology settling accounts with
philosophy, which runs throughout this study. Much of what philosophers say is
about the limits of one kind or another which they claim to perceive in the
inquiries of others. My chapter title is a conscious oxymoron which alludes to a
particular sense of the term. The conception of limits (*Grenzen*) as categoreal
presuppositions, ontological preconditions, 'that which makes possible X or Y',
etc., is the leitmotiv of neo-Kantian and other transcendental philosophy, particularly in the German tradition. By using the same term as a criticism of the
explanatory limits of sociologies that exhibit this structure, I am making the transcendental epigones dance to their own tune. I will undertake this task by
comparing the Parsonian strategy with that of Elias's developmental, figurational
approach, which will also help to clarify its particular character as a model of how
to build a sociological paradigm without a transcendental structure and, indeed,
without any philosophical foundations whatsoever, which is the thrust of my argument. The excursus provides a discussion of the limits of the most influential form
of transcendentalism in sociology, in addition to the Parsonian theory – that of
social phenomenology.

My way into the topic is initially through a critique of the Parsonian fideism of
the German neo-Parsonian Richard Münch, which has already absorbed the overstated criticisms and tried to present a balanced model of the theory and its
promise. His rigorous two-volume study (Münch 1987 and 1988) is probably one
of the most thoroughgoing defences of Parsons in recent sociology. Here we see all
the characteristic features of an advanced action theoretical scheme decisively
displayed in a way already adjusted to the objections of the critics and tailored to
the contemporary world. At the same time, Münch is particularly sensitive to the
Kantian dimension of Parsons' work. Thus, for my purposes, which are to focus on
the consequences for a general theory of society of working with a transcendental
philosophical dimension, this paradigmatic exemplar provides a reliable and
sympathetic account to use as a point of departure.

Back to Parsons

According to Münch, Parsons offered a theory that explained both the
'dynamizing' and 'controlling' aspects of modern societies, against which other
one-factor theories, with their one-sided emphasis on a single dynamic agency –
say, commodity production (Marxists), intellectual rationalization (Weberians),
monopolization of force (Elias)[2] – represent a falling back behind the advance
made by Parsons because the controlling dimension has been lost. They thus rein-
state the characteristic antinomies associated with positivism, empiricism and
idealism which had already been transcended in Parsons' voluntaristic theory of
social action. For this and related omissions, Münch raps over the knuckles just
about every important modern sociologist, living or dead. They have all failed to
deal with the crucial problem made central by Parsons: to explain, as part of a

general theory of action, how any new social order comes to be normatively stabilized over time, yet permits clashes of interest. Parsons offered a theory of the interpenetration of social sub-systems or 'spheres' such as the economy, the polity or the cultural system, and the subsequent institutionalization of such zones of overlap within one integrated social order. Münch writes:

> We can call a social order emerging in this way a *voluntaristic* order. It integrates a certain conformistic closedness based on affectual ties with the openness for individual inclinations and self-responsibility; and it combines a general identity relying on consensus, which it maintains independently of every specific change, with the ability to implement and enforce the order in concrete conflict situations.
>
> (Münch 1987: 199)

The aim of the two-volume study by Münch is 'to anchor the *sociological* theory of social order in the discipline's classical tradition' (1988: 3), which focuses the basic Parsonian idea (derived from Durkheim) of the intertwining of non-contractual, mainly affective and normative, factors with the bonds of economic exchange and interdependence characteristic of *Gesellschaft*. This aspect of his approach is least timely at the present moment: because it is this central plank of the classical legacy that has come to assume a low profile in sociology in recent years. The sociology of economic life has become increasingly dominated by a one-sided political economy or by variants that, influenced by developments in human geography, have injected concepts of time and space into an essentially reductive Marxian analysis of the dynamics of capitalism. One does not have to go all the way with Münch's Parsonianism to learn from his excellent discussions of the normative conditions of contracts and the part played in the so-called 'laws' of the economy by the struggles of groups in the compromise-oriented solidarity of collective bargaining (*ibid.*: 163ff.).

Against the tide of a good deal of sociological opinion in the 1970s,[3] during which Münch was developing his world-view, he was prepared to stand up and say that he believed the dismissal of Parsons' programme had gone too far, when in fact it was a seminal sociological advance which can be further developed. Others came to share this conviction in different degrees. Many have been prepared in recent years to give Parsons a much longer run for his money than would have been imaginable at one time. There is indeed something in the view that the dismissal of Parsons went too far, which one can accept without going over lock, stock and barrel to his transcendental action theory programme. The massive revolt against Parsons since the 1960s, coupled with the deluge of neo-Marxisms and continental philosophy which fuelled the 'war of the schools' in Anglo-American sociology, did unfortunately induce many sociologists temporarily to lose sight of the specifically *sociological* questions asked by the classical writers. These historically form the core of the discipline, which Parsons himself saw as consolidating and continuing. However, whether the range of these questions can be subsumed under a central concern with the basis of social order and whether we should follow Parsons down the Kantian road as a foundation for our sociology, are debatable points.

With hindsight, it has now become clear that many of the critiques of Parsons were often ill-informed ideological misrepresentations of his aims and intentions which put off many people from quarrying his prolific writings, particularly his more empirical articles, for the sociological insights that lie buried in them. The critiques said more about the experiences and aspirations of a generation caught up in the political events and 'expressive' revolution of the 1960s and 1970s than about the sociological issues of social integration, identity formation and the social foundations of morality which preoccupied the classical writers and which Parsons saw himself as developing. He may have been naive about some of his own presuppositions and unstated assumptions, as his critics triumphantly pointed out, but he was at least plugged into a great sociological tradition which, unlike some of his more shrill detractors, he knew intimately and took very seriously.

As has been said many times before, we mainly know Parsons through his critics Ralf Dahrendorf, Harold Garfinkel, Alvin Gouldner, Alan Dawe, Dennis Wrong and the rest who, with the best of intentions, assailed him amongst other things as a symbol of the conservative academic establishment. But who today, for example, has ever read Parsons' interesting reply to Dennis Wrong's celebrated 'Oversocialized Conception of Man' article (Parsons 1962)? Wrong's piece is reproduced in many collections with little discussion, as though it was a definitive critique. This reply shows that far from Parsons' view of socialization implying a conforming individual, submitting to society, as Wrong and many others maintained, the internalization of *cultural* norms (not social norms) is itself partly what makes individuality possible at all, and their meaning always transcends their particular embodiment in a society's institutions. Parsons carried forward this fundamental Kantian postulate which he found in Durkheim and Simmel. Hence, the more the individual internalizes cultural norms, the more he or she comes to possess the wherewithal for autonomous individual development. It does not imply that people are 'cultural dopes' at all – quite the reverse.

Having said all that, however, there is a doggedly uncritical acceptance of Parsons in Münch. As he says, he wants to make 'the strongest case possible for Parsons's theory in the face of its critics' (1987: 33). At least in his uncompromising public face on these matters, Münch will brook no doubts about the strength and comprehensiveness of Parsons' action framework in its original form. But, misguided and misdirected though many of the attacks on Parsons may have been, it is hard to believe that there could have been so much theoretical smoke blowing down the years without there being a substantial fire there somewhere. Münch has done a service in exposing the more dubious and erroneous criticisms of Parsons, but is in danger of overreacting the other way. For example, he never mentions objections raised by Giddens and others about the centrality of the problem of order in the classical tradition or the adequacy of the connection between internalization and motivation in Parsons as an important element in the explanation of the orderliness of society or the role of tacit knowledge in human action. Nor does he attempt to accommodate them.

The Kantian inspiration

Perhaps the tide of criticisms that engulfed Parsons also says something about the weaknesses of transcendentally based sociology as such and the kind of sociological knowledge that it is possible to generate by this approach and the kind of questions it suggests. That Parsons employed a mode of analysis heavily indebted to the German traditions of Kantianism and phenomenology, which he absorbed during his years studying in Heidelberg in the 1920s, is well known.[4] He himself acknowledged this inspiration quite explicitly. But Münch spells out in a particularly clear and illuminating way just how profound a parallel there is between Kant's critical philosophy and the general theory of action. What he calls this 'Kantian core' is of the utmost importance for our understanding of the transcendental structure of Parsons' theorizing. He goes so far as to say that *The Structure of Social Action* is 'the sociological equivalent of Kant's moral philosophy' (Münch 1987: 13).

However, a difficulty underplayed by Münch in his commitment to this kind of sociology is the problematic relationship between Parsons' analytic scheme and empirical reality, always the Achilles heel of transcendentally informed inquiry. Time and again Münch refers, quite correctly and consistently, to the *analytical* status of the sub-systems in the metatheory of action and in Parsons' cybernetic hierarchy. These are held to be the necessary preconditions of forms of action and are not to be taken as a direct description of the concrete world. This enables him to torpedo many of the criticisms of Parsons as simply confusing the two levels. All transcendental inquiry encourages this kind of argumentation because of its in-built philosophical distinction between the factual contingent and the categorical preconditions which make possible the cognitive organization of that factual level.

At one point Münch suggests that in reality, i.e. in concrete cases, the capacity of the analytically distinguished socio-cultural system to guide and control other sub-systems is frequently limited. He then tellingly adds that 'these are not facts which in themselves falsify the Parsonian theory of action' (Münch 1987: 218). This comment is of course correct and completely consistent with the nature of Parsons' transcendental analytic model. But it is this feature that makes it – like other forms of transcendental social science such as Lukàcs' theory of imputed class consciousness – very difficult to argue with. Advocates can always say that factual cases of individual human action are always determined *both* by their facticity *and* the unrealized transcendental conditions which limit and make that existence possible. In an odd sense the structure of Parsons' framework, the kind of abstraction it employs, has virtually immunized it against falsification.

The most powerful and relevant critique of Parsons, then, must go for the Kantian dimension, i.e. it must be an evaluation of the usefulness for developing a general theory of society of working within a transcendental framework, in this case of a Kantian kind. Many of his critics failed to understand or wilfully disregarded this dimension, because their criticisms were part of some other more imperative purpose they were pursuing. My point is, however, as Hegel put it, that no advantage is gained by attacking an opponent 'somewhere else and defeating him where he is not' (1812: 581). Their criticisms were largely off target and thus lost credibility. Hence they put back consideration of the deeper issues by a generation. They said more about them than about the object of their inquiry itself.

Furthermore, one has to get the true measure of the beast. How far is Münch correct in attributing a very direct link between Kant and Parsons, whilst bypassing *neo-Kantianism*? As is very well known, various neo-Kantian schools played a very important role in the genesis of the classical sociology of the late nineteenth and twentieth centuries, upon which Parsons drew so heavily, and continued to pervade German philosophy into the 1920s and 1930s and beyond. Parsons did not read Kant in a vacuum. As I explained at length in Chapter 2, after Rudolph Lotze in the 1870s and through to Windelband, Rickert, Cohen, Lask and many others, the original Kantian project upon which Münch focuses was considerably transformed into the dual framework of *Geltung* and *Werte*, which determined the antinomies of subsequent debate. Münch takes no account of these developments. An assessment of the relevance and importance of this question requires further research.

Transcendentalism or developmentalism?

It is important to point out that in constructing a general sociological theory of society all roads do not lead to, or indeed from, Kant, which Parsons, Münch and others in Parsons' revival would have us believe. In the Kant-drenched philosophical circles of Weimar Germany, we can note how conformist Parsons was in accepting a version of the prevailing wisdom and seeking even to found his whole sociology upon it. He reproduces the Kantian distinctions between theoretical and practical reason in sociological form. It is instructive to compare Parsons' capitulation to the critical philosophy with the rebellion against Kantianism of his contemporary Norbert Elias, who was also initially schooled in this tradition (see Kilminster & Wouters 1995). Their different attitudes towards Kant and towards philosophy in general are perfectly mirrored in their very different sociological frameworks.

From the start Elias wanted to move beyond philosophy in the direction of the sociology of knowledge and stood out against the individualism, nominalism and apriorism of his neo-Kantian philosophy teachers and the sociologists influenced by them. Neither would he have any truck with metaphysical foundations for his sociology, whether derived from Kant, Whitehead or anyone else. Elias's concept of a figuration, his developmental historical orientation and his theory of the sciences were developed in direct opposition to this orthodoxy. The pith and marrow of his approach is an attempt precisely to translate philosophical concepts and philosophically posed problems into sociological terms and render them amenable to empirical investigation. Parsons, on the other hand, built Kantian thinking and Whiteheadean analytical realism into the core of his programme. Elias was altogether much bolder.

Elias and Parsons, however, share the desire to get away from the economistic Marxist theory of society. But Parsons tries to accomplish this by *analytically* distinguishing separate fictitious 'spheres' of society, including the economy, and then positing their different modes of 'interpenetration'. This move also provides him with a way of bringing a pattern to a social reality implicitly assumed, very much in line with Simmel and Weber, to have no structure of its own. Elias, on the other hand, starts from the structured figuration of interwoven interdependent people in the plural. For him, people are bonded to each other in need, identity and antagonism because of the multiple functions that groups and individuals perform *for* each other.[5] Crucially, his depiction of the figurational compulsion of interdependencies involves no necessity to posit, in the manner of Parsons, a distinction between the factual order and the (consensual) normative order to explain the dynamizing and controlling aspects of society.[6]

Neither is Elias interested in delineating the transcendental conditions of social action as such, which make possible societal figurations. Rather, it is compatible with his theory of social processes to regard the delineation of such 'universal' conditions to be a matter of comparative historical inquiry, not quasi-aprioristic specification. Elias calls them 'process universals' in a deliberate attempt to distance his inquiry from transcendentalism (Kilminster & Wouters 1995: 91–3.) They would be seen as made possible sociologically as a developmental *result* of the cumulative momentum of a number of intertwined processes, including internal pacification, in a specific sequential order in a structured process over a very long period of time.

According to Münch, the concept of the 'interpenetration' helps us to discern the unique features of the West compared with less developed societies. The distinctive character of modernity is defined by Münch by the nature and extent of the historical interpenetration of the social spheres, not simply by its high level of social differentiation, as some evolutionists and functionalists would have it. It is the process of the interpenetration of spheres in Western societies that has made possible the unification within their institutions of seemingly contradictory components. These include individualism and universalism and rationalism and inner-worldly activism, all of which rest upon a common normative foundation, born out of the successive interpenetration of the sphere of 'communal action' with those of religious ethics, culture, politics and economy. This provides unity in diversity and permits controlled conflict.

But this theorem does not explain why such interpenetrations between analytically distinguished spheres *actually* occurred in reality, if 'occurred' is the correct word here. Why should such transfers take place? What is it that impelled people in specific societies at specific times, to transfer the manner of acting that we have come to call 'communal' into the activities of their lives that we have come to call, say, 'economic' or 'political'? Münch comes close to offering precisely the functionalist account of these interpenetrations from which he otherwise wants to distance himself (see 1988: 218–34; 1987: 28 and 67ff.). This dubiety is in contrast to Elias's theory where the process of transfer of patterns of conduct between real groups (and not analytically distinguished 'spheres') is cogently explained by the shifting balance of power between them.

Münch, like Parsons, takes for granted the concepts of economy, polity and culture as spheres of social action and they are apparently assumed to be present in all societies awaiting various modes of interpenetration, whereas for Elias the 'economy' and the 'polity' are historically emergent categories which have been given their specific meanings by people in order to explain the workings of relatively autonomous emergent social processes set in motion by the shifting balances of power between specific interdependent social groups within the wider social web. (I discussed these processes in outline in Chapter 1 when accounting for the emergence of sociology itself.) For Münch, like all Parsonians, it would be difficult to imagine theorizing in this way without relapsing into historicism, a doctrine that was also, he claims, 'overcome' by Parsons. But there are different ways of over-coming this doctrine. Both Parsons and Elias implicitly or explicitly fought historicism, each rejecting relativism as well as its teleological solution and each moved into sociology. But Parsons took the transcendental Kantian road and Elias took the developmental road.

For Parsons, social order is something to be explained by a common norma-tive framework keeping people's strivings within stable limits by providing individuals with a categorical obligation to limit their egotistical desires. Parsons' Kantian sociological theory thus has a basically *moral* thrust. As such, however, it inevitably focuses on the obligatory force of moral commitments for the *individual* in modern societies at the expense of the figurational compulsion of the complex interdependency networks of which that individual forms a part. These provide the framework in which that obligation is felt in varying degrees and played out in the relationships between many people. Parsons is mainly interested in the conditions that prevent the Hobbesian 'war of all against all' in an individualistic society, so for him, implicitly order means *orderliness*, i.e. the 'good order' of society as opposed to a feared anarchy. It seems to me that sometimes Parsonians repro-duce this sense of order when talking about the various degrees of orderedness of the different system levels in Parsons, whereas for Elias, no society, even in periods of serious social conflict and disruption, is entirely without order, i.e. *structuredness*. To grasp this structuredness from the many different perspectives that it comprises, requires on the part of sociologists, who also participate in society themselves, the achievement of a considerable degree of detachment and self-distanciation.

Parsons' sociology was of wide scope and ambition, was firmly committed to the sociological tradition, was an attempt at a general theory of society and has dominated Western sociology since 1945. For all those reasons, it has to be reck-oned with. And to be properly grasped and evaluated, its transcendental structure has to be understood. The social action approach of Parsons and the figurational approach of Elias certainly share wide scope and ambition, both in their different ways offering a paradigm of the 'human condition'. But otherwise they differ very fundamentally and will therefore generate different types of sociological knowl-edge with different practical implications. This discussion of one in the light of the other has hopefully illuminated the character of both.

Excursus: social phenomenology as proto-sociology

By way of a technical procedure which he called the transcendental reduction, or *epoché*, Husserl hoped to show that it was possible to reach a realm of purified consciousness, or 'transcendental subjectivity', held to be a self-contained realm of experience outside time and space. This philosophical method would produce non-empirical, apodictic truths, a priori, which would, he hoped, be universally valid and *free from presuppositions*. As a philosopher in the Cartesian tradition, Husserl sought nothing less than absolute truth. These universal truths would potentially provide a solid bulwark against sceptical doubt, historicism, relativism and political irrationalism. In this respect, phenomenology was a humanistic *Weltanschauung* as well as a technical philosophy. Husserl made this explicit in his last work, *The Crisis of European Sciences and Transcendental Phenomenology* (Husserl 1938).

The *social phenomenology* of Alfred Schutz, on the other hand, leaves aside the aim to build a presuppositionless philosophy and sidesteps the resultant Husserlian problem of the how the 'transcendental Ego' (which Husserl was forced to posit to avoid subjective idealism) is constituted in the individual 'empirical Ego'. Schutz assumes at the outset that people encounter each other in an already constituted, meaningful, intersubjective lifeworld (*Lebenswelt*), which is held to be the 'paramount reality' for human beings. This version of phenomenology – which has left many traces in sociology – advocates the study of the ways in which people experience this everyday lifeworld. The characteristic common-sense posture people take in this sphere Schutz calls the 'natural attitude'. The existence of others is taken for granted in everyday life since we assume a 'reciprocity of perspectives'. The concept of 'simultaneity' describes the idea that our experience of the Other occurs in the same present as the Other experiences us. People orientate themselves using 'typifications', such as business competitor, student, American, jovial type, through which meaningful interaction is effected (Schutz 1932).

Schutz shared Husserl's humanistic belief, which he had set out in the *Crisis*, in the primacy of the *Lebenswelt* as the ultimate reference point and basis in meaning for all experience as well as the scientific theories that humans construct. Highly influential on ethnomethodology and on sociological methodology was Schutz's insistence, in pursuance of that principle, that to avoid reification and the dehumanizing of society, the 'second-order' constructs created in social science should be based upon the 'first-order' ones already in use in the everyday lifeworld. Social science as a 'context of meaning' was possible and *humanly* legitimate only if it effected a two-way translation between itself and the 'stock-of-knowledge-at-hand' available and in use in the meaning contexts of the *Lebenswelt*. Schutz said that one should observe typical meaningful acts and events and coordinate them with constructed models of typical actors or 'homunculi'. In social science it was thus possible to construct, as all sciences do, analytical conceptual systems (in this case of social action) of maximum anonymity, but based in real experience and, by the two-way dialogue, retaining links with the uniqueness of ordinary individuals, which Schutz takes as given.

Controversy continues within and surrounding phenomenology. Two recurring focuses of debate are worth briefly bringing out.

1. Problems arising from the transcendental status of phenomenological reflections. In the sociological versions there is an ambiguous relationship between the transcendental categories and the real world depicted by empirical social science. This relation is always the Achilles heel of any transcendentally informed inquiry, phenomenology included, to which I have already alluded in Chapter 1. Strictly speaking, Schutz was outlining only the *preconditions* for humanistic social science inquiry, not attempting an empirical description of any society, or providing concepts for direct use in social research. As Thomas Luckmann (1983: viii–ix) put it, social phenomenology is 'proto-sociology' which 'uncovers the universal and invariant structures of human existence at all times and places'. But such a claim to universality, based as it was solely on philosophical reasoning, was always challengeable. From where does the abstract catalogue of basic structures

of the lifeworld derive? What empirical evidence, if any, could change them? Are values and prejudices about human nature being smuggled in?

Moreover, the clarificatory, a priori nature of the enterprise that the phenomenologists had garnered for themselves, meant – as they acknowledged – that they were not competent to make any systematic, concrete statements about the urgent questions of social power and domination in specific societies. Such a social scientific task was outside their bailiwick. This frequent criticism of social phenomenology was in fact misplaced. Their main claim to fame thus became – in the 1960s and 1970s in particular – the humanistic critique of objectivism and positivism where they existed in mainstream social science. Once this corrective had been taken on board by sociologists, phenomenology gradually lost its appeal.

2. The 'egological' focus of phenomenology has had important repercussions for both the social and philosophical variants. This individualistic cast is obvious in Husserl, but also clear in Schutz's view of society as consisting of concentric circles around himself:

> In reference to Us *whose center I am*, others stand out as 'You', and in reference to You, who refer back to me, third parties stand out as 'They'. My social world with the alter egos in it is arranged, *around me as the center*, into associates (Umwelt), contemporaries (Mitwelt), predecessors (Vorwelt), and successors (Folgewelt), whereby I and my different attitudes to others institute these manifold relationships. All this is done in various degrees of intimacy and anonymity.
>
> (Schutz 1940: 181, my emphasis)

Such a nominalistic starting point for social science has been the subject of considerable criticisms in sociology from Marx and Durkheim onwards, but recently notably in the theoretical and empirical work of Norbert Elias, where it has been seen as an unacceptable form of monadology (Elias 1978a, 1978b and 1991b).

The same egoism has meant that philosophical versions, particularly that of Husserl, have always been haunted by the ghost of solipsism. His solution – the universal self-experience of the 'transcendental Ego' – was assailed by existential phenomenologists (Sartre 1936; Merleau-Ponty 1945). They tried to circumvent this danger by shifting the emphasis towards ontology. They created concepts such as the 'being-in-the-world' of humankind, to try to describe the pre-theoretical togetherness of people in societies, although it is obvious that this is a sociological question. The anti-subjectivist and anti-humanist movement of structuralism in European social thought in the 1950s and 1960s was also partly a reaction to the more individualistic forms of phenomenology (see Chapter 5 below).

The individual subject, or empirical Ego, in phenomenology always had an *analytic* status, although implicitly it was assumed to be a grown-up individual. Reference to the development of this individual was made formally, for example in Husserl's distinction between the 'active' and the 'passive' genesis of the Ego (Husserl 1931: section 38). In his early work Schutz explicitly described the individual actor assumed in his analyses as the 'wide-awake adult'. This static assumption is corrected in his posthumous *The Structures of the Lifeworld* (Schutz & Luckmann 1974) which contributed to developing what has become known as 'genetic phenomenology'. In this work the fact that adults used to be children, who learned from a pre-existing culture via socialization, was acknowledged. This viewpoint can be found in a sophisticated form in Berger & Luckmann's (1967) influential work of metatheory *The Social Construction of Reality*. However, consonant with the transcendental character of phenomenological analysis in general, genesis is inevitably handled here, too, only in a *formal*, abstract way, as part of a universal framework of subjective orientation for the social sciences, with the world of real, empirical genesis placed in phenomenological 'brackets'.

Phenomenology is a preeminent product of the ego-centredness of traditional European philosophy from Descartes to Kant and Husserl. This tendency can be cogently explained by the development of a particular kind of person in complex, internally pacified Western nation-states. It can be seen as one expression of the self-experience of the highly self-controlled modern individual (Elias 1939). The dominant emerging direction of contemporary inquiries in the sociology of individuality is away from the transcendental towards the more promising task of empirical investigations, simultaneously on the two fronts of what Norbert Elias called psychogenesis and socio-genesis (Burkitt 1991; Swaan 1995 and 1997).

THE STRUCTURE OF
STRUCTURALISM

I think, therefore I am.
　　　　　　　(Descartes)

I am what I am not, and I am not what I am.
　　　　　　　　　　　(Jean-Paul Sartre) (cited in Bryant 1995: 75)

I think where I am not, therefore I am where I do not think.
　　　　　　　　　　　(Jacques Lacan) (cited in Bénoist 1970: 43)

Preamble

The sociological point of view from which I will be arguing in this chapter has been established in Part I, so does not require further explanation here. I will therefore take it for granted in my discussion of structuralism that sociology is a well-grounded scientific discipline with a unique subject-matter of its own – the structure of human interdependencies – and one that constitutes a break with philosophy. In sociology, the epistemological, ontological and ethical concerns of European philosophy have already been absorbed and transformed. I will consider the main contours and basic principles of structuralism from the point of view of its cognitive value for such a sociology. I will argue that the explicit or implicit philosophical layer in structuralism drags it back behind the ground already gained by the ongoing sociological revolution in knowledge. As sociologists, therefore, we have to approach para-sociological enterprises such as structuralism with these considerations in mind, correcting for its philosophical hangovers, epistemological overstatements and the evaluative preferences that have been smuggled into the work of many of its practitioners.

Structuralism: a first approximation

Structuralism descended on to British sociology as part of a wave of cognitive approaches, mainly in the late 1960s and into the 1970s. This is the period that I call the conflict phase of British sociology (see Chapter 8). Structuralism promised much: an interdisciplinary orientation; an all-embracing method; a general theory of society and culture to replace the dominant functionalist paradigm; a new approach to cultural universals; an alternative to the history of ideas; a resolution of the culture/structure dualism; and even a solution to the vexed problem of cultural relativism (Bauman 1973b; Glucksmann 1974). It had a considerable impact on Marxism as well in that period, in the writings of Louis Althusser (Benton 1984). Many sociologists were drawn to the paradigm with varying degrees of enthusiasm and interest and its presence has continued to be felt. Structuralism did have a revitalizing effect in the sociology of art and literature and in the study of culture. A selection of works introducing structuralism or evaluating its relevance for sociology published in Britain during this period includes Lane (1970), Bauman (1973a), Glucksmann (1974), Badcock (1975), Coward & Ellis (1977), Bottomore & Nisbet (1979), and Giddens (1979). This reflects the flourishing interest in this movement at this time. An appreciation of the influence of structuralism is basic to an understanding of the character of contemporary sociology.

As in the case of many other schools and paradigm communities competing in the sociological arena at that time, concepts derived from structuralism and post-structuralist trends have moved imperceptibly into sociological usage, their origins forgotten. However understood, structuralism has also been blended in complex combinations with other theories in adjacent fields such as feminism and cultural studies. Its continuity can arguably also be detected in postmodernism, particularly in the antipathy towards general theories of society, now called 'metanarratives', which include theories of developmental social change such as the dialectic of history in Marxism, or theories of social evolution.

Anyone writing about structuralism has to start with a large number of qualifications. It is a vast field, overlapping with semiology, and no sanctioned definition of the subject exists that would satisfy everyone. Structuralism never was a unified school, or movement, but rather it is the name applied to a distinctive, *synchronic* way of studying culture which systematically underplays the role of the individual or knowing subject. Although forerunners can be traced in nineteenth-century British and French anthropology and in the work of the linguist Ferdinand de Saussure at the turn of the century (Boyne 1995: 194ff.), structuralism as it has been encountered in sociology in recent times originated in France in the 1940s and 1950s. The movement was manifested in a number of fields, including anthropology, literature and Marxism as well as sociology, from the 1960s onwards. Roland Barthes described structuralism as 'an *activity*' (in DeGeorge & DeGeorge 1972: 149). Jean-Marie Bénoist said it was 'a method, and not a doctrine. . . . [It] would be more appropriate to speak of structuralism*s*, in the plural' (1970: 32). Ino Rossi (1982a: 3–4) distinguishes between the systematic and post-systematic phases of structuralism. The first was language based and inspired by Saussure, and embraced the earlier work of Lévi-Strauss, Barthes and Lacan. This work dealt largely with the syntactic structures of sign systems; whilst in the post-systematic phase, the writings of Julia Kristeva, Michel Foucault and the later Barthes shifted the focus in a more sociological direction towards the social processes behind the sign systems, the social usage of language and the role of power.

The topic is further complicated by the fact that many of the programmatic writings in the field are intensely polemical and allusive of political and moral debates between the various authors in the context of French intellectual and political life. It is in the course of these debates that many of the writers whom we think of as structuralists have at some time tactically disavowed the label (for example, Foucault in 1970: xiv). Deciphering all the nuances and locating the unspoken addressees and political positions in the various texts and controversies would require a far greater knowledge of the overlapping intellectual and political circles peculiar to French, indeed even more specifically, Parisian, cultural life than I possess (see Vaughan 1978; Poster 1975; Gardner 1981: ch. 6; Soper 1986: ch. 4). In any case, it would provide a picture of structuralism too intricate for my purpose here, which is to discuss the cognitive relevance of structuralism to sociology as a science of human social interdependencies. My interest is in the main contours of structuralism as part of an argument about the nature of sociology and its subject-matter and its relationship with philosophy, seen in a long-term perspective.

Bearing these considerations in mind, what I intend to keep in my sights in the discussion that follows is that French structuralism, for all its complexity, nevertheless possesses a characteristic orientation towards society and towards the study of culture. As such, its basic organizational pattern as a style of thinking – common to all its applications and arguably across the work of all its practitioners – can be detected through the layers of polemic, political rhetoric and empirical data assembled using the method in a variety of fields. It has a historically conditioned cast (not a timeless one), rooted in specific philosophical ingredients and antecedents. Once these have been grasped and we have understood against which philosophical targets the structuralists have pitted their efforts and at what stage of social development, then I think we can better get the measure of its cognitive value and usefulness to sociology. I think that this strategy is better in the long run than simply lifting isolated structuralist concepts into sociological theory in a magpie fashion, as is the wont with a number of sociological theoreticians in the present period (e.g. Giddens 1984 and Mouzelis 1995).

All versions of structuralism, whether their adherents claim the label or not, share a common concern. Stated at its most abstract, it is that in the study of human societies the aim is to seek out the invariant patterns embodied in social and cultural activities, some or many of which are unbeknown to the human subjects who constitute them, but which are decisive in shaping human perception and social relations. The structuralist credo was stated by Lévi-Strauss in the overture to *The Raw and the Cooked* in relation to mythology as the ambition 'to discover the conditions in which systems of truths become mutually convertible and therefore simultaneously acceptable to several different subjects, [and how] the pattern of those conditions takes on the character of an autonomous object, independent of any subject' (Lévi-Strauss 1969: 11).

All structuralists have defined themselves, explicitly or implicitly, as being opposed to four prominent principles, doctrines or trends in the Western philosophical tradition: (a) the epistemological centrality of the conscious ego or individual subject; (b) the metaphysical dualism between consciousness and being and various other dichotomies associated with it, such as subject/object; (c) positivism and empiricism as models of science and/or principles of knowledge; and (d) theories of diachronic, developmental or evolutionary change in the human sciences. The next four sub-sections will expound some of the basic principles of structuralist analysis by addressing each of these themes.

The individual ego or knowing subject

Challenging this motif in Western social and political thought has constituted almost a crusade in structuralist writings. The characteristic phrase 'the de-centring of the subject' captures this basic anti-individualistic impulse. As an intensely urgent task, this is one that structuralists share with Norbert Elias, although their strategies for trying to solve the problem are very different. This trenchant anti-individualism (often couched in terms of an opposition to 'bour-geois' individualism) has its origins in the reaction of structuralists to the ego-centredness of Husserl's phenomenology and that part of Sartre's existen-tialism that retained the primacy of the choosing individual's 'project'. Lévi-Strauss scathingly described existentialism as shallow 'shop-girl's meta-physics' (quoted by Pace 1983: 203). The zeal with which structuralists have wanted to write off as mere sentimentality the self-experience of modern individ-uals, including their own, suggests that there was something more going on emotionally for individual structuralists than simply the assertion of the epistemo-logical limitations of the ego-centred model of human knowing. One can only speculate on why they would want to devalue the completeness of their own sense of self. It takes a certain sort of person to say and mean it, that 'I never had, and still do not have, the perception of feeling my personal identity. I appear to myself as the place where something is going on, but there is no "I", no "me"'(Lévi-Strauss 1979: 3–4).

Leaving that question aside, the overwhelming – some would say excessive – swing of explanatory emphasis is, then, away from subjectivity, i.e. away from the consciousness of intentional, individual knowing subjects, considered as unitary. The focus is virtually entirely on that which precedes or includes the individual subject or ego in whatever field of inquiry or activity that may be under scrutiny. The approach proved itself to be a revitalizing influence in linguistics and the study of culture generally, but also included attempts to apply it to social struc-tures. So, what precedes or includes the individual may be a discourse, a language, a code or other structure of elements in social relations, i.e. any set of relations held to be extra-subjective and to provide the autonomous preconditions within which the utterances or behaviour of individual people take place and which they inevitably exemplify.

Within a discourse or other structure of related components expressed concep-tually, the investigator deals with the primary elements 'not [as] *terms* but *relations* perceived between these terms' (Lévi-Strauss 1968: 469). For example, what can be said about economic activity in the discourse of political economy is said to be conditioned by the way in which the components of the discourse are interrelated, something that is outside the control of any individual user of the discourse. What can be said (and hence also what cannot be said, or even visualized) has already been decided in advance by the way in which the elements of the discourse are combined or are combinable.

This accentuation is the basis of the so-called 'anti-humanism'[1] of struc-turalism. This has often been construed, not without good reason, as being, if not synonymous with misanthropy,[2] certainly as implying it. Structuralism does conjure up a rather bleak way of thinking about the condition of being human.

The structuralists believe that excessive individualism, particularly that associated with existentialism, has blinded us to the inexorable extra-individual parameters of our human fate and consequently to the limits of effective action to change society and culture. Structuralists of the generation of Lévi-Strauss, Lacan and Foucault 'despaired of influencing events which they saw as under the control of remote and impassive forces' (Gardner 1981: 214). In the context of French politics in the aftermath of the Algerian crisis of the late 1950s, it is plausible to suggest that there was a subterranean connection between this pessimistic sensibility and the structuralist programme (Soper 1986: 122). Note, for example, Lévi-Strauss's strong statement that he has always aimed at 'drawing up an inventory of mental patterns, to reduce apparently arbitrary data to some kind of order, and to attain a level at which a kind of necessity becomes apparent, *underlying the illusions of liberty*' (1969: 10, my emphasis). All sociology could in one sense be seen as undermining the illusions of liberty, but my point is that what is distinctive about structuralism was the shrill and trenchant way in which the constraints on individual thinking and acting were pointed out and the missionary zeal with which the programme for the pursuit of extra-individual cultural and societal constants was pursued.

More generally, it has often been said that there is an affinity between structuralist ideas and the modern experience of bureaucratic institutions which possess an autonomous functional logic, devoid of meaning and impervious to individual wishes or aims (Gardner 1981: 215). Althusser's insistence that individuals are merely the 'bearers' of the structure of the social formation makes sense in this context. For him, it is the way in which the various social practices are articulated that is decisive in defining the social conditions within which individuals imagine the place they occupy and which circumscribe their apparently planful, self-initiating actions (Althusser 1969).

It is this feature of the structuralist way of seeing society that challenges our common-sense experience as individuals and makes structuralist statements about individuals often sound counter-intuitive and paradoxical. In their most extreme formulations, structuralists will go so far as to say, for example, that a discourse – as an autonomous structure of mutually defining elements – effectively 'speaks' through the verbal or written utterances of the individual.[3] In his novel *Nice Work* (which was also made into a TV drama), David Lodge exploits the comic possibilities of this paradox. Having had sex with a poststructuralist female lecturer in English literature, the other central character, a down-to-earth managing director of an engineering firm, declares that he has fallen in love with her, although she sees their encounter as simply a night of pleasure, of no lasting significance. He beseeches her: 'Haven't you ever been in love, then?' She replies, with impeccable epistemological accuracy: 'When I was younger . . . I allowed myself to be constructed by the discourse of romantic love for a while, yes' (Lodge 1989: 293). It will be a theme of this chapter that in attacking the ego-centredness of Western philosophy, the structuralists were aiming at an important target, sociologically speaking, but that they remained within the assumptions of philosophy and over-reacted to a point of absurdity.

In pursuing this anti-individualistic quest, the structuralists pitted themselves against two further philosophical targets.

1. Hermeneutics, or similar enterprises that try to understand documents and

texts from the past by a process of bringing out the presuppositions that the investigator inevitably brings to them. This activity assumes that the text only has one meaning, that of the author considered as an individual, and that it is possible to recover it. Rather, the emphasis is on texts as 'polysemic' or 'multi-vocal', i.e. as carrying simultaneously multiple meanings. Texts are seen as linked to other texts produced in the same period within a particular linguistic or pictorial code which operates through them all. The goal of the structuralist critic is to decipher from the text this 'network of *relational invariants*' (Bénoist 1970: 38).

2. The phenomenologists' focus on the meanings and intentions of the creative, skilful actor was put in its place by the structuralists' assertion that no amount of analysis of intentional meanings, as experienced by individuals, would reveal the structure as the relations between the components of the invariant code being employed by individuals. Phenomenology had aimed to get away from naive subjectivism by drawing upon layers and levels of meaning, seen as constituted and reconstituted by people. But, as is well known, phenomenology could not get from the constituting consciousness of the individual subject to the collective level, despite its promise, and fell back into solipsism. For the structuralists, this feature of phenomenology was further confirmation of its sentimental attachment to the sovereign individual, a conceit now historically exhausted. As Vincent Descombes pointed out, in dealing with language, phenomenology placed itself on the side of the speaking subject, whereas, in contrast, semiology switched emphasis on to the receiver and hence on to the language code they both share. The meaning of a speaker's message is not the meaning of experience. 'It is the meaning that experience can *receive* in a discourse which articulates it according to a certain code – that is, in a system of signifying oppositions' (1980: 98). Then comes the structuralist paradox: 'If language is a code, it is language which speaks each time that the speaking subject delivers a remark, of whatever kind' (*ibid.*). Within philosophy, structuralism was hailed as a revolution in the theory of meaning.

Metaphysical dualisms

In one way or another, all structuralists have been seeking ways of circumventing the pitfalls, as they perceive them, of the Cartesian *cogito*, the subject/object dichotomy and other antinomies synonymous with the great fault line in Western rationalistic philosophy associated with the dualism between consciousness and being. Particularly in the various strands of the phenomenological philosophy against which the structuralists were partly reacting, the dualism and the egoism were related.

To recall a point made in the excursus to Chapter 4, Husserl's philosophy was haunted by the ghost of solipsism, which he made a number of attempts to circumvent in the direction of a trans-individual standpoint. One solution was the universal self-experience of the posited 'transcendental Ego', an argument often acknowledged in the secondary literature to have been less than convincing. It was assailed by existential phenomenologists of the next generation (Sartre 1936; Merleau-Ponty 1945). They tried to stave off this danger of solipsism by shifting the emphasis towards ontology. They created concepts such as the 'being-in-the-world' of humankind, to try to describe the pre-theoretical togetherness of individual people – the isolated egos – in social existence. This was held to be a level of being that grounded both subject and object and thought and reality. In other words, the dualism was overcome by an abstract ontological appeal to the 'Is-ness' of its two components which grounds both, a conception that has implications for the traditional definition of truth as the correspondence between the subject and object of knowledge (Mannheim 1922; Kilminster 1992c). In Heidegger's classical formulation:

> Thus truth has by no means the structure of an agreement between knowing and the object in the sense of a likening of one entity (the subject) to another (the Object). Being-true as Being-uncovering, is in turn ontologically possible only on the basis of Being-in-the-world. This latter phenomenon, which we have known as a basic state of Dasein, is the *foundation* for the primordial phenomenon of truth.
>
> (Heidegger 1927: 261)

Bénoist (1978: 222ff.) was quite correct to point out that although the concept of structure in structuralism is not synonymous with ontology, the philosophy of Heidegger is nonetheless its distant ancestor.[4] The burden of Heidegger's work, particularly his earlier writings, including *Being and Time*, was to expose the limitations not only of the subject/object dichotomy, but also other dualisms associated with the rationalistic philosophy of knowledge: perception/intelligibility, intuition/category and understanding/concept. The related dualism of form/content epitomizes this dimension. Structuralists claim to have abolished this dualism, which is also associated with certain forms of empiricism and positivism. The structure is held to be an objective mode of combination of parts or elements, present in the 'content' itself. Lévi-Strauss contrasted the structuralist position with that of positivism, in which: 'Form is defined in opposition to a content that is foreign to it; but structure has no content: it is the content itself apprehended in a logical organization conceived of as the property of the real' (quoted in Bénoist 1978: 210).

The embodiment of this position in the study of culture involved abandoning the idea that structure determines the shape of culture, or that base determines superstructure (vice versa being idealism). The search was for the generative rules of the *co-emergence* of empirical phenomena falling into both categories. Implicitly, the targets of the structuralist polemic here are the elaborate theories of the economic determination of culture as part of the superstructure, associated with the Marxian analysis of art and literature by Georg Lukács and the later writings of Lucien Goldmann (Wolff 1981: 57). The structuralist argument outflanks the sophistications of intercausality between the two postulated entities or determination by the economic *Unterbau* 'in the last instance', by denying the dualism between the two which lies at the heart of the theory (Bauman 1973a and 1973b; Williams 1973).

Coming out of European philosophy, the structuralists took for granted conceptualizations born out of the epistemological and ontological controversies of that tradition and then tried to blend them with empirical data in the study of language, culture, myth and social relations – but with little recognition of the incongruity of doing so. Although the concept of structure had an affinity with fundamental ontology, it was one that in fact subtly slid away from the philosophical notion of Being towards a method amenable to the handling of empirical data. In this sense, they allied themselves with one of the central tenets of the scientific tradition: the imperative of submitting generalizing statements to the citing of corroborative or falsifying evidence. But in the end the only way of reconciling the contradiction at the heart of this incongruity was to imply that there was such a thing as the empirical instantiation of a structure's *possibilities*, a position that is often implicit in structuralist writings. But this device simply reinforces the latent metaphysics of the paradigm.

The work of the structuralists had located important issues surrounding a number of key dualisms but, following my overall argument in this book, my view is that for all its grandeur and prestige, and the intellectual brilliance and awesome erudition of many of its practitioners, structuralism nevertheless falls back behind the sociological revolution which demands the development of a dynamic sociological theory of knowledge. Even though it may illuminate certain issues and its exaggerations did have a galvanizing and stimulating effect in some fields of sociology, it is, in the end, a paradigm couched in the language of philosophy and designed to solve specific problems within that tradition. These origins also go some way towards explaining its orientation towards the pursuit of what is apparently timeless in human societies and culture.

Positivism and empiricism

Like almost every other paradigm community in contemporary and recent sociology, structuralists have also, in their different ways, been opposed on epistemological grounds to these two related doctrines. Positivism suggested that in whatever area of investigation in the social and natural worlds, there was one kind of scientific method of inquiry and explanation applicable to all of them. This was the pursuit of empirical laws. Structuralists have insisted, however, that these can only be legitimately said to be found in the realms of the physical world investigated by either physics or chemistry. In other fields, say, in linguistics or in the study of kinship or myths, regularities are to be regarded not as exemplifying laws but as *transformations* of basic relations in the many variants observed.

Lévi-Strauss's ingenious study of the Oedipus myth (1958: 213ff.), however centrally he may have regarded it to his work in general, is instructive in this respect and can also serve to introduce the structuralist method. Myths generally are sacred narratives which usually explain how something came to be as it is – for example, how birds came to have coloured plumage or where fire originated or the origins of human beings. In the case of the famous Oedipus myth of ancient Greece, it is important to know that one background belief in the myths of the culture was that humankind is autochthonous, i.e. born out of the earth. This sacred belief obviously stands in stark contradiction to the known fact of childbirth. There are various versions of the myth, but Lévi-Strauss says that it does not matter which is the most authentic. We must abandon the search for the true version because it is the substance of the myth that is the key: 'A myth remains the same as long as it is felt as such' (*ibid.*: 181).

The story of how Oedipus, the son of Jocasta and Laius, comes, without realizing that they are his parents, to kill his father and marry his mother, as predicted by the oracle, is well known. It is a tragic and fateful tale that Freud used analogously in his psychoanalytic model of the development of the boy child caught up in competition with his father for the love of his mother. Full versions of the myth are rich with intensely symbolic acts and events like Oedipus killing the sphinx (if he had failed he would have died); the plague that rages as the punishment of the gods for Oedipus's unwitting crime of incest; Jocasta's ritual suicide when she learns what she has done; and Oedipus, consumed with guilt, blinding himself. The tension of the complex and detailed narrative partly derives from the reader's knowledge that all of this was the intricate playing out of a predicted fate that the players neither knew nor could avoid.

Drawing on structural linguistics, Lévi-Strauss draws up four columns in which he lists downwards, with no regard for chronology or diachronic sequence, events or items in the myth that (i) overrate blood relations; (ii) underrate them; (iii) deny the autochthonous origins of humankind; and (iv) affirm their persistence. These events or items are paradigmatic associations, i.e. involving interchangeable elements. For example, events that underrate blood relations include the Spartoi killing each other and Oedipus killing his father. Events doing the opposite, that is showing blood relations to be triumphant, include Kadmos seeking revenge for his ravished sister. Events denying the autochthonous origins of humankind, that is events that celebrate human power over monsters of the earth, include Kadmos killing a dragon. And the linguistic derivation of a number of names of characters in the myth (lame, swollen foot, etc.) and references to walking difficulties, signify in column (iv) the persistence of the autochthonous origins of man because in all the tales of humans coming out of the earth, they at first cannot walk properly.

The four columns of paradigmatic associations stand in two contradictory pairs: overrating versus underrating of blood relations; and denial versus persistence of the autochthonous origins of humankind. Horizontally, the method has revealed a syntagmatic chain (i.e. a combination of words in a chain of speech) in which two *kinds* of contradictory relationship stand side by side. The basic contradiction between human origins being in childbirth versus being from the earth, is replaced by the assertion in the myth that two pairs of contradictory relationships are identical inasmuch as they are both self-contradictory in a similar way. Lévi-Strauss's argument is that merely *telling* the myth is not the same as *understanding* it. Through the transformations between the two axes it is revealed that the myth is trying to resolve by analogy the main contradiction between the observed fact of childbirth and the sacred belief in the autochthonous origins of human beings. The myth functions to dissipate the contradiction by spinning out new oppositions and pairs of oppositions which replace it. In the myth the original problem is related to a derivative one to escape the fundamental insolubility of the problem.

Returning to the issue of empiricism, let us expand the question. Instead of remaining on the level of what can be observed empirically (implying sense data) as the final cognitive arbiter of valid knowledge, structuralists seek out – as we saw above – the invariant generative rules that produce the properties of the objects observed.[5] In the case of the Oedipus myth, what can be observed is a diachronic sacred narrative. Its generative rules involve the creation of new contradictions which are revealed through a classification of paradigmatic associations lying within the narrative. It is an example of what structuralism generally seeks – the universal regularities (inaccessible to direct observation) that constitute the conditions for the production and reproduction of various kinds of phenomena in different fields. In the guise of cross-cultural socio-cultural studies, this constitutes the philosophical pursuit of *necessity* within *contingency* and, as such, it is a feature that permeates all structuralist work in different ways (Bauman 1973a: 69ff.).

Once these features of the point of departure of structuralism are appreciated, then the specific meaning of the concept of structure in structuralism and semiology begins to move into sharper focus and its philosophical genesis becomes clearer. Structure in this context is not simply the arrangement of social relations or other cultural data as observed. Neither is it an aggregate or composite of units of independent status brought together inductively. Nor is it an essence hidden behind or realizing itself in appearances.[6] Nor does the metaphor of a deep structure beneath the surface completely capture the correct meaning of the concept of structure in structuralism, even though it is commonly used in the secondary literature and commentary. Rather, structure embraces the objective relations between the units which give meaning to any element in the network or system concerned. The objective configuration of the elements is held to embrace a structure that delimits the relations between them; it is something known indistinctly but not measurable in an empiricist sense. As Foucault wrote, delicately stepping between all the relevant dualisms: 'Structure is that designation of the visible which, by means of a kind of pre-linguistic sifting, enables it to be transcribed into language' (1966: 138). (By language here I take him to mean also theoretical language.)

Theories of diachronic social processes

Structuralists have bidden farewell to a range of theories and paradigms, each involving in different ways a conception of diachronic historicity, including social and cultural evolutionism, historicism, the Marxian dialectic of history and Hegelianism. The overwhelming stress of structuralist analysis has been on *synchrony*. History and diachrony are not denied, but simply put in their place because temporal order is not regarded as establishing any kind of privileged intelligibility (Lévi-Strauss 1962: 256). It constitutes a form of naive ethnocentrism, deified by historians and some philosophers, but which simply reflects our mundane experience of temporal succession in everyday life.

Although the general issue of historical explanation is at stake here, this aspect of structuralism is, like many of its features, redolent of political debates, particularly within Marxism and between liberals and conservatives. And it is also bound up with anti-humanism. As Bénoist, a devoted structuralist, tellingly proclaimed: 'we have dared lay our hands on a sacrosanct dialectic, on a moribund and embalmed Marxism' (1978: 227). Jean-Paul Sartre declared that the aim of Foucault's *The Order of Things* was 'to demonstrate the impossibility of historical thought. ... Behind history, of course, the target is Marxism' (quoted by Descombes 1980: 110). Descombes takes issue with this statement, suggesting that the structuralists were not repudiating history. Rather, he says, with obvious Nietzschean overtones, they were trying to reach a more sober conception 'after the twilight of the Hegelian idol' (*ibid.*). Needless to say, this was of course only a problem for those who were committed to either Hegelian (or Marxian) dialectics in the first place. Within the sociological tradition as a whole, their flaws had been noted for example by Sorel, Pareto, Simmel, Weber, Scheler and Mannheim at least, a very long time before the structuralist controversies of the 1960s and 1970s reinforced them once again. Much of the structuralists' proposed solutions to key problems *repeated ground already gained, but simply in new forms of overstatement.*

For the structuralists, particularly the later writers in the 'post-systematic' phase, the notion of the identity of contradictions was synonymous with Hegelianism and Marxism, both of which in their different ways took seriously the cultural or social possibility of the *Aufhebung* of contradictory oppositions or forces. Or, if those paradigms did not look forward to that, they at least avowed the coincidence of opposites. The principles of difference and dissymmetry were to replace the unity of opposites found in dialectical thought. For Bénoist, this opens up heady possibilities:

> It is the economistic Marxists and their impenitent humanist confreres who have refused to see the epistème of our era evolve towards that enigmatic site where a liberated science rediscovers its roots in the imaginary order, and where a polemical, eristic, and *non-dialectical* thought, i.e. one that is not a slave to any logos, returns in all its splendour.
>
> (Bénoist 1978: 222)

Lévi-Strauss's critique of Sartre in *The Savage Mind* (Lévi-Strauss 1962: ch. 9) became celebrated mainly because it focused three dimensions of structuralist disputation – epistemological, ethical and political – into one issue. According to Lévi-Strauss, Sartre believes that people make themselves through their acts, so Sartre continues to believe in the power of political practice. For Lévi-Strauss this is a myth, something based in individual egos, or knowing subjects who act on the basis of political consciousness. For him, it is not possible, as Sartre thinks in the *Critique of Dialectical Reason*, to redeem the past sufferings of humankind through political action. This cannot be done within the confines of political activity within one society, because this view fails to take cognizance of humankind as a whole, which exists cross-culturally. Sartre's view that history is made and hence can be re-made, by people, is a myth. Sartre partakes of this Western tradition of transcendental humanism – in fact he represents for Lévi-Strauss the last-ditch stand of metaphysics in this sense.

More radically still, for Lévi-Strauss (and in different ways for other structuralists) there is no history as such; all that passes as history is but a partial catalogue of events elaborated for people's specific purposes in the present. 'History is therefore never history, but history-for' (*ibid.*: 257). There is no such thing as history as a continuous development, because it is only a code of dates and events – it is a myth, in the sense discussed earlier. Sartre disregards the structures or generative rules revealed by structuralists, which are prior to all initiatory political practice. These structures bespeak limits to the illusion of absolute human freedom, a belief that the structuralists such as Lévi-Strauss thought they had found in the works of writers like Sartre.

Diachrony emerges as part of the analytic, abstract, Western style of thinking that Lévi-Strauss calls domesticated thinking, which he opposes to the analogical, combinatory, concrete thought – *bricolage* – of simpler peoples. 'Primitive' thought is timeless, in the sense that within it diachrony and synchrony are united. Simpler peoples work analogically, from what is at hand, building images of the world that resemble it, whereas Western science seeks explanations of origins, builds up new theories from small problems and looks for emergence and continuity. The two types of reasoning led to two types of science: practical theories of the natural world that informed animal husbandry and agriculture which helped to satisfy basic human needs; and contemporary science. Hence, there is no 'pre-logical' (Lévy-Bruhl) mentality in simpler peoples, contrasted with the logical scientific mentality. Both are equally logical. Both types of thought are part of the same 'closed system' of human knowledge (*ibid.*: 269) but have hitherto moved along different paths. In the twentieth century they have come together: 'the most modern form of the scientific spirit will have contributed to legitimize the principles of savage thought and to re-establish it in its rightful place' (*ibid.*). Hence, structuralism takes us forward, according to its advocates, towards the reaffirmation of a synchronous thinking and the unity of 'man' as such, both of which are held to have been temporarily submerged by the wave of historical, evolutionary and individualistic thinking of modern times.

Structuralism as para-sociology: Lévi-Strauss and Foucault

Virtually all of the major practitioners and influential expositors and advocates of structuralism were schooled in European philosophy and hence took their unquestioned point of departure from traditional epistemology, ontology and ethics, as adapted by recent schools. It was both the inertia of the philosophical tradition – which tends to push analysis towards the pursuit of timeless, apodictic truths – and the ulterior politics of the structuralists that combined to account for the weight of their investigatory effort being considerably tilted in the direction of the pursuit of that which is apparently changeless in a world of change and flux. Frequently this orientation is expressed in philosophical, transcendental argumentation of one kind or another.

In this section, in relation to the work of Lévi-Strauss and Foucault, I will explore the way in which this feature of the programme is played out in concrete research. Whatever other intellectual or social scientific influences may be at work in the syntheses of the two writers (see respectively Pace 1983: 161ff.; Smart 1985: 12–17) it is, I would argue, variants of the philosophical way of thinking that are decisive in determining the cast of their work and the ways in which they both employ empirical data. For all its inventiveness and intellectual bravura, the work of these two writers is, strictly speaking, on the periphery of sociology (Lévi-Strauss's more so than that of Foucault). From the point of view of the sociological programme that this study tries to anticipate, it is work still weighed down with philosophical abstractions and ethical–political overtones. From that point of view, in the structuralist writings being discussed here, those dimensions are insufficiently controlled for through detachment. We learn some something from them.

Their works are not devoid of insights. But they are ultimately case studies in para-sociology.

Claude Lévi-Strauss

As an anthropologist and unusually for French ethnologists of his generation, Lévi-Strauss undertook fieldwork in the traditional manner (Pace 1983: 212). He states that this is always his starting point in drawing up inventories of what he calls, despite its individualistic connotations, 'mental' patterns (Lévi-Strauss 1969: 10). At the same time, he was initially schooled in philosophy. In his Massey Lectures broadcast on the BBC in 1977, he claims that he moved into anthropology because he was 'trying to get out of philosophy' (Lévi-Strauss 1979: 11). But he is ambivalent about his relationship to philosophy and does not always realize how saturated in its concepts, assumptions and ways of thinking (particularly transcendentalism) he actually is. He explicitly states that he was always determined 'never to encroach on the only too closely guarded preserves of philosophy' (1969: 9). He nevertheless concedes that in his studies of myth he was proceeding 'in the manner of Kantian philosophy' to search for constraining structures of the mind (ibid.: 11). But he then tries to reassure us (in my view unconvincingly) that he did not assume their existence prior to studying the data (ibid.).

A very strong case can be made out that his work is, in its basic structure, philosophical. It is possible, for example, to detect in his remarks about temporal succession reported in the previous section, his philosopher's aspiration to reach a higher truth hidden in the flux of history and cultural variety. Implicitly, this is a level of truth held to be on a more elevated plane than that of everyday life. It is a classical example of the 'two truths' (the mundane and the supermundane) theories of knowledge that have proliferated from Plato to Hegel, to Husserl, to the young Lukács' theory of actual and 'imputed' class consciousness and which resurfaces in Habermas's 'ideal speech situation'. At the same time, on a more prosaic level, his work is couched in or assumes in its organization of data, the specific philosophical pairings of necessity/contingency, Reason/unreason and universality/particularity.

A great many other influences in Lévi-Strauss's intellectual development in fact also point in the same direction, that is, towards a preference for the discovery of what is not only a hidden order in a particular field but also its most fundamental level, i.e. something substantively changeless. In *Tristes tropiques*, he says that 'Understanding consists in reducing one type of reality to another' (1955: 57). He also mentions there geology, psychoanalysis and Marxism as formative influences, from all of which he derived the belief in an order behind what can be observed on the often chaotic surface of things. More generally, as an anthropologist concerned with cultural differences, he inevitably has an interest in their meaning for humankind as such, hence he works with the category of 'man' (ibid.: 58), a concept that, in the way in which he employs it, universalizes his inquiries. My point is that it is possible to work with humankind as the focus of research in such a way as to dissociate the inquiry from the absolutist associations that pervade Lévi-Strauss's approach. In this connection, the work of Norbert Elias provides an interesting sociological alternative which in my view has gone a long way towards showing how this can be accomplished (see Mennell 1992: ch. 9; and Chapter 6 of this volume where the issue arises in connection with the study of globalization).

The method in Lévi-Strauss's early anthropology was indebted to Saussure's model of the synchrony of *la langue* within the diachrony of *parole*, with the former brought polemically to the fore against cultural evolutionists. Unlike *parole*, which exists in a 'non-reversible' sequence, *langue* belongs to 'reversible' time, so in the study of myth this analogy enables us to balance the 'historical and the *ahistorical*' (Lévi-Strauss 1958: 209–10, my emphasis). This opens up the field for the discovery, not of the progress of the human mind, but its '*unchanged and unchanging powers*' (*ibid.*: 230, my emphasis). He agrees with Ricoeur's characterization of his work as 'Kantism without a transcendental subject', which he says is an inevitable philosophical consequence of his ethnographic approach (*ibid.*). My view would be that it is not so much a consequence of his approach, but more a feature inter-twined with it from the outset, shaping the whole framework. It is precisely this theoretical straitjacket that is, I am arguing, inimical to the development of soci-ology and needs to be moved beyond.

In the study of the Oedipus myth referred to earlier, Lévi-Strauss showed how the myth functioned to dissipate the contradiction between the known fact of childbirth and the sacred belief in the origins of human beings as coming from the earth. This was a social-psychological problem, as it were 'external' to the myth. In his *Mythologiques* volumes, on the other hand, there is an attempt to show that the same paradigmatic association and substitution of signs is going on across the field of hundreds of myths, but each is now seen as also constrained by different *ecolog-ical* factors in the environment of the peoples elaborating the myths. At the same time, the oppositions that each myth seeks to mediate and to transform are within the myths themselves – the implication being that people think in myths. The system of symbolic contrasts thus has no intrinsic significance, but only a 'posi-tional' one, i.e. it is only the context that endows it with an 'operational value', as Lévi-Strauss puts it (1969: 56).

> [E]ach matrix of meanings refers to another matrix, each myth to other myths. And if it is now asked to what final meaning these mutually signi-ficative meanings are referring – since in the last resort and in their totality they must refer to something – the only reply to emerge from this study is that myths signify the mind that evolves them by making use of the world of which it is itself a part. Thus there is simultaneous produc-tion of myths themselves, by the mind that generates them and, by the myths, of an image of the world which is already inherent in the structure of the mind.
>
> (*ibid.*: 341)

The categorizing, combinatory mind is homologous with nature. Myths express laws of the mind, exhibiting a structure of binary oppositions which express – perhaps 'embody' would be a better word – a pre-cultural structure, perhaps something even unconscious. The assumption of the homology of the mind and nature leads inexorably towards the linking of the structure of mythical thinking with the structure of the human brain. Put this way, this conception appears to be very close to the reduction of culture to nature. Indeed, in the preface to the second edition of *The Elementary Structures of Kinship*, Lévi-Strauss says that the contrast of culture/nature is itself 'an artificial creation of culture' (1966a: xxix). In the course of scientific discovery, he predicts, culture will ultimately emerge as a 'synthetic duplication of mechanisms already in existence ... permitted by the emergence of certain cerebral structures which themselves belong to nature' (*ibid.*: xxx). The issue of reductionism is a controversial one in structuralism, particularly in relation to the work of Lévi-Strauss, but is one that I cannot take further here.[7]

Returning to the *Mythologiques*, there are myths of origin, myths of migration and others that have the character of village tales (*ibid.*: 333). The master opposition of nature/culture is found expressed metaphorically in the oppositions of raw/cooked and wild/tame. The further oppositions of earth/sky, land/sea and dry/wet express aspects of the non-living world which have been socially imported into the myths. As one moves from the matrix of myths of origin or migration to the more concrete village tales, the great logical or cosmological contrasts are toned down to the manageable scale of social relations, whilst the binary structure is found to have been retained.

The myths of the origins of fire and of rain of the Brazilian Sherente and Bororo tribes, respectively, are on the face of it dissimilar because they are about the origins of two different things, although both myths possess a hero who is a deceiver and a bird-catcher and both play with the themes of death and resurrection. In the Sherente myth, fire symbolizes death and water symbolizes life. In the Bororo myth, water is associated with death and fire with life. There is a basic structure of inverse symmetry between these pairings and Lévi-Strauss correlates this with the dry and drought-prone territory of the Sherente contrasted with the watery environment of the Bororo. The latter group immerse the flesh of their dead in rivers or lakes which they believe are the habitat of souls. In myths of the origins of fire, typically the jaguar saves the hero and teaches him the art of fire and of cooking. Man and jaguar are polar opposites, one eating raw food, the other cooked. The myth solves the problem of the fire being on the earth in a plausible account that posits an archaic reciprocity between man and jaguar. The myth permutates and reproduces formal properties of nature in the binary oppositions of wild/tame, sky/earth, raw/cooked and fire/no fire (Lévi-Strauss 1969: 188–95; Yalman 1967: 77–81).

It is possible, Lévi-Strauss claims, to verify empirically, i.e. ethnographically, the facts of the ways of life and environment of the tribes as well as other images of reality conveyed in the myths. The philosophical structure of his thinking is clear, however, when he says that another procedure can be carried out to construct what he tellingly calls an 'absolute order', assuming that all the first-, second- and third-tier myths are basically transformations of one simple type (*ibid.*: 334). This myth has a '*logical*' priority – not a 'historical' priority, he adds. Lévi-Strauss is not simply attempting some speculations or generalizations on the basis of empirical work. Rather, the procedure is the specific one of carrying out the philosophical method of 'second-order' or 'systematic' analysis – this time on his own findings. Moreover, he is doing it clearly with what he perceives as the vaunting individualism of the phenomenological or existentialist view of the mind as a polemical target:

And so, if it were possible to prove in this instance [in the study of myths] ... that the apparent arbitrariness of the mind, its supposedly sponta- neous flow of inspiration, and its seemingly uncontrolled inventiveness imply the existence of laws operating at a deeper level, we would inevitably be forced to conclude that when the mind is left to commune with itself and no longer has to come to terms with objects, it is in a sense reduced to imitating itself as object; and that since the laws governing its operations are not fundamentally different from those it exhibits in its other functions, it shows itself to be of the nature of a thing among things.

(Lévi-Strauss 1969: 10)

The remarkable and ambitious work of Lévi-Strauss is on the borderlines of ethnography and philosophy. One is entitled to ask how far this grand philosoph- ical synthesis is, strictly speaking, testable, in the sense of empirical materials being deployed with a view to confirming, or refuting and amending, the theory. Are his investigations 'anything more than fascinating and flashing displays of Olympian chess games, brilliant displays of logical forms?' (Shalvey 1979: 111). Particularly in his studies of myths, examples seem to be selected and varied so as to exemplify a preconceived, philosophical and ethical world-view in which contrary cases are regarded as supplementary dimensions of the theory, rather than disproving it as such (Leach 1970: 115). He is not so much trying to settle old philosophical disputes using the empirical operations of modern science, as it might appear, as exemplifying the older categories and metaphysical ways of thinking that are at the heart of his whole inquiry, particularly the later works on myths.

Lévi-Strauss makes the dubious romantic (Rousseauian) assumption that 'prim- itive' peoples in the societies he discusses are at one with nature (Clarke 1981: 205). Furthermore, the opposition of nature/culture, so important to the structuralist, may not be important in the lives of the peoples concerned. The focus on the structure of the human mind diverts attention from other features of human soci- eties which might be more decisive in explaining the patterns in their myths. Clarke (*ibid.*) cites a study of myths in the republic of Georgia in central Asia in which the basic opposition is found to be between respect and the violation of prohibitions. That is, in Lévi-Strauss's terms, the social or cultural *content* is relevant to the *form* of the myths, i.e. the basic opposition in this case arises out of the struc- ture of Georgian society, not from this people's relationship with nature. And Ricoeur has commented that Lévi-Strauss has little to say about Semitic and Indo- European cultures, where there is further evidence running counter to his assumption of the content of culture being irrelevant to the generative structure or form (cited by Shalvey 1979: 110).

Lévi-Strauss is a prolific writer of prodigious erudition, ingenuity and origi- nality, after whose revolutionary work anthropology was never the same again. Few would gainsay his influence and contribution. As Yalman (1967: 88) said, Lévi-Strauss's work signalled a move away from a long-held view that forms of social organization are the main, if not the only, area of inquiry worthy of serious attention by anthropologists. Lévi-Strauss said that we can no longer regard the world of 'mental' life as a mere epiphenomenon. This is correct, but who, apart from a handful of very orthodox Marxists, ever did? There are surely *other* socio-logical ways of studying the world of mental life or culture in relation to social groups and power relations which are closer to the reality of social interdependencies in a variety of societies than the static universalism of Lévi-Strauss.

It is not my intention to attempt a full-scale critique of Lévi-Strauss. This is beyond my scope. But I would like to make two preliminary remarks of relevance to my sociological argument in this chapter and more broadly in this study.

1. To anticipate a theme of Chapter 8, the work of Lévi-Strauss, though based exclusively on simpler peoples and concentrating mostly on kinship and myths, nevertheless dazzled the new generations of sociologists in the 1960s and 1970s in Western countries such as Britain and France, for reasons that can be explained sociologically. These countries were in the course of giving up their colonial empires. It is reasonable to surmise that radical sociologists were drawn partly to the apparently liberating and democratizing possibilities of Lévi-Strauss's idea that there was little significant difference at the deepest cognitive level between the thinking of people in the industrialized West and so-called 'primitive' peoples of the Third World. Structuralism, and Lévi-Strauss's work in particular, was widely seen as 'anti-imperialist' (Glucksmann 1974: 230). This aspect of his work had an appeal to the generation who were part of the far-reaching functional democratization and informalization processes of the 1960s and 1970s, for whom identification with the underdog became a dominant sensibility.

2. Sociologists also noted approvingly Lévi-Strauss's pedigree in the tradition of Durkheim and Mauss, but probably did not always appreciate how much he departed from them. Initially his work was seen as promising to solve the structure–agency problem which, in the post-Parsons theoretical tumult of the late 1960s, was perceived as *the* central problem. It only became apparent gradually that his work had only marginal relevance to the study of advanced societies, their development and the structure of power associated with industrial capitalism – the staples of the sociological tradition. Going down the structuralist road also meant paying the high price of severing links with diachrony, social organization and conscious social actors (Martins 1974: 287; Giddens 1979: 25).

Michel Foucault

Here we encounter another basically philosophical thinker who addresses interesting epistemological, political and sociological issues, but in a philosophical mode which blurs comprehension. Both he and Lévi-Strauss share a fundamentally transcendental cast of mind which has been translated into versions of the structuralist programme, construed as empirical social science. For Foucault, people are formed as individuals at the intersection of trans-individual discourses which – combined in a characteristic way in a particular period and suffused with institutional power – are diffracted through them as subjects. However obscure that sounds, Foucault's work as a whole is in fact less universalistic than that of Lévi-Strauss and closer to sociological concerns. Some of Foucault's formulations, particularly his intuitions about power, whilst not new, are within a whisker of sociology;[8] but their usefulness is impaired by the philosophical awkwardness with which they are expressed.

Foucault's earlier work concentrates on the analysis of discourses and discursive practices and his later work deepens this through the infusion of the themes of power and domination (Smart 1985: 47, 73). As is the case with many other contemporary French intellectuals, the watershed appears to have been the 1968 events in France, which finally sealed Foucault's disillusionment with Marxism as well as politicized his treatment of sexuality (Sheridan 1982: 113; Walzer 1986: 65). Barry Smart (1985: 47) argues that that there is not so much a break in Foucault's work at this point, as a reordering of priorities. One of the important continuities underlying this reordering around the themes of power/knowledge, sexuality and human subjection, is that the structuralist hue never leaves his orientation. Neither does it lose its fundamentally philosophical character, something from which we are diverted by his tendency to redescribe what he is doing as a new 'discipline' of his own creation, say, genealogy. In a neat formulation, Foucault's development moves from Kant to Nietzsche, but never beyond them.

For all its rhetorical flair and dazzling displays of conceptual artistry, Foucault's work as a whole is a paradigm case of para-sociology, to be approached with caution and scepticism. Smart (1985: 136) rightly notes how difficult it is to place Foucault within the usual social scientific pigeonholes. This is because Foucault is at pains to present himself as being outside all conventional disciplines, but somehow inclusive of all of them. He presents us with what he claims is a non-privileged 'discourse about discourses', as he puts it in *The Archaeology of Knowledge* (1969: 205). But nevertheless, I would argue that Foucault's enigmatic work remains ultimately a form of philosophy, despite his attempts to prevent it being so assimilated (*ibid.*: 205–6). As I will show shortly, his work is an example of philosophical 'metacritique' (see Rose 1981: 22–47; and Chapter 2 of this volume).

In *The Order of Things* Foucault explicitly accords an autonomy to 'the philosophical dimension' in the modern epistème, that is the configuration of different discourses in the present period (Foucault 1966: 347). Significantly, though, philosophy is one major subject that remains unanalyzed as an institutional discursive practice, or form of power/knowledge, anywhere in Foucault, even though his work is drenched in its terminology, points of departure and assumptions. *Could questioning its autonomy be for Foucault the abyss into which even he is not prepared to jump?*

Foucault wants to write about social relations and human history without falling into what he sees as the undesirable (largely political) consequences of Comteanism, Durkheimianism, Marxism, positivism, scientism, the history of ideas and evolutionary theories that imply progress and continuity. So he has successively invented two new fields of inquiry of his own, which he has called *archaeology* (in his pre-1970 works) and *genealogy*, adapted from Nietszche (in the works after that) and identified himself as their pioneer. For each, he has defined its subject-matter and approach negatively, as avoiding all the pitfalls, fallacies and fatal extremities of argument that befall all those previously mentioned forms of inquiry, at least. Each of these new 'fields' has provided him with a new world-view and a new metalanguage, which immunizes him against criticism from those who still use the conventional moral, political and sociological concepts. In other words, he protects himself from opponents coming from every direction simply by the clever redescription of what he is doing. It is an ingenious, but highly idiosyncratic strategy. As Michael Walzer put it, Foucault 'doesn't play . . . any . . . game whose rules the rest of us might know' (1986: 51).

However, I think it is possible to understand Foucault a little better than he understood himself. From the sociological point of view from which I am arguing, it seems to me that he naively tries to blend empirical data with what are ultimately philosophically derived concepts, so as to address somewhat deficiently what are staple sociological questions to do with power, institutions, scientific differentiation and the origins of the modern personality. But he has no conception of how this incongruity might be a handicap to the understanding of the complexities of society and knowledge. It is this hybrid nature of his theories of discourses and power/knowledge that partly accounts for their indeterminacy and vagueness (Layder 1994: 107)

In his earlier work, Foucault was pursuing nothing less than a description of the relationship between all sciences, social sciences and humanities (as discourses or discursive practices) in a given period of history. He used the term 'archaeology' for the discipline he created that undertakes the 'differential analysis of the modalities of the discourse' (1969: 139). Here his approach was defined again largely negatively, as being against the assumptions, amongst others, of historians, Marxists, phenomenologists, existentialists and hermeneuticians. His overall ambition to understand scientific differentiation and specialization was not a great distance from the aims of the sociology of knowledge, although Mannheim, Merton and Elias have gone about the task in very different ways. They, too, were highly conscious of the presuppositions of forms of inquiry as well as the problem of ideology versus science and the role of power. For Foucault, they would be just further examples of the objectifying modern sciences of 'man' which helped to regulate and normalize conduct in modern societies. But he does share with sociologists of knowledge the desire to displace the history of ideas, the dualistic economic determinism of Marxism and the ego-centred thrust of Western thought. But unlike their broadly socio-genetic orientation towards these problems, he adopts a strategy that has a lot in common with the basic tenets of structuralism, construed as a philosophical metalanguage.

Foucault seeks to demonstrate empirically the 'mode of combination' of the discursive practices such as political economy, natural history or grammar, in a given age. The totality of this set of practices, articulated in a particular configuration of relations, he calls an epistème, avoiding alternative conceptualizations such as world-view or spirit of the age. In *The Order of Things* he analyses the Renaissance, classical and modern epistèmes which are each held to be self-contained and to have succeeded each other in a *discontinous* fashion, for reasons that are not always clear. Each one provides the 'conditions of possibility' of knowledge in a given period, which will be reflected in the objective, impersonal relations between institutionalized discursive practices. And it is these practices that are held to inscribe themselves in individuals, unbeknown to them.

Interestingly, Foucault claims that his approach 'separates itself off from all the philosophies of knowledge' (*ibid.*: 192) because it does not question the right of science to be such. It only questions the fact of the existence of science *vis-à-vis* other discourses. In other words, Foucault is here effectively subverting all the epistemological issues that arise about ideology by refusing to set up science as a privileged discourse through which one can adjudicate on its veracity. The issue of what is valid knowledge is thus transformed into one of the structure of the relations between equipollent truth-defining discourses in a particular episteme, not the question of validity in relation to a privileged standard of truth. In Sheridan's words, 'Knowledge is not so much true or false as legitimate or illegitimate for a particular set of power relations' (1982: 220). Foucault thus *apparently* moves away from the traditional philosophy of knowledge.

But the direction in which he is travelling is not, despite the talk of power relations, towards a sociological epistemology which, on my argument, is the overall tendency of the development of the sociological tradition in relation to philosophy. Foucault remains within Kantian philosophy, tacitly taking the road of 'metacritique' (Rose 1981: 22–47). This is a kind of transcendental inquiry in which a wider range of historical 'conditions of possibility' or presuppositions than simply the traditional Kantian a priori categories of the understanding, are entertained: say, 'life' (Dilthey), *Dasein* (Heidegger/Gadamer), or society (Durkheim). Its major drawback, argues Rose, is circularity:

> However, these radical approaches to the question of validity remain within a Kantian transcendental circle: the condition of the possibility of experience (meaning) is likewise the condition of the object of experience (meaning), whether the condition is 'life', 'social situation', '*Dasein*', or 'history' [*or discourse or episteme*]. The analysis revolves within an hermeneutic or transcendental circle, that is a circle without result.
>
> (*ibid.*: 23)

One can see clearly how this metacritical stance is played out in Foucault. The whole way in which he sets up the issues is entirely in the philosophical mode of transcendental argumentation. He says that the episteme is 'what ... makes possible the existence of epistemological figures and sciences' (1969: 192). The episteme is a constantly moving set of articulations and shifts between related discourses which limit and constrain what counts as scientific or any other form of truth at any point in time. He even calls this the 'historical *apriori*' of a given period (1966: 157). For Foucault there is not *a* science or *a* unified totality of discourses, but rather shifting points of intersection between discourses. Each discursive formation has its own rules, its own unity, which defines the 'mode of being' (1966: 158) of objects and *enables them to appear* and be recognized as objects. In other words, in typical Kantian fashion, any unity or regularity in the world does not reside in the object, but rather is shaped by the a priori conditions, in this case discourses. For example, for Foucault mental illness in the nineteenth century *was* all that was said in all the statements that made up the discourse. It was, and still is, the interplay of the rules of the discourse that make it possible for the 'object' of mental illness to appear at all.

In Foucault's later writings, this picture of discursive formations combined in an episteme, making possible the discontinuous structure of experience of an age, is infused with Nietzschean ideas which bring to the fore the embeddedness of the discourses in institutional power. This addition makes no difference to the fundamentally transcendental character of his inquiries as a form of 'metacritique'. The prominence of Nietzsche in Foucault's later works is well known (Sheridan 1982: 114ff.; Smart 1985: 56ff.). Nietzsche provided for Foucault, as he did for Max Weber more than fifty years before, the inspiration to reject once and for all utopian thinking and finalist theories of history and face the ubiquity of power and domination in human societies.

In his often quoted essay 'Nietzsche, Genealogy and History' (in Bouchard 1977) Foucault adopts the term 'genealogy' from Nietzsche to advocate a kind of historical analysis. It is one in which one abandons the search for absolute origins and does not assume a teleological process of history towards freedom, because both assume that there is an essence to history that can be uncovered. History is simply the discontinuous succession of one form of domination after another, driven by accidents and multiple causes, with no meaning and no end. Social knowledge is inevitably perspectival. Genealogy also embraces the investigation of commonplace, mundane bodily activities as well as the more usual lofty historical topics to do with the state and abstract ideas.

These ideas are of course hardly news to sociologists who have read Weber, Mannheim, Goffman or Elias, although they might have seemed daring and novel in the late 1960s and into the 1970s to philosophically minded people coming out of a discredited Marxism, but who could not go over to sociology because for them it was still compromised as intellectually deficient and justificatory of the inequalities of the bourgeois *status quo*. There is more than a hint of this view in Foucault, which is partly why his work has an appeal to ex-Marxists. He will call himself a historian, an archaeologist, a genealogist, but never a sociologist. The principles said to constitute the subject-matter of genealogy (i.e. abandoning the search for origins, teleology and meaning and insisting on accidents and multiple causes) are stated only negatively by Foucault, that is, as things to *avoid*. As Rorty says, they are nothing more than simply 'helpful hints on how to avoid being trapped by old historiographical assumptions' (quoted in Hoy 1986: 47). Furthermore, the infusion of these themes into Foucault's anti-humanist, structuralist form of inquiry constitutes the adoption of a revised kind of philosophy of history, disguised as the enigmatic, *self-defined* 'discipline' of genealogy. In doing this, Foucault falls further back behind the sociological revolution, which was constituted precisely by the transcendence of this genre.

It is difficult to expound Foucault's rather fuzzy analysis of the power/knowledge syndrome in his later works, *Discipline and Punish* (1975) and *The History of Sexuality* (1976) and various interviews (Gordon 1977) without reproducing its tendency towards reification. Power is treated as though it were an entity with plans and intentions, in formulations such as power 'establishes a network through which it freely circulates', 'installs itself and produces its real effects', 'surmounts the rules of right' and 'extends itself beyond them' (in Lukes 1992: 232–4). The analysis is further vitiated by the relentless rendering of power relations in the terminology of people's 'subjugation' and 'subjection' in structures of 'domination' and 'discipline', all of which carry the pre-judgement of a degree of unwarranted severity or harshness. Foucault confirms that in his work he has wanted to give due weight to 'the fact of domination, to expose both its latent nature and its *brutality*' (*ibid.*: 231, my emphasis).

Without wanting to deny the existence of this kind of oppression, this conceptual pre-judging deflects our attention from seeing the different *kinds* of power relations between interdependent individuals or groups as power *balances* (Elias 1978a; Burkitt 1993). Foucault talks about power as (a) endemic in social relations and (b) having a relational character (1976: 95), as though he was the first to reach these insights. For a sociological reader, it hardly needs saying that these are staple sociological ideas found in different forms in a variety of writers from Simmel, Pareto, Weber and Mannheim to Bourdieu, Elias and Giddens. Not surprisingly, in Foucault, because of his basically philosophical outlook and training, they are stated with little sociological precision. And his plainly erroneous statement that 'Power comes from below' (1976: 94) is a giveaway comment which contradicts the aspiration of his relational theory.

Following Foucault in close paraphrase, he argues that pre-modern sovereign power was exercised intermittently by the monarch, who did not subjugate people continuously in their day-to-day lives. The disciplinary power that is said to have succeeded it is anonymous, ubiquitous and effected through surveillance and physical punishment. The claim is that as they became aware that they were being observed (in factories, barracks and asylums in particular), individuals began to oversee themselves and regulate their behaviour. In the modern *epistème*, carceral networks, surveillance and the regulation of the bodies of subjugated people to render them docile, are part of a new modality of power, which he refers to sometimes as bio-power (Foucault 1976: 140–2). Power operates in every nook and corner of society and is 'exercised through a net-like organization' (in Lukes 1992: 234). This 'capillary' modality of power corresponds to the rationalized, 'disciplinary' society of modern times which made possible the new social sciences, which were geared to the observation, classification and objectification of persons. 'Knowable man (soul, individuality, consciousness, conduct . . .) is the object-effect of this analytical investment, of this domination-observation' (Foucault 1975: 305).

I would agree with much of Layder's (1994: 106–11) evaluation of Foucault as someone who underestimates the power of the state and fails directly to address the question of who exercises power. He also shifts his emphasis arbitrarily between the self and that which is said to constitute the self (discourses) and between micro and macro social patterns, without ever achieving a synthesis. If these points are coupled with the obvious shortcomings I discussed earlier, which arise out of its philosophical provenance, one wonders: what is the source of appeal of this flawed and imprecise theory at the present time?

Foucault's work makes a great deal out of the ways in which illegitimate, institutionally marginalized knowledge has in the past been denied, burked or otherwise repressed. (Again, all of this was discussed by Gaston Bachelard, who developed the concepts of 'sanctioned' and 'lapsed' knowledge (Bachelard 1972; Wassall 1990)). Whilst it leaves a lot to be desired sociologically, Foucault's work does have an appeal *politically* in certain phases of functional democratization and informalization (see Chapter 8). The constructivist theory of power/knowledge and the idea of 'resistance' find a resonance in the emancipatory movements of marginalized groups, such as women, gays, lesbians and ethnic minorities in recent years, who have been struggling to establish their own cultural norms against the dominant ones, in a situation of relatively unequal power chances. Foucault will have an appeal particularly in the early stages of such movements where the power balance is tilted more in favour of established groups and consequently the struggle to establish an autonomous identity and to throw off self-images imposed by the established are being more tenaciously fought. In such phases, the Foucauldian theories of marginalized knowledge and resistance speak to the condition of advocates of and participants in such movements. In these circumstances, the weaknesses and vagueness of these theories as contributions to an empirical sociological programme will go unnoticed.

Summary

1.   In drawing attention to the theoretical consequences of the ego-centredness of Western philosophy, as a symptom of the highly developed individualism of modern people, the structuralists had homed in on an important target. As is well known, it is an issue that has also exercised sociologists at every stage of the development of the discipline and in all national traditions. The leap of imagination and detachment needed to visualize ourselves as forming part of social networks extending beyond us, and forming part of regularities that exceed the scope of individual action, is one of the basic hurdles over which every budding sociologist has to jump. The issue that the structuralists were addressing is a thus a basic one. The pendulum of debate about individual and society has swung between methodological individualism on the one side (which carries the dangers of psychologism and ultimately reduction to biology) and sociological reification on the other, as in some of Durkheim's more exaggerated statements about society as a reality *sui generis* in his manifestos for sociology as a science (Frisby & Sayer 1986; Elias 1991b).

2.   The structuralists, who were politically and polemically committed to refuting the individualism of existentialism, overreacted. Through utilizing categories such as 'discourses', 'practices' and 'codes', they massively exaggerated the efficacy of extra-individual (but individual-including) processes, particularly in the field of culture. Unbeknown to individuals, discourses, codes and structures supposedly operate 'through' them. To state, as many sociologists have in different ways, that people's intended actions take place in webs of unplanned interdependencies that have properties and exhibit long-term regularities and patterns, which are outside the control of any given individual, is one thing. But to state, as the structuralists have, that extra-individual practices or codes are somehow *active in their own right, through the medium of individuals* who have no choice in the matter, is quite another. Such a view falls into hypostatization and ultimately collapses into metaphysical or animistic thinking.

3.   Furthermore, in the act of refuting the individualism of existentialism in this particular way, the structuralists inadvertently gave credence to the existentialist conception of the individual and thereby reproduced the individual/society dichotomy. On the issue of individual and society, the mutually antagonistic critiques generated by the two paradigms of existentialism and structuralism are inextricably bonded to each other. The structuralists' interest was impelled by the desire to win political points against the humanism of their rivals. They did this spectacularly through provocative posturings about the limitations of the power of

the sacrosanct individual whose end was imminent as part of the forthcoming 'death of man' (Poster 1975: 334). Where this motif was less prominent, in the field of the study of cultural codes, the structuralists have probably left their strongest legacy.

4. Arguably, Elias's notion of figuration has avoided the pitfalls of exaggeration to either side of the dualism (Elias 1991b). In this model, the indubitable self-experience of the modern individual is acknowledged in its authenticity and relative autonomy and explained sociologically. At the same time, but without the reification of 'society', the figurational compulsion of the networks of human interdependencies of which that individual is a part are shown *empirically* to possess regularities which in the long term exceed the scope of individual actions, even though inclusive of them. Instead of starting with individuals and trying to bridge the gap to that which is apparently 'beyond' them – 'society' – Elias deals from the outset with interdependent people in the plural (Elias 1978a: 125; 1991b: part 1). Working from this starting point makes it harder for ideological over-extensions – say, the assumptions of the uniqueness of each individual as the centre of the world or the total impotence of the individual in the face of the autonomous action of discursive practices – to be smuggled into the analysis.

5. The structuralists nevertheless made an important contribution in their critique of the hangovers of dualistic metaphysics to be found in Marx's theory of base and superstructure and in other theories that separate culture and structure as though they were two entities. The philosophical dualism of being and consciousness is one that has tacitly insinuated itself into the sociological tradition, despite its practitioners' many attempts to overcome it. Not only have they and Heideggerians fought against dualistic metaphysics in various ways, but so have writers within or sympathetic to the sociology of knowledge (Mannheim 1925: 142–4 and 162–3; Tillich 1933: 116; Elias 1971: 155) as well as Max Weber who was also on a similar track (Thomas 1985). The structuralists have helped to augment this innovatory movement away from dualisms of this kind.

6. The influence of Nietzsche was mainly on the poststructuralists and, indeed, the increasing prominence in the writings of the French structuralist tradition of Nietzschean themes from about 1968 onwards marks the watershed between structuralism and poststructuralism. But his influence was a mixed blessing. He was an important source of inspiration for breaking with the Marxian idea that all forms of domination and social alienation are derivative of power relations of an economic kind. This insight was not, however, translated into systematic sociological form, as it was in Weber, Mannheim and Elias, say, but rather remained simply a critical stick with which to beat Marxists. Furthermore, the world-view of the structuralists, particularly that of Foucault and Lévi-Strauss, was also affected by Nietzsche's idea of *ressentiment*, which gave their work a rather negative and dismal undertone. As Pace wrote of Lévi-Strauss: 'His work is marked, not by the affirmation of what is good, but rather by the rejection of what is evil' (1983: 199).

7. The structuralists' view of the human social condition is therefore the rather gloomy and overstated one of the continuous suffering of humans at their own hands. People are objectified and subjugated by impersonal forces outside their control, including the human sciences, and their initiatory volition as indi-

viduals is illusory. They have no unitary self, but exist only as diffractions on the surfaces of the tectonic shifts of discourse that constitute the epistème and construct them as individuals. This is a process in which naked power and domination are central. Foucault said that not only is God dead, but also that man, the murderer, 'is in the process of disappearing' (1966: 385). The idea of man as conscious creator was a product of the arrangement of knowledge in the modern epistème and all such configurations eventually unpredictably disappear. (Foucault is careful not to say 'are transcended', which would sound too Hegelian or dialectical.) If that occurred, then 'man would be erased, like a face drawn in sand at the edge of the sea' (*ibid.*: 387). The portentous cadences of the final pages of *The Order of Things* reproduce as metaphysical, even apocalyptic, a view of the human condition as any that the structuralists wanted to supplant.

8.   The undertones of tragic pessimism, misanthropy and fatalism are the result of the coming together of a number of moral and political factors in the structuralist world-view. But a significant part was played by the structuralists' failure completely to break with philosophy and its close relative, theology. In both traditions prophecy is legitimate and has a more or less free role, unencumbered by the controls of empirical evidence so basic to the culture of science. A number of writers have drawn attention to the similarities between Lévi-Strauss's writings and Buddhism (e.g. Pace 1983: 198, 204). Gillian Rose notes Foucault's use of the theological imagery of body and soul (1984: 174 and 178); and Jean-Marie Bénoist saw that the thesis of the death of man contained a subterranean return of dogmatic, 'theistic affirmations'. He concluded: 'one cannot help being seduced by the closeness of the Foucauldian notions of the death of man and the subsequent modifications in the concept of history ... to the Pascalian position of a Jansenist God who does not intervene in history' (1978: 218).

6

GLOBALIZATION AS AN EMERGENT CONCEPT

With the passage of time, nations, hitherto living in isolation, draw nearer to one another.

(Turgot 1750: 37)

An emerging area of inquiry

In the last decade, social scientists have become more and more aware of the impor-tance of transnational social processes. This chapter itself is symptomatic of the flourishing interest in this level of inquiry. The term 'globalization', increasingly used in the 1980s and 1990s in a number of fields, in fact first appeared in Webster's dictionary in 1961. This marked the beginnings of explicit recognition in the contemporary period of the growing significance of the world-wide connectedness of social events and relationships. In 1972, the OED Supplement recognized the word 'global' as being in current use meaning world-wide, complementing the pre-existing sense of pertaining to the totality of a number of items. There has also been a transformation over the last twenty-five years or so in the meaning of the word 'global' in sociology, from meaning total, as in total society, to meaning a focus on the globe as a unit of analysis in its own right (Albrow 1992b: 5–6).

In contemporary discussions, the extending interdependency chains between nations have been variously referred to as the 'global human circumstance', 'the transnational scene', 'the compression of the world', 'the global ecumene' or simply as the world 'becoming a single place'. Martin Albrow has offered a socio-logical definition which rightly emphasizes that it is the changing nature of human bonding that is implicated in the process of globalization: 'This is the process whereby the population of the world is increasingly bonded into a single society' (Albrow 1992a: 248). This definition has echoes of Hobhouse, who wrote in 1906 that 'humanity is rapidly becoming, physically speaking, a single society' (cited by Robertson 1990: 21). Neither of these definitions claims that the world *is* a single society, nor that it will inevitably become one. Both of them hint at a process, perhaps a trend, but without any commitment to a timescale.

The reality of the growing interdependence of nations has been further thrown into relief by detrimental environmental effects such as global warming and pollution as well as by the danger of nuclear war, the perilous consequences of both of which respect no national borders. Knowledge of the seriousness of these effects for all humans, irrespective of national allegiance or cultural identity, has heightened the awareness of the process of the growing interconnectedness of national societies which had been going on apace anyway. It has thus reinforced the growing awareness of our common human fate. The environmental effects, the threat of nuclear war and globalization are related. The more extensive and intensive people's dependence on each other becomes globally, the more it is in their mutual interests to mitigate the unintended harmful environmental effects as well as reduce the risk of a nuclear war.

In sociology, political science, international relations, economics and applied fields such as marketing, the process of globalization is now taken for granted. The global dimension of human experience and 'global issues' generally are routinely presented in sociology textbooks (e.g. Kerbo 1989: 355–79; Brinkerhoff & White 1991: 608–34; Giddens 1997: ch. 19), with perhaps Joan Ferrante's *Sociology: A Global Perspective* (1992) being the most thoroughgoing attempt at an internationalized textbook that I have seen so far.

Recent studies and discussions of globalization have been legion and I cannot do justice here to the vastness and complexity of the rapidly developing literature. However, for my purposes in this chapter, it is not incorrect to say that the recent sociological discussions of the globalizing process fall into three groupings, investigating the problem area in three different ways:

(a) The effects of the international division of labour in the generation of a structure of inequality between nations Research has gone ahead into global economic interdependencies using the 'world-system' model developed by Immanuel Wallerstein (1979, 1991; Chirot 1977). This influential theory has become the leader in the field, establishing a model for further research and a benchmark for subsequent critique and theoretical development. As is well known, this neo-Marxist theory posits a developing, tripartite, interconnected world structure of nations: the core, periphery and semi-periphery and stresses the importance of the activities of transnational companies and movements of capital across national frontiers. In this paradigm, it is the economic logic of capital accumulation in the larger capitalist world economy that is assumed largely to determine social events and political changes within nations.

(b) The role of culture, including the globalization of information and communication, in shaping the world reality The part played by symbolic representations, political culture, information technology, the global media and religious counter-movements is the focus here (Robertson & Lechner 1985; Robertson 1990; Bergesen 1990; Hannerz 1990). Global communication, in particular television, has played an important part in bringing people instantaneous images of distant peoples and events, thus broadening and relativizing local experiences (Featherstone 1990). The contradictory interplay of 'particularism' and 'universalism' (Parsons) in the emerging consciousness of humankind as a whole brought about by these cultural developments, has also been a prominent theme (Robertson & Chirico 1985; Garrett 1992). The argument of this tendency is that a more unified picture of the globalizing process must embrace the counter-movements and traditional communal reactions, which are organic to the process, for which we need a concept of culture. At the same time, we must look at the level of transnational

institutions and the creation of international legal norms for any observable harbingers of the emergence of a genuinely global human solidarity.

(c)   Research areas opened up by regarding the network of interdependent nations as a figuration, i.e. as an emergent transnational level of social integration with a specific orderedness of its own   Following the lead of Norbert Elias (1987a, 1987b, 1991b), research in the figurational paradigm has proceeded into areas such as the consequences of the cold war superpower confrontation under conditions of mutual nuclear threat (Benthem van den Bergh 1992); the effect of the competitive survival and status struggles between nations on the formation of We- and I-identities (and/or we- and I- self-images) and codes of interpersonal behaviour (Wouters 1990); and the effects of globalization on identity formation, particularly the effects of the widening of sources of identification and disidentification (Swaan 1995 and 1997). This paradigm has also stressed the importance of humankind as a whole as a subject for empirical investigation, viewed in the long term, as well as the related conception of social integrative levels *sui generis* (Goudsblom 1989; Mennell 1990 and 1992: ch. 9; Kilminster 1994). The present chapter is intended as a theoretical contribution to the research effort of this grouping.

The work in the field of culture (paragraph b) is a reaction to the perceived economic reductionism of the Marxian-inspired world-system approach (Robertson & Lechner 1985: 107; Robertson 1990: 16). As Robertson puts it, 'I try to turn world-systems theory "on its head" by emphasizing *culture* and the *agency* aspect of the making of the global system' (1990: 28). Because of its origins in political economy, world-system theory does indeed tend to stress only the capitalistic, *Gesellschaft*-like dimension of the interrelations between nations across the globe. This approach is a variant of Marxist theories of imperialism of Lenin and Hilferding (Arrighi 1978) and later theories of dependency.[1] A polarized model of class struggle is mapped on to the world's nations. There are the upper-class, rich, exploiting nations of the core and the lower-class, poor, exploited nations of the periphery, with a 'middle-class' stratum in between, the semi-peripheral nations (Chirot 1977: 8; Ragin & Chirot 1985: 298). Inter-state rivalry and the global territorial conflict of the twentieth century are explained as expressions of the market-seeking logic of Western capitalism. This process is also held to explain the apparent obstacles to the imagined internationalization of revolutionary socialism via the world's underprivileged classes.

It is a commonplace that an important point of departure for the sociological pioneers of the last century and the early years of this century was to insist that economic regularities had to be understood sociologically. Economic patterns are only a species of social regularities in general. As Karl Mannheim later put it: 'when the Physiocrats and Adam Smith demonstrated the important role of competition in economic life, they were in fact only discovering a *general social relationship* in the particular context of the economic system' (Mannheim 1928: 195). For generations of sociologists it was necessary to fill in the cultural and social-psychological factors without which structured, repeated economic relations would not be possible – the 'non-contractual' aspects of contract, in Parsons' words, paraphrasing Durkheim. So, the mainstream sociological tradition has always regarded Marx as in error when he tried to read off politics and culture as 'spheres' determined in some way by a separately conceived economic base and to reduce all forms of alienation to expressions of economic alienation.

The recent work of the cultural critics of Wallerstein emphasizes people's sense of solidarity, their reflexivity, the meaning they give to their lives and their identity formation, as also crucially implicated in the globalizing of social life. This accentuation forms a corrective to the analysis of globalization solely in terms of international trade and capital flows emanating to and from the core countries. These responses to Wallerstein thus reiterate an important formative dialogue in the development of sociology, but this time in relation to theorizing at the global level. Robertson has acknowledged this: 'I have set out to provide, as Weber did in his Protestant Ethic thesis, an "equally plausible" cultural account of globalization, in the face of the "materialism" of world-system theory' (1992: 320).

Much of the recent work of the cultural critics of Wallerstein draws on the once much maligned, but now to some extent rehabilitated, Parsonian paradigm, albeit construed in an adapted fashion so as to remove the naive functionalist connotations (Münch 1987; Holton & Turner 1986; Robertson 1990: 18; see also Chapter 4 of this volume). Following the general thrust of the sociological tradition, in which he was well versed, Parsons also distanced himself from the economistic Marxist theory of society. He tried to accomplish this by analytically distinguishing separate, fictitious 'spheres' of society, including the economy, culture and communal life, then positing their different modes of 'interpenetration' as a device for explaining subsequent patterns (Münch 1987: 28, 67, 199). As Robertson also says, 'I am insisting that both the economics and the culture of the global scene should be analytically connected to the general structural and actional features of the global system' (1990: 18). This manoeuvre also provided Parsons and the later writers in this tradition with a way of bringing a pattern to a social reality implicitly assumed, very much in line with Simmel and Weber, to have no structure of its own. However, this ingenious artifice carried the danger of reproducing the dualism of culture/structure, which is a distant echo of the subject/object and thought/reality polarities of Western philosophy. Robertson is clearly aware of this problem, when he says that his (neo-Parsonian) strategy 'is only a prologue to a statement which transcends the cleavage between "material" and "idealistic" approaches' (1992: 320).[2]

Arguably, the processual approach of Elias can be seen as a synthesis which, amongst other things, tries to do just that, i.e. to move away from action theory and its attendant dualisms such as culture/structure, as well as its voluntaristic overtones (see Chapter 4). Like Parsons, Elias moved beyond political economy, but rather than positing analytically distinguished social 'spheres', he starts from the structured process of interwoven interdependent people in the plural, for which he coined the concept of figuration. For him people are simultaneously bonded to each other in various ways because of the multiple functions (affective as well as economic and political) that groups and individuals perform *for each other* (see Elias 1978a: 134ff.; and note 5 to Chapter 4 of this volume).

The next two sections comprise two short excursions into some of the forerunners of global thinking from the eighteenth and nineteenth centuries, including Turgot, Condorcet, Herder, Hegel and Marx. Of necessity this coverage is somewhat schematic, but hopefully sufficient for present purposes. These are to illuminate the current sociological controversies about globalization by showing how the character of ideas on the subject of humankind as a whole as well as more systematic models of the functioning of social relations on a world level, are closely bound up with the nature of the phase of development of national differentiation and international integration at which they are articulated. This should help us to guard against uncritically employing today theories or concepts on this subject that were developed at earlier stages of development. Without these references to the balance of social forces in the societies in which these forerunners lived, and between nations at the time, I do not think it is possible fully to understand the character of their ideas on the subject of nations and their interrelations.

These excursions are thus an organic part of my argument about the concept of globalization being an emergent one developed to capture the contours of the recent integrative spurt in the level of social integration comprising the bonds between nation-states. Even though I have consulted the works of historians of ideas in writing these sections, it would be a misunderstanding of my sociological approach to assume from that fact that what follows is simply an interesting exercise in the history of ideas tacked on to the analysis of contemporary theories of globalization so as to provide some historical 'background'. Nothing could be further from my intention.

I will return in the two sections after that to the basic sociological questions that have come to the surface again in the current debate about thinking and theorizing at the global level. I will conclude with some reflections on orientation and disorientation in the present period of extensive and bewildering change and the relevance of my preceding discussions as a contribution towards our better orientation.

Forerunners

Even though they consist largely of adaptations to theories handed down to us as part of sociological traditions, the models of global social structure discussed in the previous sub-section are still nevertheless a product of the current phase of the development of national and international dependencies. It is in the present period that the need to elaborate global sociological models has been perceived as an imperative. It is no accident that it is a period where accelerating global interdependence is more clearly visible around us and is shaping our fate in more compelling ways. However, as Johan Goudsblom has pointed out, 'global interdependence is far less recent than we may have been led to believe' (1989: 25). At no point in the past, he argues, has the history of any people been unaffected by that of their neighbours and theirs by their neighbours, and so on. These interconnections have been obscured in the earlier attempts by, say, Herodotus in the Ancient world or by St Augustine in the medieval period, to write histories of humanity as whole, which were in fact disguised histories of particular peoples or other selective trajectories.

I discovered by simply looking in the dictionary that the word 'humanity', derived from the Latin *humanitas* and corresponding to the French *humanité*, is first recorded as being in use meaning the human race in 1579 (*OED*). Today, the word 'humankind' has come into currency as the non-sexist alternative to mankind, but in fact it is not a neologism but a revival. As a synonym for humanity, the word humankind dates from 1645.

Philosophers in the European Enlightenment such as Herder, Turgot and Condorcet, as well as later social scientists such as Marx and Comte, prefigured (which is not the same thing as anticipated) current debates about humankind as a whole and the relations between nations. The same is true of the writings of Hegel, particularly his *Philosophy of History* (1830b). They addressed somewhat abstractly the fate of the human species and the linkages between nations, linguistic groups and civilizations and the development of human knowledge as a whole. Even if they were not always successful in their attempts, they all genuinely tried to transcend specific national allegiances and preferences. But they did so in different ways, according to different national traditions, such that it is misleading to specify one eighteenth-century view on the subject of nations and their linkages as being that of *The* Enlightenment. They also did not have the benefit of the enormous growth of knowledge about human societies that is so easily available to us. Hence, their attempted syntheses of the perceived trend towards human unification and the development of human knowledge, were rather premature (Elias 1991b: 89, 120; Goudsblom 1989: 11–12).

Philosophies of history, such as those of Herder, Vico or Hegel, are, as William H. Dray (1964: 59) pointed out, attempts to find meaning or significance in the historical events studied empirically by historians. They are often shot through with preconceived values or unconscious wishes and fears, stemming from the political hopes of their authors or from their national or class habitus. In the writings of Johann Gottfried von Herder in the 1770s and 1780s,[3] particularly his *Also a Philosophy of History* of 1774, the nation is regarded as the only relatively stable entity in the flux of history. It is an organism, a non-rational, vital centre of human association and the source of all secular human truth. It was to be understood not through reason, but through empathy. For Herder, history is benevolent: all that has grown naturally, historically, including nations, is good. All nations are of equal worth and all contribute to the richness of humanity as a whole (Iggers 1968: 34ff.).

This romantic–conservative view was relativistic and suffused with metaphysical and theological undertones (Baumer 1977: 295). However, what is interesting from the point of view of my argument is that Herder, like many of the other German 'historicists' of his time, had a conception of a common humanity which expressed itself in those national manifestations. His nationalism was not of the exclusive or chauvinistic kind that we find in the late nineteenth and twentieth centuries, but was, rather, a 'cosmopolitan culture-oriented nationalism' (Iggers 1968: 30) undergirded ultimately by a theological view of human unity. The *Humanitätsideal* that Herder shared with Winckelmann, Humboldt and Goethe specified – contrary to the more rationalistic view of humankind found elsewhere in the Enlightenment, particularly in France – that humans are diverse, the rational and irrational aspects of the human personality being unified in a harmonious whole. Humboldt declared that 'Mankind as a whole exists only in the never attainable totality of all individualities that come into existence one after another' (quoted by Iggers 1968: 38).

These formulations, I would argue, represent a way of visualizing humankind as a whole when national self-images were strong in people's thinking, particularly in that of aristocratic élites, but not so strong as to block their prominent articulation of what they have in common with people of other nations (Elias 1968: 240ff.). At this stage, such commonality was expressed rhetorically and at a high level of generality, largely by representatives of aristocratic strata whose confidence of their status and their *real international bonds* enabled them to visualize peoples of other nations with a cosmopolitan magnanimity. As Hans Kohn (1971: 120) has pointed out, the internationalist consciousness came from the European educated upper classes of the eighteenth century. Turgot's statement, quoted as the epigraph of this chapter, visualizes nations developing closer ties with each other in a similarly visionary and hence rather unspecific way.

During the French Revolution, Condorcet distinguished between intra- and international social relations, as well as raised the question of judging the improvement of humankind as a whole. In keeping with the more politicized nature of the French Enlightenment compared with that of Germany or England, Condorcet felt compelled to express the issue in the high moral tone of social criticism:

> Our hopes, as to the future condition of the human species, may be reduced to three points: the destruction of inequality between different nations; the progress of equality in one and the same nation; and lastly, the real improvement of man.
>
> (quoted by Baumer 1977: 232–3)

The kinds of nations that all these writers have in mind are still dominated by dynastic and ecclesiastical élites – they are not yet nation-states dominated by industrial classes and characterized by highly exclusionary and competing nationalistic ideologies. They talked about the unity of all nations in the most lofty and general terms, long before the territorial rivalries of this century and long before harbingers of its real possibility (but not its inevitability) had begun to be observed, without anyone planning it, more tangibly around us, thereby generating the concept of globalization. It has been the nineteenth- and twentieth-century inter-state conflict and rivalry that has produced the more exclusionary and chauvinistic forms of modern nationalism, blinding us to the developing international interdependencies that those ideological antagonisms belied. Herder's internationalist consciousness was, and still is, somewhat ahead of its time:

> The scholars who study [the] customs and languages [of the European nationalities] must hurry to do so while these peoples are still distinguishable: for everything in Europe tends toward the slow extinction of national character.
>
> (cited by Kohn 1971: 120)

At the later stage of the twentieth century, the inter-state conflicts have, in a series of waves, raised the level of social tension within and between nation-states, generating fear images in people's thinking. From the point of view of people in richer, more powerful, higher status nations, the peoples of other, poorer, less powerful, lower status nations can be often regarded as subhuman, as ethnically inferior or in other ways as of low social worth. It is only in these circumstances that, at the level of inter-state conflict, the conditions for the achievement of 'mutual identification' (Elias) between conflicting international antagonists becomes both a practical and a sociological problem. At the earlier stage, the lower level of international tension and the domination of loosely integrated European nations by pre-industrial élites, produced, depending on national context, conditions more conducive to cosmopolitan internationalism or to generalized theories of the moral or political progress of humankind, such as those of Condorcet and Turgot (1750).

Marx's synthesis: global aspects

Marx is an important actor in the drama because he was one of the first to try to develop social scientific concepts systematically to deal with the social regularities and patterns set in train by the rapidly extending global trade networks of his time. It is worth dwelling on the global aspect of his theory of capitalism, since it has provided the framework upon which later exponents of the most influential contemporary model in the field – the theory of the world capitalist system – have, in their different ways, built. His work can be seen as a synthesis of Enlightenment ideas about humanity as a whole with a theory of the emerging global market which he found discussed in the works of political economists (Gay 1973: 344–68). He combined the two in the utopian projection of a world communist society, a vision he shared with many other socialist radicals of his time (Evans 1951).

The gist of the early sections of *The German Ideology* on this subject (Marx & Engels 1845a: 39ff. especially) is that communism is the empirical realization of the oneness of the human species, made possible by the development of social bonds of cooperation on a world scale. Communist society will put 'world historical . . . universal individuals in place of local ones' (*ibid*.: 47). Marx also suggests that social processes within nations will tend to become increasingly determined by the relationships *between* nations. He describes this process cryptically as the contradiction between 'national consciousness and the practice of other nations, i.e. between the national and the general consciousness of a nation' (*ibid*.: 43). Marx argues that this process could only be expressed metaphysically by Hegel because the productive forces and modes of human cooperation were insufficiently developed on a world scale to permit the realization of human unity in reality. In the *Economic and Philosophic Manuscripts*, written just a year before, he projects into the communist society 'the complete return of man himself as a *social* (i.e. human) being – a return become conscious, and accomplished within the entire wealth of previous development' (Marx 1844: 95).

Invoking Hegel and Adam Smith, Marx says that international trade and exchange and the whole world economic process appear to operate independently of individual people, setting up empires, causing nations to rise and fall and to rule the earth with a 'hidden hand'. He concludes that Hegel and his followers had mistaken these alienating effects of the broadening of the division of labour and modes of human cooperation across the globe, as the existence of an external spirit-force driving the history of the world's peoples. Marx revels in making these basic sociological points over and over again against the Hegelians.

> In history up to the present it is certainly an empirical fact that separate individuals have, with the broadening of their activity into world-historical activity, become more and more enslaved under a power alien to them (a pressure which they have conceived of as a dirty trick on the part of the so-called universal spirit, etc.), a power which has become more and more enormous and, in the last instance, turns out to be the world market.
>
> (Marx & Engels 1845a: 49)

Marx genuinely tried to render the issues of the structure of history and the possibility of human global unification amenable to empirical investigation. He looked for what he called the 'anatomy' of this process, which he variously terms – in his dualistic, philosophical way – the material 'substratum' or 'substructure', in political economy, the only developed social science at his disposal. At the stage of the differentiation of social functions at which he stood, self-regulating, autonomous economic activities had outstripped the integrating social and political institutions, thus producing the illusion that the economic 'sphere' was a separate entity, independent of the state. Economic activity was so prominent and its representatives so powerful, that it probably seemed indubitable to Marx that the patterned human activities analysed by political economy – production and consumption – constituted the basic determining level of society and the driving force of all historical change. It was understandable that he should have seen society this way. He was not the only one in his time who did so – it was a model that he shared in essentials with the liberals.

However, the whole way in which Marx integrated scientific concepts from political economy into his theory was shaped by his confrontation with the philosophy of Hegel. And this, in turn, was overwhelmingly coloured by Marx's communist politics. He takes as his starting point Hegel's philosophy of history and claims, as we saw above, that it was a disguised representation of a real historical process of alienation. Marx's science of the development of historical modes of production purported to show empirically that international socialism and communism were the assured outcome of history: indeed they were written into it as its *telos*. What Hegel called the Absolute Ethical Life, that is universal human freedom, Marx implicitly translates into real-world communism, or democratic cooperation on a global scale, which progressively manifests itself in world history (Marx & Engels 1845a: 49–50; see also Chapter 2 of this volume).

Marx's synthesis gave him a 'scientific' version of socialism which politically subsumed all other versions. It was Marx's political commitments to socialism (and ultimately to communism) that fatefully drove him to translate one 'universalizing' philosophy of history into another, thus failing to make a clean break with the genre. Marx's social scientific theory was thus burdened with the same teleology as that of the metaphysical theory he was claiming to supplant.[4] Few who have followed Marx in developing theories of imperialism, dependency and world system out of his observations on the global, market-seeking logic of capital accumulation, have also used the dialectical–categoreal method in which his work was couched. This is the method whereby (like Hegel) he moved in his inquiries from the abstract to the concrete, using concepts and empirical materials to construct the concrete totality of bourgeois civilization – including its world-wide manifestations – 'in thought', as he puts it.[5]

I cannot go into this obscure subject here, but suffice it to say that this method was integral to the way in which Marx investigated bourgeois civilization and its tendencies on a global scale. It was not a purely technical matter, or an optional extra. The later Marxist writers have probably left it out because they wanted to jettison the metaphysical baggage in Marx, whilst retrieving the basic theory of economic power and exploitation for their own political purposes. However, by so doing, they by no means eliminated that baggage, but only obscured it. It remains true that Marx conspicuously failed completely to break with the philosophy of history. Hence, to appropriate his work uncritically, without correction for this, carries a number of risks, one being teleology.

It is worth bearing this in mind when considering Wallerstein's theory of the functioning of the world capitalist economy which comes packaged, not in the highly wrought categoreal sequences of Hegel's *Logic* or Marx's *Capital*, but in the wrappings of contemporary empirical social science, including standard theories of economic cycles and a veneer of rigorous methodology. Wallerstein, like other contemporary Marxists, *appears* to have jettisoned the metaphysical hangovers that pervade Marx's work and salvaged the 'rational kernel' of his theories of economic power and of world capitalism. However, despite appearances and his disclaimers to the contrary (Wallerstein 1991: 225ff.), at a deeper level of tacit assumptions, Wallerstein's theory still carries teleological overtones, which are the marks of its origins in Marx's partial overcoming of metaphysics. Wallerstein writes:

> It is precisely because [the world system] will continue to function as it has been functioning for 500 years, in search of the ceaseless accumulation of capital, that it will soon no longer be able to function in this manner. Historical capitalism, like all historical systems, *will perish* from its successes not from its failures.
>
> (Wallerstein 1991: 15, my emphasis)

Developing a sociological theory that can deal with the shape of the present stage of the global integration of nations, without falling into the economism and finalism of Wallerstein or the relatively high level of abstraction of the cultural corrective of Robertson, is the sociological task in this field at the present time. The Marxian tradition and later elaborations broadly within this paradigm have been looking decidedly unserviceable for some time. The reasons for this lie not just in recent events such as the collapse of communism in the European revolutions of 1989 which have had the effect of finally undermining the credibility of Marxism. They also lie a long way back in Marx himself, who left us the legacy of a one-sidedly economistic theory about the developing global human circumstance which was skewed not only by metaphysical but also by mythological elements. The way in which his work is often portrayed today in summaries of his theory of class power in sociological textbooks and the ways in which it has been developed on the global level in world-system theory have hidden from view just how arcane it actually was.

The one line from Hegel that every sociologist knows is that 'the Owl of Minerva spreads its wings only with the falling of the dusk' (Hegel 1820: 13). Never was this phrase more applicable than to the empirical research of Marx into the dynamics of bourgeois civilization on a world scale. In a profound discussion of Marx's method, Joseph J. O'Malley (1977: 26) pointed out that Marx's later writings and letters are studded with references to new crises and developments and to economic and political phenomena entering new phases, but which are not yet developed enough to a point where their significance could be grasped. As a good Hegelian, he knew that only when an institution or sphere had reached its nodal point of world-historical development and was in decline, could we fully understand it and its genesis. Changes in the national and world economies thus prevented, or delayed, Marx's work of scientific synthesis. It is possible that this was one reason that Marx's masterwork, which he called *The Economics*, was never finished (*Das Kapital* was one small part of it). O'Malley asks: can we in the later letters of Marx detect 'a growing awareness that the world which he was seeking to grasp and to depict in its totality and in a scientific way had not yet grown old enough for him to do so?' (1977: 26).

Thinking globally

The formation of sociologists' 'we' and 'I' identities within one or other of the mostly richer and more powerful nation-states unconsciously shapes the ways in which they fashion sociological concepts. During the period of intense European national territorial rivalry from the late nineteenth century onwards, to which the theorists of imperialism were responding, national self-images became entrenched in the consciousness of most people living in European countries. Hence, the macro sociological concepts such as social system, social structure and total society which sociologists and other social scientists have subsequently developed, though of some explanatory usefulness of course, were none the less effectively synonyms for 'nation' (Elias 1968; Tiryakian 1986). This has made both the intellectual and emotional leaps into developing concepts adequate to the emerging level of integration above the national one, formidably difficult. The integrity of the personalities of people living in nation-states is to a very large extent still dependent upon the emotional security of a national 'we-identity', because 'nations were born in wars and for wars' (Elias 1991b: 208). Nation-state based thinking seems therefore indubitable and provides for most social scientists the outer horizon of what is sociologically visualizable. Thinking about humankind as a whole or even new transnational regional identities has little or no emotional significance.

It *may* be getting a little easier, during the current intensification of globalization, to begin to think about human association, bonding and patterning at the global level, as the process impinges on us in reality in a more pressing, rapid and unavoidable way. The conditions for greater 'mutual identification' between peoples may be becoming more favourable. But it nevertheless still represents a challenge to the sociological imagination. In this respect Wallerstein has to be

given credit as a pioneer. He has contributed much to the collective leap of imagination and detachment that is needed to begin to think about (and thence to
develop concepts adequate to) social reciprocities and interdependencies integrated at a level above that of the nation-state.

Unfortunately, however, as in the case of his predecessor Marx, the cast of
Wallerstein's thinking has been very considerably shaped by a strong sense of political mission. Following Ragin & Chirot's penetrating analysis (1985: 301ff), the first
priority of Wallerstein's theory from the beginning was to inform a political and
ideological programme, which they convincingly trace from his biography. Only
secondarily was it intended to be a contribution to the comparative scientific
understanding of historical origins of contemporary societies. From the model of
the world capitalist system it can be predicted, to the satisfaction of its adherents
anyway, that the system will be transformed into a socialist world system. The
theory is not, they maintain, based on propositions that can be proved or falsified.
It can only be illustrated. Furthermore, considered from a social scientific point of
view, it is this political impetus that is the source of many of the lacunae of the
theory. These include not only its radical externalism and teleology, but also in
particular its neglect of culture.

For the most part Wallerstein's model explains all important internal changes in
countries, particularly economic changes, 'exogenetically' by their relative power
position in the wider world system that produces such events. But this does not
always explain why economic development affects extensive areas of the world
with similar cultures in very similar ways, despite profound differences in their
power position in the world system. To explain these cases, they argue, a concept of
culture is necessary because clearly some countries are culturally more conducive
to successful economic development than others. For Wallerstein, however, it is not
a question of explaining the causes of change using a variety of concepts tenta-
tively in close conjunction with evidence, but of finding more and more
illustrations of the functioning of the world capitalist system. This is carried out
solely in the service of demonstrating over and over again the exploitative nature
of the capitalist world system in order to prepare the intellectual and political
ground for the coming world socialist system. As Ragin & Chirot put it: 'those who
make politics the first order of their intellectual agenda know what they are doing.
It is unlikely that anyone could attempt as grand an enterprise as Wallerstein's
without a powerful ideological vision of the world' (*ibid.*: 302). The parallel with
Marx is striking.

The internationalist consciousness so typical of socialists such as Marx, and
taken for granted by Wallerstein later in the tradition, was not created by either of
them. It arose from the cosmopolitanism of eighteenth-century thinkers such as
Herder, that is from the confident magnanimity of the educated, privileged upper
classes who had international links and experiences. It also depended heavily on
new views of nature, society and man produced by the scientific outlook so prominent among the *philosophes* at the time (Wagar 1971: 114; Buchdahl 1961: 27; Gay
1973: 126–87). From the seventeenth century onwards, science was no longer
subordinate to theology or metaphysics, reflecting in part a lessening of the relative power of the church *vis-à-vis* other groups. At the same time, the abstract ways
in which these forerunners visualized international linkages and the lofty and

rhetorical way in which they discoursed about humankind as a whole and its progress, also corresponded to the properties of the stage of development of the integration of nations at which they, within their own nations, stood.

Sociological issues

The recent debate about the problem area of global interdependence has been dominated by a reprise of the traditional confrontation between political economy and sociology, but played out in relation to building models to understand global processes. Marxian political economy, as represented by Wallerstein's model of the world capitalist system, has become the leader in the field. Despite its flaws, even its sternest critics will concede its usefulness for explaining certain comparative patterns of historical change. However, it must be remembered that it has also become prominent partly through Wallerstein, driven by the monumental political mission that lies behind his theory, establishing a strong institutional base for its development and dissemination.

Quite understandably, given the pervasiveness of dualistic thinking, as sociologists became aware of the materialistic cast of the theory, it has generated various cultural correctives. Most of these have been informed by the Parsonian social action approach, whereby culture is analytically distinguished from the economy as a structural feature of the global social system. Much of the current research and discussion in this area revolves around positions taken within the framework of this time-honoured encounter and in terms of the antinomies thrown up by it.

Social relations at the level of integration above that of nations do not, however, represent in principle any particular technical difficulty of concept formation, provided a model of levels is employed to avoid reductionism (Elias 1987a). The main challenges to overcome in developing such models are: (a) the achievement of relative distanciation from political convictions; (b) going beyond political economy and the related materialism (structure)/idealism (culture) confrontation; (c) developing an interdisciplinary and cooperative approach towards the formidable task of data collection in this field; and (d) rising above nation-state based thinking. The overcoming of these challenges is, however, not entirely in the hands of sociologists themselves, no matter how talented they may be. It is partly bound up with the precarious institutional autonomy of communities of sociologists as well as the professional closure of disciplinary boundaries, which militates against grasping the connectedness of social events and processes. At the same time, the raising of the level of tensions in the global interdependencies themselves and/or within nation-states, can reinforce national self-images, hence the retrenchment of national and emotive thinking of all kinds, which spills over into sociological concept formation.

This chapter is partly an attempt to offer a programmatic 'third way' for sociological inquiry into globalization, moving between the economism of Wallerstein and the culturalism of Robertson. Or, to employ another metaphor, to proffer an alternative which comes up behind both of those approaches and goes round them. This is attempted by swinging the explanatory emphasis on to the conception of social relations as an emergent level of integration *sui generis* in the evolution of humankind out of physical, chemical and biological nature. The orderedness of the transnational level appears to be becoming increasingly autonomous and self-regulating, such that processes at the lower integrative levels (nation-state, region, community, kinship) are in the present period becoming increasingly governed by the order of the higher level. This means that increasingly the range of decisions that can be taken at the nation-state level is decreasing as the continental and global levels increase in size and complexity (Elias 1987a and 1991b).

Like the self-regulating, autonomous and impersonal nexus of events that came to be referred to at the national level as 'society', these higher, continental and global integrative processes are also operating, as it were, 'behind the backs' (a phrase of Hegel's) of the people whose intentional actions constitute them. But as such they by no means represent 'external' forces outside the effects of reciprocal human association and its unintended consequences. It would be a grave misunderstanding of my argument to read the terminology of levels of integration as indicative of metaphysical residues lingering in my own approach, even as I attempt to expose them in the work of others. The model is intended to be of use in *empirical research* and the concepts adequate to observable levels of the integration of human groups and the functions they perform for each other. The interdependencies between groups within nations and between nations across the globe, which has to be investigated much more on the empirical level, have properties that are the result of the unplanned consequences of those compelling relations, which exceed the scope of individual actions but are nevertheless only the result of those actions and the cumulative effect of the historical order of their development. My point is that their existence and concrete effects are empirically demonstrable and not a metaphysical assumption.

The venerable sociological issue upon which this matter ultimately turns is that between sociological nominalism and sociological realism, played out this time in relation to higher integrative levels than that of the nation-state. Over and over again in the history of sociology, writers who have tried to develop theories to explain the properties generated by one or other type or level of the widespread patterns of the interdependent relations of human groups, have been accused of metaphysics. And so often the counterposed alternative has been some form of individualism, carrying the danger of reduction to either psychology or biology.

The more sophisticated analytic approaches to sociology (e.g. Weberian, Simmelian, Parsonian) have wanted to preserve sovereign individuals at all costs, but at the same time to acknowledge the structured, patterned character of society. They have achieved this only by regarding society as in part the product of the cognitive organizing capacity of human beings (forms of sociation or culture) without which it would be structure*less*. The important work on globalization in the Parsonian tradition by Roland Robertson, however, shows equivocation on this issue, oscillating between nominalism and realism. Sometimes, consistently with the general transcendental cast of this approach, he feels compelled to put reality in inverted commas. For example, talking about transcending materialism and idealism he writes: 'In any case, "reality" has made it increasingly easy to do this, since economics and culture [analytically distinguished] have become increasingly intertwined in the contemporary world' (Robertson 1992: 320). Similarly, in other places he says that 'the concrete patterning of the world' is a 'heavily contested problem' and that 'the world' is 'the most salient *plausibility structure* of our time'

(Robertson 1990: 20–1, my emphasis). Then, on the other hand, we find realist statements: 'there is a general autonomy and "logic" to the globalization process – which operates in *relative* independence of strictly societal . . . processes' (*ibid.*: 27–8).

Globalization is, then, viewed in this chapter as an emergent concept, which was created spontaneously to reflect people's experiences of the properties of an accelerating phase of the level of social integration comprising the bonds *between* nation-states. The sociological concept of globalization is a more systematic version taken up from everyday usage and employed as a scientific concept. As I argued earlier, this emergent level of integration would appear in the present period to be beginning to canalize the levels below to a *greater* extent than before. The reasons for these unintended effects, brought about by the pressures being put on interdependent nations by each other, and by groups within them, is at present either reductively understood by Marxist political economy or attenuated by the abstract analytic sociology of the cultural corrective.

However, taken together, those two paradigms have located important problem areas and have begun to shift to an explanatory level above that of the nation-state. But in so doing, they have thrown up some characteristic antinomies, which need to be overcome. Once one enters the field attempting to correct, via 'culture', for the 'material' emphasis of world-system theory, then one has automatically repro-duced the culture/structure dualism and its correlates. At the same time, Robertson has transferred the classical Parsonian 'problem of order' on to the global level, looking for cultural norms that would ensure the regulation of conflict at this level. He points to the importance of 'global norms' concerning national sovereignty, distinguishing the actual operation of state institutions from 'the development of regulative norms concerning the relationships between states', such as international law (1990: 23).

Following the figurational approach, on the other hand, there is no necessity to posit, on the lines of Parsons, a distinction between the factual order and the normative order for the purpose of explaining social cohesion, let alone to transfer this to higher levels. Rather, the focus is on the figurational compulsion of the web of social interrelations at the national, regional and global levels. It is the particular nature of the relatedness and interdependence of groups within nations and between them, that exerts constraint over each one. Clearly, differing power ratios between the participants play an important part in structuring the options and possible outcomes of struggles. For example, Elias (1987a: 74ff.) traces the poten-tially dangerous consequences of the fact that at the inter-state level there is no effective equivalent of the monopolization of the means of force by state institu-tions which exists within most internally pacified nation-states. Each individually armed country feels much less inhibited in using violence internationally to settle disputes than do individuals or groups within nation-states. Whether they do or not, depends not so much on the existence of international 'regulative' norms, as their place in the structured network of national and international power, which determines the 'price of violence' at any stage. As Elias (1978a: 78ff) has pointed out, in trials of strength between groups of antagonists it will depend on whose potential for withholding what the other requires is greater and who, accordingly, is more or less dependent on the other.

Applied to the level of transnational processes, the figurational approach antic-ipates the focus on economic power of the world-system analysis, as well as the accent on lived experience in the cultural corrective. It extends the former into other forms of the monopolization of means of social power and incorporates as a matter of course their embodiment in the structure of the interpersonal relations of everyday life. In this paradigm, the global structure of economic and political power is seen from the outset as intertwined with the monopolization of the means of force by nations as another source of power. Elias takes for granted the simulta-neous embodiment of all three dimensions at the level of personality and interpersonal relations and in international communications, i.e. at the level of 'culture' (see discussions in Arnason 1987; Kilminster 1989b; Wouters 1990; and further glosses in Chapters 4 and 8 of this volume).

The proponents of the world-system model have, however, made an important contribution in highlighting the global inequalities between nations, considered from the economic point of view. True to the history and tradition of this form of inquiry, however, its accent is on international inequality seen *from the point of view of the weaker, exploited nations*, with an eye always on developments that could be construed as leading towards greater equality between nations and a 'democratic world order' (Wallerstein 1991: 134–6).

However, it has been pointed out by a number of writers (e.g. Lenski & Lenski 1987: 313, 333; Wouters 1990: 69ff.) that whilst the long-term trend this century *within* Western industrialized nation-states has been towards a *decrease* in power, status and wealth differentials between social groups, the trend in the relations *between* nations across the globe has been towards an *increase* in the gap between powerful rich and less powerful poor countries. It is clear that it is a phase of this latter polarizing international economic trend that has attracted the attention of the world-system theorists in recent times. The problem of inequality and the hope of revolution has been transferred to the international level. The underprivileged (often still referred to by the older, mythical word 'proletariat') were now seen as a potentially unitable world-wide stratum.

The growing economic inequality gap between nations was of course real, but my point is that the Marxists were drawn *politically* to it, once the long-term, *intra*-national trend towards relative social equalization had given the lie to hopes of increased class polarization producing proletarian revolutions within Western nations (leaving aside short-lived polarizing phases.) There is evidence that this impetus was certainly behind the genesis of Wallerstein's programme (Ragin & Chirot 1985: 278–84).

The explanatory fruitfulness of looking at the intertwining of economic and non-economic factors in globalizing developments, rather than analytically distin-guishing them, is brought out in the work of Wouters (1990) in the figurational paradigm. He sees structural parallels between social developments that took place between groups within Western nation-states in the last 300 years and processes occurring subsequently in the relations between nation-states. If one looks beyond the criterion of income when assessing the gap between the rich and the poor nations, a more nuanced – and, in view of current orthodoxies, controversial – picture emerges. Since the end of colonialism between the 1940s and the 1980s, so far as power and prestige are concerned, the gap between them has in fact *diminished.* The rich nations are now less likely to use violent means to settle disputes between themselves and the poor nations: they have been compelled to show them more respect than in the days of colonialism. Why is this, when they still have overwhelming power and military force on their side?[6]

The increasing restraints on military intervention world-wide brought about during the cold war by the nuclear threat (Benthem van den Bergh 1992) created favourable conditions for remarkable commercial and financial growth in this period, hence raising standards of living in the richer countries. This helped to produce the well-known gap between rich and poor countries, upon which the world-systems theorists relentlessly focus. This process parallels the cumulative effect of the internal pacification of European nation-states from the sixteenth century onwards on the efficiency of organized work, which was considerably to increase it, thus contributing one of the conditions necessary for the origins of capitalism and the subsequent conflicts between social groups that flowed from it. Within Third World countries, the growth of institutions and organizations of administration has meant that more individuals have been compelled to regulate their conduct in a more even and stable manner, in ways comparable with the pattern of foresight and self-restraint that came to dominate personality formation of people in the industrial nations of the West.

The mechanism that led to the end of colonialism was therefore the beginning of a shift in the balance of power in favour of the colonized, paralleling the democratization between strata which – after an intense polarization shortly after the French Revolution – has accelerated *within* Western nations. Within these nations functional democratization[7] has closed social distance between people to a greater degree, producing greater mutual identification and a sensibility more conducive to taking the side of the international underprivileged. This, in turn, has fed into the economic and military dimensions of the relationship between the richer and the poorer nations. Put another way, the augmentation of the power potential of the poorer nations cannot be grasped without considering the relations between interdependent people in the round, not just economically.

Controlling the world market is beyond the power of any nation on its own, whatever its ideological hue or degree of wealth. In this context, the countries heavily in debt to the richer nations can still exercise constraint on them. The more serious the debt crisis, the more strenuous have become the loan conditions and the collective, cooperative policies for stimulating economic development. The poorer countries need the loans and the transnational companies operating within these countries are dependent upon the loan-demanding governments of those countries.

The process whereby in the West there was a reduction in the contrasts between groups, but an increase in their differences, via democratization and the informalization of behaviour codes, is likely to be repeated on the global level, producing, argues Wouters, a commingling of patterns of conduct. What seems to be a formalization of conduct and behaviour and manners in Third World countries, with the adoption of Western formal dress and orderly meetings, is in fact, in relation to the older traditional codes of these countries, an informalization, thus reproducing again one of the trends of Western nation-state formation.

The point is that the present informalized pattern of self-regulation of Western people *functions as a power resource*, an instrument of dominance, at the negotiating tables of the world and is a great advantage in a situation whereby the balance of power is shifting towards the outsider nations. It is not just an adjunct. It is *constitutive* of the balance of power. The older, formal codes of conduct of the colonial administrator now seem ridiculous because they reflected an earlier phase where the dividing lines between classes, generations and the sexes were much stronger within Western nations and were played out in the colonial context by upper-class representatives of those nations.

Orientation and disorientation

1.   Speculating about future societal scenarios is not illegitimate, if it is done realistically. It forms a valuable part of the contribution that sociology can make. Following on from the previous argument, I would argue, along with Wouters, that the tendency in the relations between rich and poor nations has been for the poorer ones to be attracted to the products of the industrial economies, as well as to the models of behaviour and feeling characteristic of people living within them. The dominant direction of change at the international level, brought about by the structural compulsion of the power relations between nations themselves, is towards the more 'modern' models of behaviour, conduct and organization. If the development of inter-group relations within European nations is anything to go by, the compulsion to adopt the aspirations, lifestyle and modes of conduct of the more powerful is very strong and probably will, in the long run, prove irresistible at the global level as well. Sociologically speaking, in contrast to what people might or might not wish to happen, this seems, from a purely sociological point of view, a very likely long-term scenario.

2.   The counter-trend towards fundamentalism in beliefs and lifestyle has been highlighted by the culturalist theories of globalization and is undoubtedly important. This counter-current has arisen in opposition to the intermingling of Western and traditional attitudes and behaviour. It is likely to be prominent in nations that find themselves, through no fault of their own, structurally at the lower end of the international stratification ladder which is dominated by the Western and Western-orientated nations.

3.   In the present period, national disintegration goes hand in hand with transnational reintegration at a higher level, particularly the continental, with an accompanying reinvigoration of ethnicity. In my view to concentrate on the fragmentary – or centrifugal – movement alone corresponds with a pluralistic conception of many different nations, which informs the so-called 'postmodern' world-view. This outlook is a symptom of disorientation brought about by people's experiences of the logic of the current phase of the continental and global levels of integration, which are disturbing national societies and individual identity formation more rapidly than hitherto, confusing people's orientation generally.

4.   Since 1945, in the advanced countries, our orientation has been profoundly shaped by the relatively stable cold war phase of international tension and the related economic prosperity thus made possible within the richer countries. As Hans Joas has aptly said, recently we have seen 'the return to a multipolar world after decades of bipolarity' (1991: 63). The postmodern outlook represents

the sensibilities of younger generations of intellectuals and radicals in Western societies, which have undergone far-reaching democratization and informaliza- tion processes internally during this period. The conviction that the nations of the Third World have now increasingly to be taken into account, to be shown respect, suggests that a shift in conscience formation has gradually occurred in the domi- nant countries. Hence, in the current phase people are searching for an alternative to the self-satisfied model of civilization associated with European colonialists and are experimenting with alternative ideals and moralities. The postmodern world- view is partly a product of this search for alternatives – an overreaction to European–American hegemony in the direction of cultural pluralism, elevated to an almost absolute status. The author of a paper for an international conference on culture and identity which I recently read, situated himself 'within the discourse of critical or insurgent multiculturalism'.

5.   In sociological and related debates in adjacent fields in the current period, this new sensibility plays itself out in the Lyotardian aversion to the 'grand narra- tives', such as Marxism or evolutionism. These are associated with the older civilizational ideal of the dominant European colonialists and the stage of the polarization of group conflicts and accompanying greater social distance, that they represented. This aversion would rule out in advance the development of any general theory of globalization in the name of the highly 'informalized' concept of *narrative*, as opposed to *theory*. But this criticism simply overlooks that theories are not narratives, the advocacy of the latter marking a lapse back into the pre-scien- tific modes of thinking associated with traditionalism, myth and folklore.

It is perfectly possible to have a general *theory* of global integration (without tele- ology) for the 'next step' in the process which, at the same time, acknowledges the extent of ethnic/national autonomy continuing at a given stage. The postmodern sensibility simply picks up on the cultural consequences of the centrifugal (rather than the centripetal) side of the current phase and infuses it with positive ethical–political evaluations. I think it is plausible to argue that this reflects the sensitivity of democratized and reformalized younger intellectuals and others within Western nations, the structural position of which nations in the world network of interdependent nations is shifting.

6.   My belief is that, now the dust has settled from the explosion of interest in globalization, some clear theoretical and empirical stocktaking is needed, particu- larly on the issue of developing new sociological concepts and models to capture the emergent global level of integration. This does not mean, however, as Tiryakian (1986) seems to think, that the *whole* of sociology has to be 'internation- alized', root and branch. This seems to me to be, at this stage, an overreaction. Sociologically speaking, the apparently fragmented character of national societies and the world circumstance in general in the contemporary period could simply bespeak a *phase* and not an end-state of international pluralism. Many recent commentators have made this mistake. For example, in the influential writings of Zygmunt Bauman we find the following diagnosis of the contemporary situation: 'The main feature ascribed to "postmodernity" is ... the permanent and irreducible *pluralism* of cultures ... or the awareness and recognition of such pluralism' (1992: 102, emphasis in original; see also *ibid.*: 64). This statement confuses the moral and political ideal of cultural pluralism with its permanent

empirical actuality. It rules out the possibility of longer-term continental, or regional alliances, or mergers of nations, which could considerably reduce cultural plurality or lead even to further episodes of territorial expansion and conquest by a relatively few new hegemonic centres of power, during which cultures and even whole nations could be, in the longer run, assimilated or destroyed. The future consolidation of three power blocs on the lines of, say, the fictional super-states of Eurasia, Oceana and Eastasia of George Orwell's *Nineteen Eighty-Four*, or something resembling them, could in the long run prove to be a real structural possibility (though not necessarily with the same totalitarian features as he depicts).

7. The doctrine of cultural pluralism presupposes a level of 'mutual identification' (Elias) between people, brought about by far-reaching democratization and informalization processes within the Euro-American nation-states we call the West (as does the postmodern sensibility.) In the longer term, however, the hegemonial struggles involved in the development of emergent, larger, regional centres of international social power could throw these democratization and informalization processes into reverse, steepening power gradients and social distance between groups within those new units. This would thus create social conditions conducive to *new* doctrines of civilizational superiority over lower status groupings or nations. The current assertion that cultural pluralism is the final shape of the world reality and its enthusiastic advocacy as an absolute doctrine, or goal to work towards, is surely naive and unrealistic. At a future point it could seem as quaintly anachronistic as cosmopolitan internationalism seemed during the inter-state rivalry of the period of European colonialism when chauvinistic and exclusionary nationalisms were so prominent. These remarks are intended only to be a sober sociological judgement of real possibilities, nothing more.

8. Some, at least, of the apparent harbingers of 'social chaos' (Loye 1991: 12) discovered in the contemporary world are probably a matter of a faulty conceptualization, skewed by fear images.[8] But insofar as strife, conflicts and crises of various kinds are discernible on an increasing scale in the present period (more clarificatory work is needed in this field), my guess is that they are manifestations of complex realignments of social forces and behavioural readjustments taking place as the pressures that nations are increasingly putting on each other are unintendedly pushing the ordering principles of social development on to the higher regional and global integrative levels. These are then canalizing the levels below. It may be that on the global stage at the present time the centrifugal movement towards national and ethnic fragmentation just has the upper hand over the centripetal tendencies towards regional alliances of nations. The European Union suggests an incipient continental integration. Maybe others will emerge in the Far East. There is also the pact for a free trade zone consisting of Canada, the United States and Latin America recently entered into under US leadership.

9. There are also international institutions such as the World Bank, United Nations, Red Cross, Amnesty International and the World Health Organization. In the absence of a world polity these bodies are not yet, strictly speaking, 'world' organizations, but could be seen in that regard as nascent, though still skewed by US dominance, particularly in the case of the UN. But it is a question of keeping a longer-term view of these developments and not jumping to conclusions as to outcomes, which might be centuries in the future. The assumption of the opposite

outcome to pluralism and endemic fragmentation, i.e. that of central political institutions and the pacification of the whole planet, is just as one-sided and utopian. As Elias writes of such institutions:

> But anyone who has studied the growth of central institutions knows that integration processes which are precipitated in the setting up of central institutions at a new level often need *a run-up period of several centuries* before they are somewhat effective. And no one can foresee whether central institutions formed in the course of a powerful integration may not be destroyed in an equally powerful disintegration process.
>
> (Elias 1991b: 227, my emphasis)

10. New hegemonic regional alliances or even coalescences of nation-states could emerge in the longer term, but the dominant shape of the next phase is just not clear enough at present to warrant the hasty judgement about cultural pluralism. The longer view suggests that any *relatively* stable and enduring new regional or global integrative patterns of nations (including possibly the long-term death of nations through absorption) could take a very long time to crystallize, well beyond the lifetimes of all of us living today.

11. The current situation is a thus disorientating one, which encourages unsubstantiated speculation and rash social diagnosis. A further example is that some contemporary social scientists have uncritically applied to social development varieties of disequilibrium theory and 'chaos theory' taken from the biological and physical sciences. In doing so, they have assumed that what they take to be widespread 'crises and discontinuities affecting increasingly larger segments of the world population' (Loye 1991: 12) are indicative of a novel situation of *chronic* crisis. Others have assumed, without an assessment of empirical evidence, that the current national and global situation is 'underpatterned' (Bauman) and have even gone so far as to say that it necessitates therefore wholly new sociological concepts, theories and assumptions (e.g. Bauman 1992: 65, 191ff.). In my view both of these judgements are somewhat premature.

12. When discussing the possibility of the globalization of manners, Stephen Mennell asks rhetorically:

> What are the implications now for a world-wide civilizing process, considered as changes in ways of demanding and showing respect, when Europe and Europe-over-the-ocean no longer occupy the hegemonic position? Or do they?
>
> (Mennell 1990: 369)

The force of my previous discussion leads to the definite answer of 'yes' to the last question. In the present phase and for the foreseeable future, the relative power potential of the United States is, and will probably remain, decisive in social developments on a world scale. The rise of newly industrializing countries (the so-called NICs) in what we in Europe call the Far East and the break-up of the former Soviet Union are symptoms of a shift in the global balance of power between nations which involves the relative decline (but by no means total fall) of American global hegemony. The former superpower confrontation of the cold war has been transformed, but the Gulf War of 1990 was a telling reminder of the continuing power of the alliance of nations led by the United States. As Susan Strange has rightly said, 'The decline of U.S. hegemony is a myth – powerful, no doubt, but still a myth. In every important respect the United States still has the predominant power to shape frameworks and thus to influence outcomes' (1989: 169).

13.   It is noticeable that whilst sociologists of the first rank have emerged in poorer, so-called 'peripheral' countries (Albrow & King 1990: 101ff.) they are not yet institutionally strong. There still exists a powerful, US–European led, English-language, global hegemony in social science. This preeminent sociological archetype originates in the dominant world bloc of rich, powerful, high status nations (Oommen 1991). This bloc also provides the standards of living, lifestyle and behaviour to which, as a matter of sociological fact, people of other nations (no matter what their ideological persuasion) seek to aspire. It is likely that the compelling force of this structure of power will, in the long run, prove irresistible. This sociological diagnosis is not synonymous with the prophetic 'triumph of capitalism' or 'end of history' scenarios that have become prominent in the present period, nor does it carry an evaluative preference.

14.   The global migration of people across borders has become an issue in many countries. The problem for many governments is how to open borders for global trade and at the same time to keep them closed for those whom they perceive as unwanted immigrants. This illustrates very well the paradox of internationalization going hand in hand with the protection of nationhood. Globalization both fosters forms of cosmopolitan consciousness *and* stimulates feelings and expressions of ethnicity. It is not surprising, therefore, that the dominant contemporary sociological conception of globalization is of a Janus-faced process of global incorporation and local resistance. The changing global structural position of the dominant nations in which the younger generations of those social scientists who argue that way currently work, is one that is conducive to the sociological reproduction in these groups of psychological ambivalence. This may account for why a strong evaluative weighting has become attached to the resistance component of the conception of the Janus-faced tension, as well as to the ideal of cultural pluralism.

15.   Both tendencies correspond to a sensibility at least partly explicable by the changing conscience formation of these highly democratized social scientists and intellectuals based in the Euro-American hegemonic bloc of nations. These social scientists are operating in a new situation where the nations in which they have grown up and in which they live and work are being increasingly put under pressure to show respect for and restraint in relation to the weaker, poorer, lower status nations, with which they are interdependent. At the same time, these social scientists cannot escape the fact that although, from the point of view of prestige (if not wealth), the gap between the richer established and the poorer outsider nations has narrowed, taken *overall*, the hegemonic group of nations of which their own nation is a part nonetheless still possesses the higher power ratio, whether they as a group approve of it or not.

7

STRUCTURATION THEORY AS A WORLD-VIEW[1]

Syntheses ... do not float in an abstract space, uninfluenced by social gravitation; it is the structural configuration of the social situation which makes it possible for them to emerge and develop.

(Mannheim 1928: 225)

Parsonian affinities

Contrary to the misgivings of some commentators, for example Hirst (1982), Giddens' theory of structuration, as elaborated in *The Constitution of Society* (Giddens 1984), is an example not of eclecticism, but of theoretical synthesis. As an exponent of synthesis, he shares the sociological stage with other synthesizers, including Parsons (1937), Lenski (1966) and Collins (1993). As Stephen K. Sanderson (1987) has usefully pointed out, eclecticism involves a mechanical juxtaposing of elements of research traditions, whereas theoretical synthesis combines elements in such a way that the recombination produces a novel fusion, structurally distinct from any of the combined components. The new combination then acquires assumptions, concepts and principles of its own, forming a new basis for research efforts. Eclectics, on the other hand, always advocate using multi-theoretical approaches in principle (e.g. Merton 1981).[2] Giddens says explicitly, and reasonably in my view, that he cannot see the force of the objection that his work is unacceptably eclectic (Giddens 1984: xxii). His involvement with the various schools of sociology and philosophy is entirely for the purpose of extracting the relevant guiding thread, concept or core insight in order to recombine it with other elements. He writes:

> The theory of structuration was worked out as an attempt to transcend, without discarding altogether, three prominent traditions of thought in social theory and philosophy: hermeneutics or 'interpretative sociologies', functionalism and structuralism. Each of these traditions, in my view, incorporates distinctive and valuable contributions to social analysis – while each has tended to suffer from a number of defined limitations.

> (Giddens 1981: 26)

In this respect he shares the *method*, at least, of Parsons' research project in the

Structure of Social Action (1937), even if he does distance himself from Parsons' systemic determinism, functionalism and naturalism (Giddens 1984: xxxvii; 1976: ch. 3). There is extensive discussion of Parsons in Giddens' works because in many ways Parsons provided the theoretical point of departure for his reflections, as he did for a number of other sociologists in the 1950s and 1960s such as David Lockwood (1956), Alan Dawe (1970), Percy Cohen (1968) and Harold Garfinkel (1967). Obviously, Giddens is operating in a new context, with a different range of theorists and philosophers from those upon whom Parsons drew to build his general action theory in the 1930s and 1940s. But like Parsons, Giddens proceeds from the raw material of diverse theories to erect a scaffolding of synthesized concepts for the purpose of informing further research; and both resultant schemes are forms of action theory. Neither theorist builds his theory in direct cross-fertilization with evidence as he proceeds; rather, empirical examples are appended illustratively or suggestively.

Parsons wrote that the *Structure of Social Action* was a 'study in social *theory*, not *theories*' (Parsons 1937: v) and that what unified the discussion was that each author discussed was held to have made, in a different way, an important contribution to 'this single coherent body of theory', i.e. Parsons' theory of social action. Giddens does not see the same kind of immanent convergence in all the recent writers he discusses, but they are nonetheless described as 'working on a common range of problems' (1982a: 175) and 'they come together in the following conclusions' (1976: 52); or there are 'affinities between' (*ibid.*) various ideas from different traditions. In other words, Giddens too borrows valuable contributions from diverse schools to forge what is effectively another 'single coherent body of theory', i.e. structuration theory. He explicitly describes this theory as an example of 'social theory in general' (1984: xvii). (NB: Giddens denies that his *New Rules* was a work of synthesis because of its selectiveness (1976: 20), but I do not think this is true of *The Constitution of Society*, which integrates into the theory concepts derived from many more sources, including human geography and existential phenomenology, and which he describes as a 'summation' (Giddens 1984: preface) of his previous work on this subject.)

Despite its level of abstraction and method of construction, the theory of structuration is not, however, as divorced from relevance to empirical research as it might have appeared in the earlier versions. Giddens sees his theory as theoretically linking a number of levels of the total social process in time–space which can guide empirical research both in general and at each level: 'Structuration theory will not be of much value if it does not help to illuminate problems of empirical research' (Giddens 1984: xxix). The concepts 'should for research purposes be regarded as sensitizing devices . . . useful for thinking about research problems and the interpretation of research results' (*ibid.*: 326–7). The action concepts in Giddens are more sophisticated than those of Parsons, as are the recommended research techniques for each level. This is because of Giddens' insistence on the reflexive character of the constituting social action of knowledgeable agents and the methodological consequences of the 'double hermeneutic'. But the overall ambition that the theoretical framework should inform empirical research is something he shares with Parsons, who wrote of his own generalized action theory: 'It . . . constitutes a crucially important guide to the direction of fruitful research'

(Parsons 1938: 89). I appreciate that there are also a number of discontinuities with the work of Parsons, and aims that Giddens does not share with him: for example, Giddens does not pursue universals or other societal constants; and he is critical of Parsons' 'cybernetic hierarchy'. But the comparison does serve to put structuration theory into perspective as a species of action theory with the characteristic assumptions and limitations that implies.

It is a theme of this chapter that there are tenets in structuration theory the presence of which are not explicable entirely by Giddens having been rationally or intellectually convinced of their soundness, as well as other tacit assumptions of which he is hardly aware. Structuration theory is, on the one hand, a metatheory of action and, on the other, a pulling together of a selection of concepts, tenets, assumptions, emphases and normative elements, the unity of which constitutes a world-view. As we will repeatedly see, some of these features derive from the traces within structuration theory, as in sociology in general, of the great ideologies of the nineteenth century – liberalism, socialism and conservatism, and their later developments. Others derive from the institutional location of the project and still others from the moral and political convictions of the author.

New liberal affinities

Let us begin the topic of liberal assumptions and residues in Giddens' work by looking at the significance of some of Giddens' guidelines for empirical research in *The Constitution of Society* in the light of the above considerations. Giddens wants to direct research towards: (a) hermeneutic concerns, that is in this context the mediation of frames of meaning; (b) the skills of knowledgeable actors; and (c) the time–space constitution of social life. These proposals are intended to supplement the more customary sociological focus on institutions. He says that it is the concerns of the researcher that determine the emphasis on any one of these levels and the consequent methodological bracketing of the others. For example, in analysing the strategic conduct of actors the focus is on the modes in which agents, in their plans and intentions, draw upon knowledge of the structural properties of institutions. For this purpose these institutions are methodologically regarded as 'given'. But he adds:

> There is, of course, no obligation for anyone doing detailed empirical research, in a given localized setting, to take on board an array of abstract notions that would merely clutter up what could otherwise be described with economy and in ordinary language.
>
> (Giddens 1984: 326)

The oddity of this comment will be apparent. In the theory of structuration Giddens expends a lot of effort trying to establish theoretically the links between 'social integration' and 'system integration', i.e. between the face-to-face encounters of co-present actors and the wider social formation of which they form a part. In addition to the hermeneutic research advocated, he also commends research into time–space constitution; but then, in the above quotation, he seems to throw away this thrust of his work by devaluing its theoretical expression as mere clutter.

An unintended consequence of the methodological 'bracketing' recommendation, and this way of representing it, is to provide a legitimation for researchers to remain in their 'localized setting' or to continue to focus on a small corner of the total societal web. It discourages researchers from any ambitions they may have to make the linkages to the wider and more far-flung social interconnections implied by the metatheory itself.

However, if sociologists are substantively, and not just at the level of metatheory, to take this aim on board, then they need to be developing ways of presenting their findings that show these simultaneous linkages. (They would have to go beyond Giddens, though, if they wanted to represent society as a *figuration*, in Norbert Elias's terminology. This would incorporate the interpenetrating view-points of groups across the whole social network, something not envisageable within structuration theory: more on this later.) Clearly, reaching this goal is not an easy task, but is not beyond the sociological imagination: it is an ambition that unites works as diverse in aims, period and subject-matter as Hegel's *Phenomenology*, Marx's *Capital* and Elias's *Civilizing Process*. This piece of Giddens' methodological advice, together with the stress on meaning frameworks, legitimates the frag-mented, if scrupulous, empirical research efforts in the institutionalized settings of contemporary sociology.

The methodological recommendations seem to embody a liberalistic timidity about the possibility of representing and theorizing 'social wholes', lest this proce-dure erases individuals. This uncertainty is reminiscent of the diffidence generated by the publication of Karl Popper's *Poverty of Historicism* in the 1960s and indeed Giddens' recommendations would seem compatible with Popper's strictures against holism (Popper 1961: 79).[3] It is noticeable how many pages Giddens devotes in the *Constitution of Society* to refuting the arguments of the methodological individualists, whose work he takes very seriously: 'they are quite justified in being suspicious of the aspirations of "structural sociology"' (Giddens 1984: 220). He is not content to let the debate rest where it was left by Steven Lukes in the 1970s, but further worries over exchanges between Perry Anderson and Edward Thompson before concluding that the whole debate presupposes a false antinomy of indi-vidual/society. This is true, but it is the worrying that is significant.

The historical involvement of the European sociological tradition with the development of liberalism, both as a political doctrine and as a style of thought, is well known (Mannheim 1928: 216ff.; 1929: 276ff.; Seidman 1983), as are the other connections of sociology with socialism and conservatism. In drawing out the liberal strand I am not implying that either sociology in general, or Giddens' theory of structuration in particular, is *reducible* to its liberal ingredient. Traces of all three of the great nineteenth-century ideologies can be found woven into the fabric of sociology (Goudsblom 1977a: ch. 5) and also into Giddens' work. Nor do I intend any pejorative judgement by this observation.

The tradition of European liberalism in various national contexts has placed the freedom and self-actualization of the individual at the centre of the doctrine. Early liberalism was all about protecting the individual from arbitrary power, that of the state in particular, but later on into the early years of this century the 'new liberalism' developed amongst other principles a broader conception of the indi-vidual (Freeden 1978). In the words of Bramsted and Melhuish, the individual was now viewed as 'potentially unique and spontaneous' , a line of thought going back to the Renaissance. They add:

> Individualism as a "habit of mind", as the right of the individual to follow his own preferences and tastes within the limits imposed by the law instead of *having them dictated by the conventions of society*, became an additional strand in the liberal attitude.
>
> (Bramsted & Melhuish 1978: xviii, my emphasis)

The new liberalism was partly a political doctrine, but it was also an ontology of the individual, seen as the unique, bounded and dynamic centre of self-activity, set against arbitrary power in the political realm and against 'society' in general. Liberalism derives much of its force from its foundation in the self-experience and type of conscience formation of individuals in the increasingly complex networks of interdependencies of urbanized, advanced societies.

It would not be too fanciful to note how easily Giddens' theory of structuration dovetails into this style of thought. One of the central tenets of the theory is that, against functionalism and structuralism, the agent is to be seen not as a 'cultural dope', i.e. not as a mere conforming, approval-seeking reflex of a central value system which the actor has successfully internalized and translated into motivations. Nor is the actor simply constructed by discourses, as the anti-humanist structuralists would have it. Giddens counters these distortions with a plea for the dignity of capable human actors who have 'knowledgeability', a reflexive self-monitoring capacity, discursive and tacit knowledge and 'practical consciousness'. Built into the theory are individual agents seen as acting knowledgeably and intentionally, bounded on the one side by objective institutions, and on the other by their unconscious. Giddens lists elaborately (1984: 90–2) the conditions that enable the differential cognitive penetration of wider societal processes to be achieved by aware agents. Like all liberalism, this dimension of the theory seeks to maximize the conditions for rationality so as to minimize, and thus control, the irrational.

Furthermore, for Giddens the action of human agents involves the possibility of 'doing otherwise', of being able to make a difference in the world – a principle that has for Giddens the status of a 'philosophical theorem' (Giddens 1982e: 30). He realizes, however, that power differentials limit agents' relative capacities to mobilize resources to make a difference. The implication is clear: the unstated value premise of this view of human action is that individual human dignity, self-expression and freedom *should* be maximized against and within institutional parameters and against unequal power chances. It makes sense of Giddens ending an analysis of worker resistance on the shop floor with the evocative words: 'precisely because they are not machines, wherever they can do so human actors devise ways of avoiding being treated as such' (*ibid.*: 45).

Obviously these commitments work at a tacit level in structuration theory and, having located them, one needs to explain how and why they got there at the time they did. I cannot go into this question here. Suffice it to say that the liberal strand is the dominant one, providing an exaggerated – even Promethean – conception of the extraordinarily skilled individual agent in social reproduction.

The scope of sociology

Giddens has been influential in establishing within educational institutions in recent years a particular construction of the sociological tradition as consisting primarily of the triumvirate of Marx, Weber and Durkheim (Giddens 1971). He gives short shrift to Simmel because his use of evidence is cavalier and his terminology loose (Giddens 1965: 143); Comte is dismissed as an eccentric nineteenth-century figure whose extravagant works betray a naive faith in science (Giddens 1982a: 68–75);[4] and one can multiply the number of other important earlier figures who are barely mentioned, let alone discussed in the same depth: Spencer, Tönnies, Tocqueville, Hobhouse, Pareto, Mannheim, Sorokin, Elias. Standing behind structuration theory is not only a thorough grounding in this tripartite 'selective tradition' (Williams 1973: 9) and its (partial) Parsonian consolidation, but also a staunch commitment to the importance of the sociological enterprise as such. Giddens has grasped that sociology in general has always had the capacity to contribute to an understanding of the feasibility of the plans and goals offered by various political ideologies and groups, despite the fact that many of its most distinguished practitioners have espoused one or other ideology themselves. In this vein he comments as follows on the work of the three nominated greats:

> The writings of both Durkheim and Weber have their origin in an attempt to defend – or rather to reinterpret – the claims of political liberalism within the twin pressures of Romantic hypernationalistic conservatism on the one side, and revolutionary socialism on the other. Marx's writings, on the other hand, constitute an analysis and critique of early capitalism.
>
> (Giddens 1971: 244)

It is noticeable that Giddens nowhere attempts to muster arguments to ground a specifically 'critical' sociology in the manner of Habermas (1972) or Bauman (1976b), because in absorbing the classical tradition he has already assumed that sociology is *inherently* critical. He said in an interview that he worked within a sociological conception which suggested 'that some things are clearly noxious and other things are clearly desirable and that it isn't necessary to ground them in order to proclaim this to be so' (Giddens 1982c: 72). Hence:

> As critical theory sociology does not take the social world as a given, but poses the questions: what types of social change are feasible and desirable, and how should we strive to achieve them?
>
> (Giddens 1982b: 166)

In later formulations of the practical implications of sociological research, he has added the new dimension – implied by structuration theory and the principle of the 'double hermeneutic' – that concepts constructed within sociology itself, through a process of 'slippage' (Giddens 1976: 162) back into the world of everyday life, can come to be appropriated by lay people whose conduct the concepts were originally coined to analyse (Giddens 1984: 348–54). Giddens does not give many examples of concepts that have become an integral feature of social life in this way, but perhaps alienation would be one. From a technical concept known and used by only a handful of sociologists and philosophers a few decades ago, it has now become a word that people living in large cities often use to describe a whole range of feelings of estrangement, frustration and loneliness which they experience (Kilminster 1992a).

Giddens served his sociological apprenticeship in the high seriousness of the Leicester school of sociology built largely from continental traditions of theory and research by Ilya Neustadt and Norbert Elias (before his world-wide acclaim) in the 1950s and 1960s (Neustadt 1965; Marshall 1982; Brown 1987). Though not intellectually unified, this department was for a long time the largest outside London. All accounts agree that it generated in its participants considerable enthusiasm for the discipline and cultivated a particularly high degree of self-confidence. Giddens' sociological commitment bears the marks of its origins here, where he taught for eight years. As far as I can discern, his absorption of a thoroughgoing sociological orientation importantly from this source, though not entirely from it, effectively immunized him against getting carried away by any one of the many perspectives, schools, manifestos and fads with which sociology was subsequently deluged. As he says again and again in his many discussions of these schools, he is prepared to learn or borrow from them without becoming a disciple or a partisan of any particular one.

An awareness of this dimension throws light on Giddens' attitude towards the attacks that were made during the 1960s and 1970s against the very possibility of a science of society, which often drew on older traditions of philosophical anti-sociology. Of the proliferating schools of recent times, the more radical exponents of three of them in particular – neo-Marxism, ethnomethodology and Wittgensteinism – have claimed that sociology was, if not impossible, then certainly suspect. Briefly, the grounds were, respectively, because: (a) sociology was a bourgeois reaction to socialism and Marxism which justified inequality in capitalist societies; (b) in its professionalized and positivistic mode sociology illegitimately bootlegged lay actors' meanings into its explanations; and (c) its subject-matter properly belonged to philosophy.

How does Giddens react to these attacks? His writings from the early 1970s are saturated with the problems raised by the then current Marxism-versus-sociology controversy, and he is clearly *au fait* with the general outlines of the debate (Giddens 1971: introduction; 1973: *passim*). But he gives it short shrift: 'I do not wish to discuss here the relative merits of these competing views' (1973: 17). Following his customary strategy, he says he will, however, take from the debate only the implications 'for the identification of the tasks with which contemporary social theory should be concerned' (*ibid.*). There is nowhere in his writings from this period a systematic discussion of the attacks made against sociology in the writings of, say, Lukács or Adorno which had been rediscovered and reworked at that time (Kilminster 1979). Giddens rises above the controversy, pointing out both the overreaction by Marxists to sociology in its shallow 'end-of-ideology' mode, and their simultaneous failure to come to terms with the lack of proletarian revolutions in the West and the legitimation of domination in the name of Marx in eastern Europe. Hence: 'we live in a society which is both "post-Marxist" and "post-bourgeois", although not in a society which is "post-capitalist", let alone "post-industrial"' (Giddens 1973: 19). The point is that Giddens' unstated warrant for transcending these misleading antinomies is a prior commitment to the stand-point of sociology as an overarching and mediating framework, even if it is only implicit.

In relation to ethnomethodology, Giddens rightly points out that the implica-tions of Garfinkel's concepts of reflexivity and indexicality, taken together, led in two directions. One was towards a kind of naturalism, resulting in conversation analysis, and the other was into the infinite regress of the hermeneutic circle. This was the more radical direction of the project of Theorizing associated with Alan Blum and Peter McHugh (Giddens 1976: 52). This philosophical project aban-doned all attempts to generate reliable knowledge of society, and instead celebrated the ongoing process of collective enquiry for its own sake into the collective ontological grounds that make possible any enquiry at all (Blum 1974; McHugh *et al.* 1974). From the interpretative sociologies, including ethnomethod-ology, Giddens borrows four basic ideas for incorporation into structuration theory. These are that (a) sociology draws on the same resources as lay people; (b) people have pragmatic knowledge; (c) sociological concepts are linked to lay ones; and (d) *Verstehen* should be treated as 'generic to all social explanation' (Giddens 1976: 52). This tenet is transcribed into the explanatory principle of the 'double hermeneutic'.

But in extracting these principles Giddens does not pick up Garfinkel's profound discussion of the distinction made in German philosophy between *Verstehen* (the state of understanding) and *Begreifen* (the process of coming to an understanding) (Garfinkel 1967: 24ff.) and neither the latter concept nor any equivalent plays any part in Giddens' theory, for reasons that will become clear. The Theorizing tendency, which picked up on the latter concept, is abandoned by Giddens without discussion, deserving only the comment that Blum and McHugh and their British followers (see Sandywell *et al.* 1975; Dobson 1979) are 'intrepid travellers all, now left swirling helplessly in the vortex of the hermeneutic whirlpool' (Giddens 1976: 166).

It is obvious, however, that this rhetorical comment does not actually engage with the essentially philosophical arguments of the Theorizers and, indeed, to my knowledge there has been no serious sociological riposte to the group's programme. Giddens' summary abandonment of them is ironic because they have made much of Heidegger's concept of 'presencing' which has also inspired the development of his own conception of time (Giddens 1984: 45; 1979: 3ff. and 54ff.). As Attewell (1974) has pointed out, Garfinkel's theory of members' accounts fuses 'doing' interaction with 'telling' about it. This fusion effectively reduces *Verstehen* to *Begreifen*. So, on the strong version of ethnomethodology (e.g. Theorizing), understanding becomes *entirely process*, which conception undermines the sociological project of trying to substitute objective, i.e. scientific, expressions for the ubiquitous indexical ones. This substitution, Garfinkel says, 'remains programmatic in every *particular* case and in every *actual* occasion in which the distinction or substitutability must be demonstrated' (Garfinkel 1967: 6). This is because sociologists' accounts (including their would-be objective expressions) inevitably remain organized features of the research settings that in organizing they describe. As Attewell rightly says, Garfinkel's statement, in this radical form, is perhaps the most extreme found in sociology: 'It is as extreme a statement as the declaration of form without content, or subject without object' (Attewell 1974: 202).

Giddens does not take on the challenge of the Theorizing tendency, which took this radical road from Garfinkel. This omission is in marked contrast to his lengthy discussion in the *New Rules of Sociological Method* of the radical Wittgensteinian ideas of Peter Winch (Giddens 1976: 44–51). 'Theorizing' is, I think, dismissed with an *ad hominem* argument because it does not occur to Giddens that so fundamental a philosophical critique of sociology even needs to be seriously discussed. He is insufficiently worried by the school to take the trouble of refuting it. This abstention is indicative of the strength of his sociological outlook and the stage of development of British sociology at which it was acquired. It may also say something about the Leicester ethos.

Winch, on the other hand, has more professional credibility, even though he was avowedly mounting what was an unsuccessful take-over bid for sociology by philosophy. In his observations on language games Winch is at least saying something relevant to the empirical understanding of forms of life. It is this anthropological core to Winch's work that interests Giddens (1982b: 22ff.). He notes with approval and grateful relief that Winch 'makes a scrambled retreat from a full-blown relativism' (1976: 50), even if it is into dubious biological universals as a bedrock for cross-cultural understanding (*ibid.*: 49).

So, there is a solid sociological commitment of a specific kind embodied in Giddens' work. But what else can we discern about its nature? Despite Giddens' advocacy in his successful textbook (Giddens 1997: xiii) that sociology should be a discipline with a fundamentally important historical dimension, a close reading of his other writings reveals inconsistency and equivocation on the subjects of development and socio-genesis. He seems to have overreacted both to the weaknesses of specifically evolutionary thinking in sociology and to philosophers' fears that appealing to the socio-genesis of concepts *ipso facto* undermines validity and rationality. This ambiguity shows itself in two ways.

1.   There is no historical, genetic device in Giddens' theory construction which could take account of how the different schools and perspectives across which he abstractly roams *came* to achieve the specificity and institutional salience they possess in the form in which he finds them. Lacking a dynamic principle, he can only logically assess the cognitive value of the perspectives and schools, which he treats as comparable and equipollent. This procedure has a levelling effect on the theories and authors. He is therefore unable, for example, to distinguish true advances in theory from revived dead-ends because in eschewing development he has left himself bereft of any theory of progression or scientific advance which might enable him to accomplish this. Put another way, he does not allow genetic considerations to play any part in concept formation. (I will return to this issue later on and in Chapters 8 and 9.) For now, we can note the fact that quite a long time ago Giddens dismissed the usefulness of the sociology of knowledge in the establishment of valid concepts and has written nothing on the subject. He bade farewell to this tradition using a standard argument:

But it needs no special perspicacity to see the *petitio principii* involved in the notion that such an exercise can in itself produce a new theoretical framework for sociology; the transmutation of sociology into the sociology of knowledge is a logically impossible endeavour.

(Giddens 1973: 15)

2.   Giddens' conception of the subject-matter of sociology is based on an a priori commitment to a ceasural, or discontinuist, view of history. He writes:

The modern world is born out of discontinuity with what went before rather than continuity with it. It is the nature of this discontinuity – the specificity of the world ushered in by the advent of industrial capitalism, originally located and founded in the West – which it is the business of sociology to explain as best it can.

(Giddens 1984: 239)

Elsewhere he writes that he is committed to this view 'whatever continuities may exist with what went before' (1982a: 107) which suggests that he is not denying that continuities exist side by side with discontinuities, but that in this balance he is simply wanting to privilege discontinuity, as a preference, for unstated reasons.

But to what form of 'caesurism' (Martins 1974: 280) is Giddens committing us here? And does this commitment go beyond mere preference or simple conviction as a reaction, or even revulsion, against archaic evolutionism? Giddens implies that he is intellectually convinced by discontinuism. He says that by a discontinuist view of history he means his belief – derived from Ernest Gellner (1964) – that the transformation of the West over the last 300 years has no precedent in history and is a break of scale with what went before, greater than any previous break (Giddens 1982c: 107; 1984: 237–8). This clearly delimited configuration of modern industrialized societies provides the terrain for sociology, which emerged precisely as the discipline *par excellence* for explaining this bounded but historically discontinuous and distinctive world. He writes: 'Human history is not, to use Gellner's term, a "world growth story"' (Giddens 1984: 237; see also 1982c: 76ff.).

A starting point for raising the problems involved here is a perceptive comment by Herminio Martins:

Gellner's version of caesurism is particularly attractive to sociologists, not least because in a sense his conception of the modern world implies a rather central place for sociology as against history, and to some extent also asociological conceptions of epistemology and ethics. ... As a general characterization of the modern world, of the paramount structure of 'our time', it remains highly plausible. ... As a forceful reminder of the strong and in some respects overriding moral obligations incumbent on sociologists and scholars in the contemporary world it remains valid.

(Martins 1974: 282)

Indeed, I think that Giddens' commitment to discontinuism *à la* Gellner is shot through with moral as well as empirical or scientific considerations. It fits very well with Giddens' oft-repeated advocacy of the 'critical' vocation of the sociologist to illuminate the structure of this singularly modern world. And it sits comfortably with his related socialist convictions: 'Here I should declare my *parti pris*, and say that my political sympathies lie on the Left' (Giddens 1982a: 227; see also 1982c) which have partly guided his annexation of much of the socialist–Marxist economic ontology into this structuration theory alongside the action components. Predictably, therefore, Giddens uses highly evaluative and emotive language to describe the character of this discontinuous modern world: 'It is much more illuminating to see it as placing a caesura upon the traditional world, which it seems irretrievably to *corrode and destroy*' (Giddens 1984: 239, my emphasis). And more strikingly on capitalism:

> A philosophical anthropology relevant to socialism must attend closely to what we can retain of the human diversity that is being devoured by the voracious expansion of the 'created space' of capitalism – for in the world that capitalism has originated, time is no longer understood as the medium of Being, and the gearing of daily life into comprehended tradition is replaced by the empty routines of everyday life. On the other hand, the whole of humanity now lives in the shadow of possible destruction. This unique conjunction of the banal and the apocalyptic, this is the world that capitalism has fashioned.
>
> (Giddens 1981: 252)

It is not surprising that, with a moral conviction of this emotional intensity driving his commitment to Gellnerian caesurism, Giddens will be uninterested in developing a more sober picture of the balance of continuity/discontinuity on various levels; or retrieving the developmental baby thrown out with the evolutionary bathwater in order to put on to the agenda structured long-term *development*. As one can see from the above quotation, capitalism sometimes assumes in Giddens' hands (as it did for Marx)[5] the character of an unstoppable force spreading like a contagion across the globe. But he has overstated the penetration and effects of global capitalistic economic relations, which he sees only as *one-way* traffic, with the result that he underplays counter-movements, for example fundamentalist religious and political movements in various parts of the world, including, in the advanced societies, movements that seek to reassert national or ethnic identities as a kind of cultural protectionism against the encroaching globalization which is pulling nations together (Robertson & Lechner 1985; see also Chapter 6).

Moreover, Giddens' world-view discourages asking what is the longer-run sequential order of processes of differentiation/integration which has shaped the present conditions and which foreshadows the next emergent phase (see Elias 1987b); but rather encourages apparently looking only at social and political processes in the national and global *present* for a diagnosis of the current situation and its possibilities.[6] The sequential order issue is suppressed because of the assumption that the study of long-range developmental change can only be evolutionist, i.e. an inquiry which he claims contains the fatal flaw of seeing modernity as an inevitable accentuation of previous trends, i.e. as their summation. But this is an overreaction.

To put the corrective briefly and abstractly for present purposes: attention to the sequential order of continuous but uneven strands of development, which provides successively newer sets of preconditions for the emergence of the next phase of societal change, can illuminate the problem of how such combinations result in the production of discontinuity and societal specificity. Continuity and discontinuity are both implicated in social development and no inevitability or teleology need be implied. A fuller and more finely tuned social diagnosis of the present situation will entail extending the analysis into non-economic bonds (see later discussion in this chapter) as well as back into the order and sequencing of longer-term continuities which Giddens' discontinuism, as a matter of principle, plays down.

Finally, another example of the way that Giddens' evaluative enthusiasm interferes with a sober sociological analysis of human social realities occurs when he is drawn in an interview on the subject of the relationship between human beings and nature. In a Romantic statement apparently inspired by reading Lévi-Strauss, he declares:

> A ... major feature of modern world civilizations is the loss of a generic relationship between human beings and nature and I think that's really a tremendous loss for the style of life we live because we just live in an essentially artificial milieu in which there is no longer any contact with nature of the traditional kind. I just think to go on holidays, tourism, to go out into the country at weekends, is different from the way in which people have always lived in dealing with nature.
>
> (Giddens 1982c: 68)

It is as though Giddens has not heard of the whole tradition from Marx, Simmel, Lukács and Elias to the Frankfurt School and many others who have in different ways established the historical variability of 'human nature' and questioned the idea that there ever was a time when human beings stood in an authentic relationship to nature. The character of the relationship between human beings and non-human nature, as well as the interplay between human sociality and the biological level which it continues, depends on the stage of social development. In the above quotation Giddens unreflectively interposes modern society as an 'artificial' milieu between man and nature, when man is inconceivable outside social relations *or* as severed from biological nature. Society was made possible by a prior evolutionary biological precondition. *'Nature' is as human-made a category as 'society'*. But we would never consider that the natural sciences were sciences of something artificial. Giddens has reproduced a value assumption that, compared with genuine, pristine, real nature, modern society is a merely artificial, synthesized and, by implication, somewhat debased concoction. We are living in a way that cuts us off from authentic communion with nature. Giddens reinforces the old dualism between nature and culture by superimposing it on the traditional/modern distinction, thereby reproducing it in a most misleading way.

Philosophy and 'social theory'

In inspecting Giddens' sociological credentials one is struck by his very conventional view of the relationship between sociology and philosophy, but one also detects a certain ambivalence surrounding this subject. As I will show below, he takes for granted philosophers' stipulations of the range of questions to be allocated to the respective academic establishments. This topic is worth attention because it bears upon the status of structuration theory as 'social theory' and affects how we evaluate the 'systematic' as opposed to historical or genetic theoretical strategy which it exemplifies.

Giddens' attitude to this issue can be gathered from these two quotations: 'both empirical social analysis and sociological theorizing involve inherently philosophical endeavours' (1982d: 175) and 'The social sciences are lost if they are not directly related to philosophical problems by those who practise them' (1984: xvii). However, as I argued in Chapter 1, the evidence suggests that with the rise of the social sciences and of sociology in particular within European social development, it became more and more difficult for philosophers to justify an autonomous area of competence for their discipline. Indeed, this problem could be said to have reached crisis proportions in contemporary philosophy (Baynes *et al.* 1987; Rorty 1979 and 1982).

Sociology, I am arguing, gradually took over and transposed on to a new level questions about the nature of knowledge and morality that were previously raised by philosophers or theologians or that were locked up in the great ideologies of the nineteenth century. These matters became embedded in the conceptual structure of sociology and are profoundly preserved within it, carried forward in a reformulated state. Meanwhile, the philosophical establishment retreated more and more into developing their logical and conceptual skills, transforming philosophy mainly into a technical discipline, particularly in the Anglo-Saxon tradition, and erecting barriers of argument and cultivated profundity around themselves to effect the professional closure of their subject.

If this general picture of the historical fate of philosophy (which I painted in greater detail in Chapter 1) has even a grain of accuracy, then we must be more cautious than Giddens in taking for granted the autonomy and cognitive value of philosophy and the range of specialisms within it which we find ready to hand in the current books produced in the field. On one level Giddens seems to grasp the profound evaluative social relevance of the sociological tradition which he sees as a 'critical' commitment, in deference to the current catchword. But there is also in Giddens a failure of nerve in not carrying this awareness through to its conclusion in relation to philosophy.

Like many other writers in the present period, Giddens brings into play the woolly term 'social theory', which he concedes is 'not a term which has any precision' (1984: xvii), derived from the Parsonian–Mertonian tradition, in order to build bridges towards philosophy. The 'field' of social theory is said to encompass issues about the nature and conceptualization of human action in relation to institutions and the practical connotations of social analysis which are deemed to be applicable to all social sciences. 'Sociological theory', on the other hand, is said to be relevant only to advanced industrialized societies and to be a species of social theory. It is social theory that is said to raise issues that 'spill over into philosophy' (*ibid.*: xvii). The dubiety of the field called social theory can readily be seen if sociology is compared with the science of psychology. In this discipline would anyone ever refer to 'psychic theory'?

The problem I am bringing into focus here is that philosophical concepts, unlike sociological ones, have not been developed in direct cross-fertilization with empirical evidence, and that the importance of this difference is blurred by the acceptance of the legitimacy of the enterprise of social theory. Oddly enough, in one place Giddens acknowledges just this difference. Speaking about divergences between Marx's conception of history and the observations of later critics, he says that he does not think that the divergences can be either validated or invalidated by a conventional empirical test: 'But neither are they refractory to empirical reference in the sense in which philosophical theories are' (Giddens 1971: x). But in *The Constitution of Society* he sees the conceptions of human action and agency to be produced by social theory as theorems which 'can be placed in the service of empirical work' (1984: xvii) – the point, presumably, being that when doing social theory one works up concepts of action and agency found in philosophy in such a way as to render them amenable to empirical research. I say 'presumably' because this is far from clear.

Furthermore, the subject is made even more vague by his casual and undiscriminating terminology. When describing the texture of the philosophical enterprise that is supposed to connect with social theory, Giddens moves freely between philosophical 'concepts', 'theories', 'issues' and 'debates'. If these terms are studied separately, however, the uncertainty surrounding the status of structuration theory is compounded. Philosophical 'concepts' have, as Giddens has clearly also seen, no direct empirical reference or intention and are hence, in themselves, of no usefulness for research purposes. Indeed, by their very nature philosophical concepts are held to be part of a transcendental, i.e. non-empirical kind of discourse. From the standpoint of the sociological view of theory as being involved in an interplay with evidence, surely the phrase 'philosophical theories' is a contradiction in terms. Furthermore, because of philosophy's dubious autonomy historically, it is by no means clear that there are philosophical 'issues' at all, let alone any relevant to the social sciences. Philosophical 'debates' certainly exist, but their cognitive value cannot be guaranteed. They are often arbitrary and of only accidental relevance to sociology.

In the light of the above one can then ask: in what does the perceived overlap between philosophers' and sociologists' treatments of issues in the study of social action consist? Both groups are said to have been working 'on a common range of problems' (Giddens 1982d: 175) but surely this is true only in an abstract sense, insofar as all the writers concerned are talking about human action generally and the ways in which sociologists have tried to explain it. Under the rubric of social theory, Giddens is able to move freely between authors as diverse as Weber, Garfinkel, Durkheim, Gadamer, Erikson, Austin, Schutz and Wittgenstein – an exercise that grossly flattens out the distinctive historical and national specificity of their work, as well as eliding the sociology/philosophy distinction. Moreover, because philosophers can only, in the nature of what they do, develop their concepts and discussions without direct interplay with empirical evidence, we can never be sure whether their assertions or conclusions are not hypostatizations of their own self-experience or that of particular groups in our society or in some other society or period. The apparent convergence observed may also be partly due to the slippage of sociological findings and concepts *into* philosophy, which are then reworked in a different and characteristically philosophical vocabulary. These are then fed back into sociology as insights that have apparently been independently arrived at.

The status of social theory and its role in Giddens' thinking has to be seen against his depiction of the proper field of sociology. As we have already seen, for Giddens sociology is the social science dealing only with advanced societies, its concepts being developed in relation to the distinctive character of the discontinuous, modern industrialized world. Hence sociology is 'not a generic discipline dealing with human societies as a whole' (Giddens 1984: xvii). But if sociology is not this generic discipline, then which is? Presumably the imprecise social theory, which is said to span all the social sciences. Social theory, therefore, as a 'second-order' range of conceptual reflections on the nature of action occupies a structurally similar place in relation to sociology as conventional wisdom has it that philosophy in general stands to all the sciences. Indeed, as far as I can see social theory is philosophizing by another name.

Structuration theory, as social theory, is born out of a style of thinking that assumes that philosophy is the master discipline unifying the sciences and, as such, it reinforces this role. Giddens cannot entertain the possibility that the master science might be *sociology*, because for him that would smack of Comteanism, scientism and positivism and similar doctrines which, together with the idea of progress, apparently celebrated the superiority of the West. This is why he so strenuously rejects all theories of *evolution* (Giddens 1984: ch. 5) because they are regarded as part of the same undesirable package of nineteenth-century ideas; but in doing so he also discards a sensitivity to *development*, which is not the same thing.

Giddens' response to the work of Habermas, as the leading exponent of 'critical' theory in the Marxist tradition, is interesting in the light of what I have been arguing in this and the previous sections. Habermas has produced a vast and weighty output over the last thirty years and has been highly influential because of the challenging way in which he has reconstructed the Marxian legacy for a generation caught up in the radical politics in the 1960s and 1970s. As is well known, he builds on the work of the earlier writers of the Frankfurt School, and the *Dialectic of Enlightenment* by Adorno and Horkheimer looms large in his intellectual development. Because of the particular German transcendental philosophical tradition from which Habermas comes and the specifically Western Marxist problematics in which his work is embedded, one can only fully understand his work once one has taken account of certain Kantian principles and traced his project back to the Hegelian structure of thinking epitomized by Horkheimer's essay 'Traditional and Critical Theory' of 1937 and ultimately back to Lukács' *History and Class Consciousness* (Kilminster 1979). Hence, when Habermas employs in his work concepts and insights derived from the philosophy of language, linguistics, developmental psychology and systems theory, these are grafted on to an already consolidated philosophical–sociological standpoint in which Kantian and

Hegelian themes are intertwined in interesting and, in my view, contradictory ways.

Much of the centre of gravity of this critical theory tradition is lost in Giddens' otherwise clear and concise discussions of the writings of Habermas. He seems to learn little from Habermas and none of his concepts are directly integrated into structuration theory. Giddens expounds Habermas in a disinterested kind of way, clinically laying out the ideas and evaluating them in the light of his own interest in the nature of knowledgeable human action. And he explains the importance of one strand of the philosophical tradition in which Habermas stands (that which located social sciences as *Geisteswissenschaften*) which is most relevant to the matter in hand. He comes at Habermas as a curious but sceptical observer who wants to take his works seriously because of their eminence, but who in the end cannot see their point.

Giddens' criticisms of Habermas are in fact standard ones, frequently made by critics. He says that the two distinctions labour/interaction and nomological/hermeneutic science in Habermas interpenetrate to such a degree in real life that he questions the usefulness of distinguishing them analytically in the first place. He also questions Habermas's analogy between the relationship of psychoanalysts communicating to patients and social scientists communicating to lay people knowledge about structures of inequality in society. And he wonders if Habermas has not exaggerated the pervasiveness of technocratic consciousness in late capitalism (Giddens 1977: 135–64).

Giddens is obviously out of sympathy with Habermas's whole endeavour and style, referring to its 'quasi-Hegelian murkiness' (Giddens 1974: 20). He sometimes makes shrewd substantive objections but often misunderstands or disregards the significance of the transcendental dimension of Habermas's work, i.e. the metatheoretical aspects, to which he gives much less attention. Clearly, if you think sociology is already 'critical', why bother evaluating philosophical arguments designed to demonstrate it? But it is not enough, however, simply to say, as Giddens does, that the ideal speech situation, because it is an ideal, cannot be used to analyse concrete linguistic situations; or that its use in evaluating distorted speech presupposes nomological knowledge of that speech situation. Of course it does, in Habermas's terms, because the knowledge constitutive interests have an analytical, transcendental status.

These comments of Giddens miss the trickier implications in Habermas (and in Karl-Otto Apel) of the ideal speech situation as a regulative principle, in Kantian terminology. As I mentioned in Chapter 3, the ideal speech situation is held to be partly realized in the distorted speech of the present, but is as yet also *un*realized. In the theory of communication its utopian status is regarded as more firmly grounded. This model serves as an ideal, a basis for critique and evaluation, as something both to work towards and to employ as a bulwark against bureaucratic socialist élites, in particular, who might claim that the utopia has been realized in the society in which they have the main power advantage. That is to say, it provides a criterion by which to see through spurious utopias or false claims to 'universality'. For this reason alone, in this frame of reference the ideal speech situation, as a utopia, cannot and should not be taken as concretely realizable. In other words, it is held to be related to empirical situations both concretely and 'potentially'.

Consequently, Habermas's theory entails that conditions sustaining some distorted communication must, dialectically speaking, *always* exist for the ideal speech situation to have its transcendental existence and thus its critical power. There are echoes here of Marx's 'realm of necessity'. For this reason, too, the ideal speech situation is unrealizable concretely. Paradoxically, once built or created, i.e. realized in practice in the world, the ideal speech situation would then lose its critical function. It follows, therefore, that in the meantime the critical theorist can only work towards achieving an idealized situation which is inherently *un*achievable. I have mentioned in note 10 to Chapter 3 the serious implications of that paradox. The point to be made here, however, is that the particular kind of prior sociological commitment of Giddens has desensitized him to the tensions of critical theory, which require sociological understanding. I too would want to reject this programme, but feel that it has to be thoroughly evaluated in its full dignity. This paradox constitutes for the practitioners of critical theory an agonizing spiritual dilemma. They are driven by their conscience to try to achieve an unachievable ideal, against which their efforts are forever condemned to inadequacy. Nowhere is the guilt-driven Protestant super-ego writ larger than in the Kantian dimension of critical theory.

Interaction or interdependence?

As a species of action theory, Giddens' theory of structuration is an attempt to bring together conceptually, through a process of reasoning, the two levels of action and system. Moving off from a critique of Parsons' theory of socialization via the internalization of norms, he sets out to show how the *actual process of interaction* by skilled, knowledgeable actors produces and reproduces the structure and widespread patterning – or degree of 'systemness' – of social relations. This strategy overcomes both Parsons' tendency to reify social systems as well as the powerful objection made by a number of writers, but notably Percy Cohen in his influential *Modern Social Theory*, that 'Parsons is scarcely concerned with action at all, but rather with the conditions that lead up to it' (Cohen 1968: 237). This observation had neatly encapsulated the central weakness of transcendental sociology.

Giddens then weaves in an action theory variant of the principle of the ubiquity of power in social relations, a human reality established in the sociology of Norbert Elias and also derivable from Foucault, Pareto, Simmel and from Max Weber's efforts to show how Marx's analysis of economic power was only one example of a generic phenomenon.[7] Without making it explicit, Giddens is conjuring up a massive weight of sociological tradition when he writes: 'There is no more elemental concept than that of power' (Giddens 1984: 283). This move enables him to correct for the assumption found in Garfinkel that the skilled interpretative exchanges of actors take place between peers by providing the conceptual wherewithal to show how they might be skewed or imbalanced by the distribution of power in society at large. And for the sake of completion (and to cover the contemporary demand for reflexivity) Giddens builds in the tenet that both the unintended consequences of action, and agents' knowledge of the mechanisms of system reproduction, can feed back into system reproduction.

The essence of structuration theory can thus be grasped from the following two quotations:

> All structural properties of social systems ... are the medium and outcome of the contingently accomplished activities of situated actors. The reflexive monitoring of action in situations of co-presence is the main anchoring feature of social integration, but both the conditions and the outcomes of situated interaction stretch far beyond those situations as such. The mechanisms of 'stretching' are variable but in modern societies tend to involve reflexive monitoring itself. That is to say, understanding the conditions of system reproduction becomes part of those conditions of system reproduction as such.
>
> (Giddens 1984: 191)

> Power is not, as such, an obstacle to freedom or emancipation but is their very medium. ... The existence of power presumes structures of domination whereby power that 'flows smoothly' in processes of social reproduction (and is, as it were, 'unseen') operates. The development of force or its threat is thus not the type case of the use of power.
>
> (*ibid.*: 257)

In a similar vein to my remarks in the previous section, a number of critics have suggested that Giddens' stress on people's knowledgeability and reflexive monitoring tilts the balance of structuration theory towards subjectivism. This line of argument is worth pursuing further. Johnson, Dandeker and Ashworth, for example, argue that despite his intention to transcend the subjectivism/objectivism dualism by reformulating it as the 'duality of structure', Giddens' ambiguous attitude towards realism means that he remains a subjectivist (Johnson *et al.* 1984: 205–13). And Margaret Archer underlines this by pointing out, from a systems theory perspective, the vaunting power that Giddens ascribes to human agency, including that of apparently generating social structural properties, which are *all* said to be instantiated by action. But she argues that not all such features are equally changeable by agents. These will include some that change quickly, such as taxation rules, others that take longer such as demographic distributions, to others that are resistant to change such as gender roles and some, like natural resources or language, that are effectively unchangeable. Giddens' overwhelming commitment to the efficacy of reflexively monitored action flattens out these crucial distinctions, leaving him unable to deal with *degrees* of constraint. She writes that he thus 'provides an insufficient account of the mechanisms of stable replication' (Archer 1982: 479).

In *The Constitution of Society* Giddens implicitly tries to counter this objection and other criticisms of a similar kind, particularly in the section 'Three Senses of Constraint' (1984: 174ff.). He acknowledges bodily and material constraints, which he distinguishes from constraining negative sanctions and from structural constraint derived from the given context of differentially empowered, situated actors. All these limit the range of options open to knowledgeable agents and some of these constraints, which include structural properties, he says *cannot* be changed, but these are not named (*ibid.*: 176). Essentially he differentiates the issue in a Weberian fashion, claiming that there are different types of constraint which work in different contexts of action; in any case, constraints on one level can also provide the enablement of individual action on another.

Giddens states that it is the *structural properties* of institutions (symbolic orders, political, economic, legal dimensions) that are objective to the individual agent. (The more deeply embedded ones he calls structural principles.) The *structure*, however, as rules and resources, has a paradigmatic existence, and is said to be only instantiated in action and memory traces, providing the 'virtual' order in the patterning of the social practices in the social system. In this sense 'structure' in Giddens' theory is *internal* to actors (Giddens 1984: 25). But do these definitions meet Archer's criticism about the problematic objectivity of constraints in Giddens' theory?

When talking about these structural properties of institutions in detail, Giddens says that this is only a valid procedure 'if it is recognized as placing an *epoché* upon (holding in suspension) reflexively monitored conduct' (*ibid.*: 30). What does this mean? Presumably that with the methodological brackets removed, structural properties are *also* – like structure – uniformly *instantiated* in reality in reflexively monitored conduct. Or does he mean that reflexively monitored conduct can go on with institutions existing as an objective backdrop? In which case, what is their ontological status? The first suggestion finds backing in an earlier formulation by Giddens (1979: 80) that seemed to imply that by virtue of the 'duality of structure' these structural properties too are instantiated in human action, both constraining and enabling it. The latter interpretation seems to square with Giddens' comment about symbolic orders in semiotics as a constraint in the realm of signification: 'Signs "exist" only as the medium and outcome of communicative processes in interaction' (Giddens 1984: 31). But these formulations are at odds with the definition of 'structural properties' given in the glossary to *The Constitution of Society* which only mentions 'institutionalized' and 'structured' features, with no reference to reflexively monitored conduct or to instantiation.

I think that the source of these inconsistencies lies partly in the specific character of the structuralists' concept he has used. (I will return to this concept in the next section.) In addition, the problem arises from the nature of structuration theory as action theory. The starting point for Giddens is the bequeathed theoretical problem of how the actions of skilled actors continuously produce and reproduce the systemness of wider patterns of social relations. Hence, Giddens has to provide a way of talking about the patterned interconnections between far-flung chains of interdependent groups and individuals that both retains the all-important skilled, knowledgeable actor but does not reify structure as an external source of constraint, thus reproducing the fallacious individual/society dualism. He is trying to deal with interdependence in the language of interaction.

Let us look more closely at this problem, in the light of Elias's comment that 'the concept of "individual" refers to interdependent people in the singular, and the concept of "society" to interdependent people in the plural' (Elias 1978a: 125). The point to be made is that structuration theory does not at any level contain a fully *relational* conception of constraint because of Giddens' failure to incorporate the reality and concept of human interdependence into this theory. Nowhere does he provide a conceptual discussion of the term 'interdependence'. The term appears occasionally in his writings, as when he is expounding the functionalists' conception of the interdependence of parts and whole, or when it is dropped loosely into discussions to mean interaction or interrelation. In other places, he is clearly aware of the socio-economic meaning of the concept in the theory of the division of labour in Marx and Durkheim (Giddens 1971; 1982e: 36) but these are the only senses in which Giddens appears to know the concept. Interdependence plays no systematic part in the theory of structuration.

Once he has started down the action theory road, then this approach defines the problems for Giddens and circumscribes their solution. Once the starting point is interacting individuals and types of individuals, rather than the plurality of people in webs of interdependencies, two features come to dominate the analysis.

1. A tendency to see unintended consequences and unacknowledged conditions of action only as consequences or conditions of *individual* actions, not as endemic to the actions of many interdependent individuals in society. Similarly, the ambiguous 'structural properties' of institutions tend also to be regarded in Giddens as objective only in relation to the individual. Despite his attempt to transcend the individual/society dichotomy by the duality of agency and structure, the ghost of the old dualism haunts the theory because his point of departure is action theory which carries the dualism at its core.

2. The interacting individuals in conditions of co-presence (social integration applies here) can only be visualized as connected to other individuals who are *not* present by using metaphors such as the 'stretching' of social practices ('time–space distanciation'), or by reference to their 'lateral' properties or to the 'channelling of time–space paths of individuals' in system integration (Giddens 1984: 142). Metaphors of stretching, laterality or of paths of individuals are inherently unrelational. When talking about social integration he sometimes refers to 'absent others' or 'those who are physically absent' (*ibid.*: 37) without further comment. The closest Giddens comes to conceptualizing interdependence is when he makes a distinction in one passage (though not sustained throughout *The Constitution of Society*) between 'social interaction' and 'social relations':

> Social interaction refers to encounters in which individuals engage in situations of co-presence, and hence to social integration as a level of the 'building blocks' where the institutions of social systems are articulated. Social relations are certainly involved in the structuring of interaction but are also the main 'building blocks' around which institutions are articulated in system integration. Interaction depends upon the 'positioning' of individuals in the time–space contexts of activity. Social relations concern the 'positioning' of individuals within a 'social space' of symbolic categories and ties.
>
> (Giddens 1984: 89)

I have quoted this knotty passage at length in order that the ambiguities and elisions of the theory can stand out in sharper relief. This quotation articulates the furthest point possible within action theory and yet it still fails to resolve the action/system dualism. Individual interactions in conditions of co-presence seem to be given precedence and form the starting point. These are said to involve reflexively applied procedures by knowledgeable agents whereby social integration is achieved. But note the vagueness of the terms 'building blocks', 'social relations', 'symbolic categories' and 'ties' to describe the way that integration is achieved on the system level. Unspecified 'social relations' are said to be involved at both levels and the differential 'positioning' of individuals in both is regarded as significant. Despite the word 'relations', individuals are seen here only in the first person, as positions. There is no conceptual grasp of the perspective from which they themselves are regarded *by others* in the total social web, nor of their combined relatedness. Structuration theory is a one-dimensional view of society which does not permit the sociologist to show this combined interplay of relations and perspectives in all its richness and complex balances of power.

The issue here is this: what is the nature of the social interconnectedness, the unspecified 'ties' which bind people both into smaller networks and into wider ones which ripple beyond their immediate milieu? To extend the question: what makes it socially possible for people to break off contacts and move on spatially to take up others, then to break these, and so on, in the manner described so vividly by Giddens (and by Simmel before him)? In all cases I would suggest it is their inescapable *interdependence* with others. Actors do indeed have intentions, plans, goals and knowledgeability and possess differentially valid discursive cognitive 'penetration' of wider social interconnections, as Giddens specifies. But they cannot escape their complex interdependence with others, present or absent, no matter how penetrative their knowledge may be. In John Lennon's haunting line: 'Life is what happens to you while you're busy making other plans.' People's rational, aware actions may have unplanned consequences, which they did not anticipate and cannot control, brought about by the repercussions of the actions of others whom they do not know but with whom they are interdependent. And this process works the other way, not as an 'interaction' or simple reciprocity, but as a functional nexus. Giddens' theorem of individuals 'making a difference' has to be rethought and cleansed of its rationalistic and voluntaristic character.

The complex intertwined nature of the social bonding that binds social and system integration, in Giddens' terminology, is left in woolly vagueness in structuration theory by the nature of its cognitive cast. As we have seen, Giddens can only visualize interdependence in its partial economic mode in his discussions of Durkheim and the capitalist wage labour contract in Marx. But even this dimension is marginal to his structuration theory, as such. He thus fails to grasp interdependence as a much more multi-dimensional and multi-levelled, complex and *relational* structure, involving human bonding of various kinds, including political, economic and affective bonds. As Elias says of the multiple functions that people perform *for* each other:

> People need each other, are directed towards and bonded to each other as a result of the division of labour, of occupational specialization, of integration into tribes or states, or a common sense of identity, and of their shared antagonism for others or their hatred and enmity towards each other.

> (Elias 1978a: 175)

In analyzing such multi-dimensional functional nexuses, one can show how the nature of bonds between individuals and groups changes over time as part of wider societal changes. For example, the parent–child bond goes through a number of stages during the lifetime of the two people, as the balance of power shifts from one to the other as part of the changing play of forces across the family network and society as a whole.

With his concept of the 'dialectic of control' (Giddens 1984: 283) Giddens has conceptualized the important fact that subordinate groups can, through making use of resources open to them, exercise some control over superordinate ones, even if the balance is highly asymmetrical. This welcome concept, though not in essence original, contributes much to the debate about the nature of social power and rightly has a high profile in the theory of structuration. But it has not the same explanatory force as grasping such a skewed balance-of-power relationship as one of functional interdependence in the above sense, whereby each group or unit is dependent on the other *for its very social existence*. And sometimes groups or larger social units will be driven into bitter conflict with each other by the structure of their relatedness, despite their mutual understanding of their relationship. Giddens can only grasp this kind of interdependency-in-antagonism in the weaker and more voluntaristic form of 'control . . . as the capability that some actors, groups or types of actors have of influencing the circumstances of action of others' (*ibid.*). But this formulation overlooks that these groups or actors are *already* locked into forms of bonding with those they are trying to influence, and they with them, vice versa, forming a functional nexus in a wider web of interdependencies. As Elias says: 'Underlying all intended interactions of human beings is their unintended interdependence' (Elias 1969: 143).

Structuration theory embodies a rationalistic image of people whose affective life – and readiness to connect with others on this dimension of human bonding – is bracketed out by the methodological prescription that the reflexively monitoring actor is bounded by institutions on the one side and by the unconscious on the other, which is said – following ego psychology – to be little implicated in practical conduct (Giddens 1984: 50). Giddens' indebtedness to this school of psychoanalysis and, within it, to Erik Erikson, helps to focus the model of the rational agent at the centre of the theory. Erikson's work, and that of this school in general, is famous for broadening the scope of psychoanalysis to include the ego's conscious interests and the individual's relationships with collective symbols and social institutions other than the Oedipal family constellation associated with classical Freudianism.

Giddens accepts much of Erikson's sociological corrective to the more mythic and individualistic aspects of Freud. In so doing he takes on board a notion of the agent very much in line with Erikson's version of Freud's 'ego ideal', seen by Erikson as more flexible, more conscious and more bound to prevalent cultural values and susceptible to change than the more thoroughly internalized super-ego of Freud (Erikson 1968: 210). There is thus an interesting consistency in Giddens' work. This model of the rational agent fits well with Giddens' fascination with the extraordinary capacities of the skilful actor derived from Garfinkel and goes hand in hand with the tacit neo-liberal impulse in the theory that people's capacities to 'make a difference' should be maximized. To quote Hoffman on Erikson's concept of the 'ego ideal': 'This definition, more than Freud's, resembles the classical liberal notion of an "inner-directing" conscience and assumes that individuals are capable of participating in the direction of their own lives' (Hoffman 1982: 140).

In a word, structuration theory articulates, with an implicit normative stress, the dominant self-experience and public code of behaviour of highly self-controlled individuals in advanced industrialized societies. But it is unable to show how this kind of individual came to develop in the first place: for Giddens, people have, apparently, always been the same since the dawn of history. I am not gainsaying the importance of ego psychology, which provides, for example, a profound understanding of individual identity formation as a series of stages, nor that the incorporation of concepts derived from it into research programmes will not illuminate at least a certain range of problems in sociology. My point is that if a theory embodying the model of the agent described is pursued exclusively, one pays a high price. It effectively closes the door to an understanding of the crucial role played in society by socially controlled and regulated instincts and drives. By its very conceptual structure and assumptions, structuration theory cannot address the *emotional 'constitution of society'*. Excluded is the study of social standards of affect control and individual self-control. Alien to the theory is the changing social regulation of pleasure, desire and aggression through shame, embarrassment and revulsion. These emotions have been systematically ruled out in advance as unsociological.[8]

Systematics or socio-genesis?

Structuration theory is conceived as a metatheory of action relevant to all the social sciences, a conceptual effort of synthetic theory construction designed to consolidate current developments in theory and reconstruct the orthodox consensus. But, I have been arguing, it is more than this. It is also the pulling together into a more or less coherent sociological package, of a particular selection of concepts, tenets, assumptions, emphases and normative elements, the unity of which can be seen to constitute a world-view. The selective principle underlying its component parts is its prescriptive force as a moral–political platform for the social criticism of modernity from the point of view of the freedom of the individual, seen as potentially self-directing and expressive. This evaluative stress, as well as rational, intellectual criteria, determines what is included within or excluded from the purview of the theory. The liberal strand is the most dominant, in a number of senses, as we have seen. The socialist current is represented by the appropriation of the Marxist economic ontology of labour and the stress on individual freedom is also compatible with forms of democratic socialism. Conservatism provides the *longue durée* of sedimented and reproduced institutions and the concept of existential contradiction, both of which have a lower profile in the theory.

I do not think it imposes too great a degree of coherence to represent the world-view implicit in structuration theory in general outline as follows. Sociology is seen as the 'critical' social science which deals with the class societies of the discontinuous 'modern' capitalist world. Its central concern is with examining which conditions of action will maximize the capacity of knowledgeable actors to make a difference in this society when they are differentially socially endowed with access

to resources. Sociology needs to be open to philosophy because here we find apposite discussions of rationality and intentional action which are appropriate for
understanding the kind of self-monitoring people characteristic of the rationalized
world of modernity. We concentrate on knowledgeability, discursive and practical
consciousness because in the modern, internally pacified nation-states the personality formation of actors is such that the unconscious is not much implicated in
their everyday action. Hence it can be bracketed out. The choice of Marx, Weber
and Durkheim as the 'selective tradition' is appropriate because they were preeminently the sociologists of discontinuous modernity and its problems. They
criticized respectively early capitalism, the later anomic aspects of economic life
and increasing capitalistic rationalization. This version of the nature and role of
sociology in the modern world is institutionally prominent in various forms. This is
because it is self-evidently plausible to the highly self-controlled, self-monitoring
people who participate in the sociological community and who find mirrored in
the programme their most deeply felt moral obligations as social critics.

For the sake of contrast and in order to open up a dialogue with this way of
doing sociology, I have counterposed a number of opposite principles. This tactic
is employed in order to retrieve from the theoretical bathwater some conceptual
babies hastily discarded. These recoveries will hopefully also ultimately transform
the normative implications by reconstituting a more realistic balance. Instead of a
narrow sociology of modernity, I counterposed a broader conception of sociology
as the unifying social science applicable to all historical societies. Instead of discontinuism, I opposed continuism. Instead of the knowledgeable actor, I substituted
changing patterns of figurational compulsion. Against interaction I pitted interdependence. Instead of embracing philosophy, I suggested that we pull away. Instead
of agents as first-person 'positions', I advocated multi-perspective relatedness.
Against the rationalistic actor I counterposed a more complete model of people in
the plural which incorporates the changing regulation of affect and individual self-
controls. And against 'hodiecentric' (today-centred) (Goudsblom 1977a: 7ff., 78,
168) socio-political diagnosis I opposed the study of the long-range sequential
order of development to help discern the general shape of the next phase that
leads from the present national and global condition.

I have expressed these oppositions starkly and pithily for effect and can only
make a couple of the qualifications needed to avoid being misunderstood. I am not
intending to create another set of dualisms, nor am I counterposing a rival world-
view, because *initially* I eschew normative considerations. My aim is simply to open
up a different range of questions. The task ultimately is to achieve a more
complete sociological picture of society than is possible via structuration theory,
illuminating though it is for some purposes. For example, it would be foolish and
misleading simply to counterpose another apriori of continuism against discontinuism. Only a conservative would see *only* continuities. Rather, it is the
assessment of the balance of these and other dimensions in tandem with an accent
on long-term social development that is the key. Similarly, it is clear that actors are
indeed knowledgeable and to some extent rational in all societies, perhaps increasingly so in our own society. But this exclusive focus is an arbitrary emphasis
coloured by the dominant rationality of our society that puts in brackets the
massively important emotional bonding in social life. It also tends to assume that

people have been the same throughout history, leaving out of account the study of the ways in which people *themselves* change during social transformations, even during the course of the short 'modern' phrase.

Giddens' appropriation of Hans-Georg Gadamer's version of hermeneutics (Gadamer 1960) illustrates very well the nature of the particular set of emphases and assumptions of the structurationist programme. For Gadamer, understanding is not a special method of *Verstehen* but an ontological condition of humankind. In the interpretation of texts written in different periods it is impossible to eliminate the prejudices or pre-understandings that we bring to them, because we cannot escape the tradition from which we enter into the subject-matter of the text. Both the interpreter and the tradition being investigated through the text contain their own 'horizon', in Gadamer's terms, so the task of hermeneutic inquiry is a circular one of integrating one's own horizon with that of the tradition concerned to produce a 'fusion of horizons'. This is an unending process whereby we test out our pre-understandings, so changing our understanding of the past and ourselves in a continuous process. Thus the present is always formed through a constant contact and interchange with the past which Gadamer calls our effective history (*Wirkungsgeschichte*). Gadamer is not offering a methodology for the human sciences, but rather his work is a philosophical attempt 'to understand what the human sciences truly are, beyond their methodological self-consciousness, and what connects them with the totality of our experience of the world' (*ibid.*: xiii).

As Outhwaite has pointed out, Gadamer's Heideggerian radicalization of the hermeneutic tradition has had a growing influence on the social sciences: 'It has become increasingly clear that social scientists can no longer pass over the hermeneutic foundations of their practice, nor consign them to the domain of an optional *verstehende* sociology' (Outhwaite 1985: 37). Like Habermas, Giddens takes hermeneutics seriously. Consistent with his individualistic sympathies, he criticizes Gadamer for overreacting against earlier empathetic versions of textual hermeneutics by eliminating the author's intentions entirely. (This is a similar criticism to the one Giddens directs at structuralism.) But most importantly he incorporates Gadamer's ontological view of understanding as the fusion of horizons directly into his prescriptions for explanation in sociology in his conception of the 'double hermeneutic' (Giddens 1976: 162). This duplex process is one whereby the sociologists mediate ordinary language meanings of actors, obtained from sociologists' immersion in forms of life, with the technical metalanguage of sociology.

So, Giddens takes existential hermeneutics into his framework, but contrary to the whole intention of Gadamer, he reformulates its essence as a method, i.e. as an explanatory prescription for sociology. This move is consistent with his customary strategy of taking from philosophies and sociological schools only what he needs for reconstructing the sociological tradition, which takes priority. At the same time, Giddens is anxious to appropriate this kind of hermeneutics without leading sociology into epistemological relativism, a known danger in this field. Such a result would, of course, undermine his commitment to the efficacy of reliable sociological knowledge in the discontinuous, modern world. In the hermeneutic debates he therefore sides with Emilio Betti's insistence on keeping hold of the integrity and autonomy of the *object*, i.e. the text as a 'situated creation of its author'

(Giddens 1976: 63). And he seizes on the distinction made by philosophers between sense and reference in order to reconcile the respect for the authenticity of mediated frames of meaning with the question of the *validity* of knowledge. He sees hermeneutic understanding as a 'condition of' (*ibid.*: 145) validity, rather than something that excludes it, although, as is Giddens' wont, for principled reasons (Giddens 1984: xx) he does not pursue this vexed epistemological question any further. For him, these kinds of debates get in the way of sociological research. It is predictable, therefore, that he would have backed Betti, although to do so runs counter to the drift of recent, more sceptical commentary. For example, Bleicher regards Betti's concern with salvaging some limited objectivity from hermeneutics as representing 'a residual of the scientistic approach to the non-natural sphere' (Bleicher 1980: 125).

Furthermore, Habermas has objected that Gadamer's hermeneutics cannot deal with *emancipation* from structures of domination and authority embedded in language and traditions. Bleicher again locates the true fulfilment of hermeneutics as lying in its emancipatory function. There is, Bleicher argues, a 'critical-anticipatory moment in understanding' which cannot be envisaged by Gadamer: 'Ultimately, the possibility of critical hermeneutics depends on the framework that Habermas is attempting to construct out of a materialist theory of society and of social evolution in conjunction with a theory of ordinary language' (Bleicher 1980: 258). On the other hand, Giddens sees Habermas's contention that language is a medium of domination as conceding too much to hermeneutics because it transmutes power into ideologically deformed communication. At the same time, Habermas is said to concede too little because, for Giddens, the mediation of frames of meaning must form a basis for ideology critique as a human activity (Giddens 1977: 153).

In a word, Giddens abandons the difficult epistemological issue of validity arising out of hermeneutics because he has a prior commitment to eschewing elaborate epistemological discussions. Thus he is able to appropriate hermeneutics in a methodological manner and still sleep at night. And he is insensitive to the Habermas–Bleicher problem of reconciling Gadamer's ontological hermeneutics with 'critique' because, as we saw earlier, he already regards sociology as an inherently 'critical' enterprise, borrowing the term's established resonances for his own purposes.

Finally, let us turn more explicitly to what I am calling Giddens' 'systematic' method and contrast it with a socio-genetic approach, in order to build up a picture of the comparative gains and losses of each for the task of sociological synthesis. The term 'systematic' in the sense I am using here is of Kantian origins and is one side of the distinction between systematic and historical inquiries, delineating a division of labour between philosophy and social scientific disciplines. 'Systematic' refers to a range of reflections of a conceptual or transcendental kind arising from the factual socio-historical data assembled by the social sciences (see Chapter 1).

The related sociological use – and this is the sense implicitly embodied in Giddens' method – was codified by R.K. Merton in his essay 'On the History and Systematics of Sociological Theory' (in Merton 1968b). By 'systematics' he referred to the substance of theories, i.e. the generalizable conceptual yield derivable independently from their history or origins. His analysis went along with a plea for not merging or blurring the distinction which sociologists, far more than physicists or chemists, tend to do. (As will be clear later on, I accept this general advice but, because of various drawbacks to the analytic systematics of Giddens' approach, I advocate a 'historical systematics'.)

Giddens only involves himself in developmental thinking marginally in his discussions of institutions and various empirical areas in his work *The Nation State and Violence* (1985). He is generally uninterested in the study of long-term processes at the level of his metatheory in *The Constitution of Society* (1984). Both works embody the erroneous equation development = evolution. And his summary dismissal of the sociology of knowledge blocks off access to the usefulness of this tradition not only for establishing the hidden interests of opponents' utterances, but also for aiding adequate concept formation itself in a developmental and historical way. As I have been arguing throughout this study, *there is more to the sociology of knowledge than its use simply for debunking*. Furthermore, his use of hermeneutics recommends the mediation of meaning frames or forms of life with the metalanguages of social science. But it is a method that seems to be geared only to the mediations between the West and other cultures, between forms of life in the society of the here-and-now or between the present and past forms of life in the shorter run *within* the 'modern' world. Giddens' hermeneutic programme seems to exclude the aim of securing a deeper and more long-range historical understanding of humankind by recovering the forgotten distant developments that have shaped our world, ourselves and our whole conceptual apparatus.

Methodologically, moving in this direction means embracing (without teleology and with other modifications) the principle encapsulated in Marx's dictum that the 'anatomy of man contains the key to the anatomy of the ape', i.e. that the structure of a later stage of development enables us potentially better to grasp earlier ones, traces of which are found embedded in the later stage. This thrust is also embodied in various forms in Hegel, writers in the German tradition of historicism, various Western Marxists, including Gramsci and Sartre in his *Question of Method* (Kilminster 1979: part III and ch.15) and in Collingwood. As the latter writer put it:

> Because the historical past, unlike the natural past, is a living past, kept alive by the act of historical thinking itself, the historical change from one way of thinking to another is not the death of the first, but its survival integrated in a new context involving the development and criticism of its own ideas.
>
> (Collingwood 1946: 226)

Apart from a very brief discussion of Oakeshott (Giddens 1984: 355–6) Giddens is, as far as I am aware, ill-versed in these traditions and consequently lacks a historical consciousness in the above sense. He significantly extracts from Marx only the appeal to the 'discontinuous' structure of capitalism, disregarding entirely Marx's equally central historical–*genetic* orientation – the so-called dialectical method. Not surprisingly, therefore, Giddens tends to assume in a Kantian fashion that concepts in general are simply abstract in relation to the concrete, or empirical. He has no conception of concepts as *synthetic*, i.e. as having embedded within them traces of earlier stages of social and scientific development. (I will return to this issue in Chapter 8.)

Furthermore, Giddens' 'systematic' strategy treats the different schools of philosophy and sociology discussed as equipollent and hence as abstractly comparable. Each is assumed to provide a substantive yield irrespective of its nature and origins. The project has been made possible by the institutionalization of sociology in recent times in which, in Edward Shils's words, institutions 'foster the production of works' and 'create a resonant and echoing intellectual environment' (Shils 1982: 279). In this resonating intellectual world Giddens (skilfully and intelligently, to be sure) discovers convergences between the schools which he finds ready to hand and side by side in theses, curricula, journals, conference papers and publications, but takes for granted their specificity and how they came to achieve their salience. The danger of over-abstraction is compounded by the lack of acknowledgement of the potentially differing status and cognitive value of each school's contribution. As Shils warns: 'Institutionalization is not a guarantee of truthfulness: it only renders more probable the consolidation, elaboration and diffusion of a set of ideas' (*ibid.*: 308). Of course, it is possible to produce theoretical syntheses at a certain level of abstraction, as Parsons and Giddens have shown, and these may be of a certain heuristic value. But each takes too much for granted.

However, following Elias and the sociology of knowledge tradition, I would advocate injecting into the process of theory formation a historical, socio-genetic way of controlling for the validity or cognitive value of synthesized components to supplement the logical criteria employed by Giddens. Perhaps this method could be called 'historical systematics'. Set out on the theory stall of contemporary sociology is a variety of theoretical products, their origins largely forgotten, some of which are philosophical and some sociological or various hybrids of the two. Structuration theory synthesizes a selection of the theoretical results of a complex social and institutional development which has thrown up the paradigms and placed them side by side. The point is that, lacking a developmental theory both of society and of scientific development (which must in my view go hand in hand), Giddens has no way of sorting them out from the point of view of whether any one theory or concept among them is an advance over a previous stage of more or less adequate elaboration.

A socio-genetic synthesis would take a different form and hopefully provide a more robust, object-adequate synthesis because it would contain only sociologically proven components. It would comprise a different kind of abstraction, because it would be a synthesis of the real perspectives in society as a whole at the present stage of development. From this point of view, I can see three further disadvantages of the systematic synthesis, particularly in the hands of Giddens. Each of these areas brings out the standpoint that I am contrasting with it.

1. To repeat an important point: because concepts are discovered ready to hand within the developed institutionalized settings of sociology, then the assumption tends to be that, just because they are there in an articulated form as part of a school or perspective, they must be credible and valid. As Shils said, however, this cannot be assumed and *nor can their usefulness for sociological purposes*. For example, there are many concepts used in the theory of structuration which are originally of

philosophical provenance – such as praxis, contradiction, presencing, historicity – which need scrutiny on this count. I will briefly look in more detail at another one, Giddens' appropriation of the concept of structure from structuralism, in order to make the point.

The concept of structure is used in structuration theory in several senses and word combinations, but one – that of the timeless, paradigmatic, virtual structure – is particularly problematic. In the works of Lévi-Strauss, typically within the structuralist tradition (Lévi-Strauss 1962; 1969: overture), the concept of structure has a particular epistemological function. For him, and others, the structure is not an aggregate, nor a composite, nor an essence or *Zeitgeist* behind the appearances of the aggregate, but the cognitive laws of relation between the units concerned. The structure is present in the observable units in the relations between them in the network, and is generative of them, including absences as well as presences (Piaget 1971: chs I and VI). Lévi-Strauss has arrived at this complex conception within a philosophical discourse. The concept is informed by an attempt to resolve an epistemological (indeed metaphysical) issue in the philosophy of perception without falling into empiricism, idealism, essentialism or subjectivism. His implicit targets are positivism and phenomenology (see Chapter 5 for a further discussion of this matter).

Now, Giddens incorporates the concept of structure, in this sense, into his synthesis, assuming that the logical philosophical idea of the existence of non-essential paradigmatic structures is a way of conceptualizing data automatically applicable to the study of patterns of social life. But why should this be so, when the structuralists' concept of structure was tailored to the solution of a problem posed by the thought/reality dualism of traditional epistemology? This concept of structure is then *made* relevant by Giddens to patterns of social life as rules and resources instantiated in social practices and found in memory traces. But surely its use by Giddens in his theory is a contrivance, the uncritical importation into socio-logical theory of a philosophical way of looking at human perception and the problem of knowledge. It seems to have been brought in simply because it is there, available as part of an academically respectable paradigm within institutionalized sociology, crying out for integration into structuration theory. But its adequacy and appropriateness to the object of sociology seem to me to be questionable. Only theory formation alert to the status and origins of concepts, I am arguing, can prevent us from going down theoretical cul-de-sacs of this kind.

2. The basic argumentation technique of Giddens is to say that *dualisms*, say, individual/society or subjectivism/objectivism, can be 'resolved' through reasoning. This procedure consists in saying that we know, rationally, that the two sides are not mutually exclusive and have been wrongly regarded as alternatives. Hence, they can be replaced by the *dualities* of agency/structure and constraint/enablement. Their resolution through reasoning in this way is an attempt to resolve the dualisms in a philosophical manner, often undertaken by Giddens with, to be sure, great ingenuity and craft. Having done this philosophical work, the way is apparently then cleared for empirical investigation unencumbered by the dualisms, which have been neutralized.

Another way, however, would be to undertake socio-genetic investigation to show, first, how the dualisms came into social and sociological currency and acquired their cognitive force; and second, to test how far they actually do articulate two sides of real social relations in real cases. Some theoretical and conceptual work will be necessary in conjunction with this empirical research, but this is not the same thing as attempting resolution or neutralization of the dualisms by reasoning prior to empirical research. Put another way, the socio-genetic approach establishes the validity and range of applicability of the dualisms *empirically and genetically*. It is a scientific as opposed to a philosophical procedure.

3. The 'systematic' method embodied in structuration theory fails to grasp that the paradigms, tendencies and schools upon which it draws were also, following Karl Mannheim (1928), interpretations of the world. They were also, and to some extent still are, the banners behind which groups have marched in a competition to impose their definition of reality in the teeth of the dominant one – the paradigm that Giddens calls the orthodox consensus.

Giddens does have some conception of the extra-theoretical group life lying behind paradigms when he remarks that 'Any generalized theoretical scheme in the natural or social sciences is in a certain sense a form of life in itself, the concepts of which have to be mastered as a mode of practical activity generating specific types of descriptions' (Giddens 1976: 162). But this is an anodyne and bloodless view of group life. For Giddens, the hermeneutic mediation of divergent forms of life, and the immersion of sociologists in alien cultures, are essentially smooth and harmonious negotiations. Nor is there any conception that the metalanguages of social science – such as structuralism, ethnomethodology, Althusserian Marxism or Theorizing – have been *fought* for, involving passion, commitment, clashes and conflict. This is because they were also interpretations of the society, espoused by conflicting groups whose social existence and identity were bound up with them. How else can one account for the passion of the challenges to epistemological authority in the tumult years of sociology in the late 1960s and 1970s, the zeal of the manifestos for new perspectives, the conflict and the strife of the *Sturm und Drang* period of the war of the schools? All the emotion of these conflicts is lost in the analytic–systematic method of Giddens, in whose hands each paradigm becomes, in Hegel's famous words, 'a corpse which has left behind its living impulse' (Hegel 1807: 69).

A theory of cognitive change based in the competition between groups for, amongst other things, the public interpretation of reality can, with some modifications, provide a starting point for a socio-genetic account that can inform the creation of a more adequate and realistic synthesis. It also enables us to deal with something impossible to envisage within structuration theory, that is to explain the conditions of possibility of the synthesis itself. Those are the tasks that I will undertake in the next chapter.

8

SOCIOLOGY SINCE 1945

Socio-genetic and psychogenetic aspects

Sociology, as a systematic study of a whole society, develops only within a nation which is beginning to be unsure of itself.

(Karl Mannheim, cited in Mitchell 1970: 129)

The greatest advances in the sphere of the social sciences are substantively tied up with the shift in practical cultural problems and take the guise of a critique of concept-construction.

(Max Weber 1904: 105–6)

Validity, progress and phaseology

The centrepiece of this chapter is a three-phase model of theory development substantiated by empirical examples taken from the history of British sociology since 1945. It is intended to show in outline the social and psychological transformations out of which have grown the current state of theoretical sociology as well as the consciousness of the nature of the sociological revolution which is embraced in this book. The presentation develops concretely the strategy that I called 'historical systematics' in Chapter 7. The issues traditionally raised under the headings of *validity* and *progress* inevitably present themselves as key problem areas in the sociology field as the result of the proliferation of sociological paradigms, research and reflection in recent times. The model of phases is also intended to provide a framework within which these problems can be *reframed*. I cannot take these cognitive questions very far in this chapter, beyond a few programmatic remarks.

On the topic of validity, our sociological culture is still dominated by the static, absolutist philosophers' concept of 'truth'. Against this, the only alternative seems to be cognitive relativism, disorientating forms of which reappear with a disconcerting regularity in each generation. Marx was one of the first not only to try to dynamize, but also to sociologize the classical definition of truth, and thus to point to the way out of the coercive relativism/absolutism antithesis. But, as we saw in Chapter 3, his theory of knowledge was burdened not only by economic overextension and utopian political overstatement, but also by metaphysical hangovers (dualism and teleology in particular) deriving from the philosophical tradition, which were possibly just as detrimental.

Static philosophical modes of thinking continue to suffuse the field of epistemology in far-reaching and subtle ways and relatively few sociologists have tried to develop their own, alternative epistemological vocabulary. Consequently, it is difficult for many even to visualize, let alone to take seriously, the proposition that sociological concepts *become* explanatory and are held to be effective, i.e. 'valid', in the same social process that their originators are trying to explain. It is in the nature of the synthetic character of sociological knowledge that it cannot be formulated without reference to its genesis, in the broadest sense. The perspectival character of human interdependencies means that we are always observing human society as a moving object from shifting points of view within the overall social network. To understand the growth of knowledge and the development of sciences, what is needed is a dynamic theory of cognitive growth as an ordered sequential change, in which controlling for the positions of social observers is explicitly and integrally embraced.

The broader strategy behind my presentation in this chapter is that once the deeper, longer-term social substructure (not in the Marxian sense) has been more or less adequately identified (I must stress *empirically*, as part of an ongoing research programme) embracing a higher level of detachment (Elias), then it is theoretically possible to detect the types of involvement bound up with other approaches and perspectives. Armed with this provisional, *working* synthesis, one can then approach the history of sociology and potentially be able to discern innovations and advances, because one has in mind a more adequate total picture of the longer-term social process and its immediate tendencies, which people have been successively trying to grasp sociologically from their differing positions within it, corresponding to differing degrees of involvement. The issue of cognitive advance thus resolves itself as the empirical pursuit of evidence of *progression*, i.e. an advance beyond a previously demonstrable point of elaboration. This concept is substituted in this area, at any rate, for the somewhat ideologically compromised term 'progress'.

Working with a model of phases does not present the history of changes in sociology (or in any other domain) as a chronology. Rather, theoretical solutions in the present phase are seen as growing out of an agenda of problems transmitted by the previous phases, each of which has, at the same time, a particular character of its own, dictated by the intersection of various interlocking social processes. Johan Goudsblom has ingeniously called this methodological strategy 'phaseology' (in Goudsblom, Jones & Mennell 1989: 16) through which it is possible, he argues, to discern in a previous phase 'precursors' of a later one, as well as 'turning points'. It is the combination of the two dimensions (internal and external) that gives each phase of sociology its particular character and stamps the majority of its products with its peculiar mark. When picking up a sociological theory text, the first questions the investigator should ask are: when was it written? What was the condition of sociological theory in that phase? What extra-theoretical developments – institutional, generational, political, social-psychological and otherwise in the wider society and beyond – can we expect to find expressed in the guise of concept formation? *Only then* can we ask: what is the cognitive value of the text?

The important wider, extra-theoretical developments implicated in the model are the institutionalization of the discipline; functional democratization; informalization; inter-generational conflict and globalization (the latter, having been dealt with at length in Chapter 6, will receive only passing references here). And for reasons of space and the manageability of data, the generational dimension is relatively underdeveloped theoretically. I will establish in the next sections the main contours of the first three paramount processes, but without reference to sociological theoretical artefacts. I will then move on to a presentation of the model itself, in which I will interlace these extra-theoretical developments with the sociological theoretical developments, so as to bring out their interrelations in the determination of the social character of each phase and its corresponding charac-teristic sociological products.

My argument is that the fears, hopes and psychological ambivalence experi-enced by people in society (albeit unevenly), particularly during intensified phases of those four processes in certain combinations, become stamped on many cultural practices and behavioural codes in society. By studying the way in which they also become inscribed in *theoretical sociology* in particular, provides us with a unique opportunity to understand the self-consciousness of an age. Let us now turn to the institutionalization of the discipline.

The institutionalization of sociology: the British case

Following the Robbins Report of 1963, there took place in Britain a major, unprecedented expansion of higher education (Halsey, Floud & Anderson 1961; Banks 1968: ch. 2; Edwards 1982). In the 1960s sociology benefited from this expansion. For the first time it entered British universities as a significant discipline, on a par with the established ones. The overall expansion of sociology was phenomenal. According to data cited by Abrams (1981: 62), in the 1960s 28 new university departments and thirty new chairs of sociology were established (with a parallel expansion in the polytechnics and colleges of education). There was a 450 per cent increase in the output of sociology graduates between 1952 and 1966. In 1966 there were 724 sociology graduates. In 1971 this had risen to 1,768. This suggests that sociology was attractive to students. Sociology also became fashion-able in a variety of cultural intellectual circles as a result of its public exposure through the institutional expansion. The founding in October 1962 and subse-quent success of the popular social science magazine *New Society*, to which many sociologists contributed, is an indicator of the level of general interest in the disci-pline in this phase. The magazine was merged with *The New Statesman* in 1988.

Like all institutionalization in any field, this one too provided the conditions for the repeated, regularized interaction of a profession, scheduled teaching and the assessment of performance. It gradually established self-perpetuating institutional boundaries, and encouraged the production of texts as well as internal peer controls regulating the activity of sociologists. A minimum degree of institutional-ization is essential for the intellectual development of any discipline. However, as I pointed out (following Shils 1982: 308) in relation to the work of Giddens in the previous chapter, institutionalization only renders it more probable that a set of ideas will be diffused and consolidated – it does not guarantee their cognitive power. This is a significant point to bear in mind when evaluating the state of soci-ological theory in the three phases and the questions of cognitive value and theoretical progression.

There are a number of peculiar features of the institutionalization of sociology in Britain which have a direct bearing on the way in which sociology developed and what came to be regarded as core sociological concepts, theories and issues. The context was unusual because the expansion was a very rapid one in a country with a well-developed tradition of studies in social administration and, to an extent, of anthropology, but a relatively underdeveloped tradition of sociology. Unlike Durkheim and the Durkheimians in France during the Third Republic (Clark 1968), sociologists in Britain did not have to fight to establish the discipline in the country's institutions – it was effectively established 'for' them as part of the expansion of universities in general. In these expanding departments, as Abrams put it, 'the new sociologists were to a quite remarkable degree left free to define sociology in any way they chose' (1981: 62). To paraphrase Parkinson's Law: in these circumstances sociological paradigms expanded to fill the institutional space available. Because of the permeable boundaries around the burgeoning discipline, it became a conduit for social and ideological conflict and a crucible for the fusion of the intense social reflection and behavioural experimentation going on in the wider society in this phase.

In a relatively short time-span, an underdeveloped tradition of sociology, until the 1960s unevenly embedded in a few institutions, was transformed by a sudden explosion in the numbers of departments and practitioners. It was this rampant growth that created an imbalance in the system. It produced the tension between the regularized practices of the limited, existing institutionalized discipline and the possibilities opened up and expectations raised by the massive and sudden expansion. Until sociologists could come to terms with the implications of the new paradigms and ideas thrown up in this process, the outcome was a period of chaotic paradigm conflict and theoretical experimentation, which paralleled similar developments in other areas of society and often overlapped with them.

The novel problem that faced sociologists was to explain not only to others, but also *to themselves*, what this burgeoning discipline was, in a situation in which their status as an academic discipline was uncertain. This could be done by writing histories of the discipline or exegetical works on classical sociologists. But the paramount way to do it was to deal with sociology's epistemological foundations. Goudsblom has succinctly described the connection between the preoccupation with epistemological problems and disciplinary ranking:

> [T]he degree to which the practitioners of an academic discipline can permit themselves to be indifferent towards epistemological problems may well be a measure of the intellectual autonomy and social prestige of that discipline. There is no urgent need for legitimation on theoretical grounds in fields which rank highly in terms of either scientific success or general social status.
>
> (Goudsblom 1990: 34)

At the same time, the exigencies of institutionalization generated the need to define sociology curricula, when few models existed. To use a theatrical metaphor, there was a public and a patron for sociology, but no play to perform. It had to be written. It was in the course of defining these curricula that the trio of Marx, Durkheim and Weber, as the 'founding fathers' of sociology, became established, *simultaneously demoting by exclusion* the significance of others such as Comte, Tocqueville, Spencer, Pareto, Simmel, Elias, Mannheim and Hobhouse. In this process of tradition formation, as we saw in the previous chapter, Anthony Giddens (1971, 1977) played a significant role. Amongst other things, he brought Marx into the pantheon, adding him to the others in the European classical tradition, such as Durkheim and Weber, who had already been established as significant by Parsons, who had, however, minimized Marx. Giddens avoided that view as well as the other prominent one of the time, which he found expressed by the New Left,[1] of Marx as the founder of a science of society against which the sociological tradition appears as merely 'liberal bourgeois ideology' (Giddens 1971: 243).

Marxism, both in political organizations of the New Left and as a paradigm community within institutionalized sociology (and other social sciences), proved exceptionally vigorous and fashionable in the 1970s as the result of the coming together of a number of developments. Historically, there has long been a British cultural preoccupation with social class and the phase in question was additionally one that saw considerable industrial conflict as well as political polarization associated with the student movement, which embodied a strong element of inter-generational conflict. Marxism has a perennial appeal to younger people and will tend to resurface in periods of intense inter-generational conflict (Elias 1996: 416).

But another reason for the predominance of Marxism in sociology in this period was that, as a paradigm community, Marxists were also able to present variants of their theory of society as a serious contender for the social scientific crown (i.e. as a *general theory of society*) in the new situation of open theoretical competition. This had been created by, on the one hand, the exceptionally favourable institutional setting and, on the other, by a pervasive uncertainty as to what this new 'science of society' (Marxism or something else) actually was. For some Marxists, working towards the capture of the central paradigm of sociology in academia was seen politically as creating an academic arm to the labour movement.

Functional democratization and informalization

Political scientists use the term 'democratization' to describe the extension of political representation and the development of democratic political institutions. The meaning of the sociological term is different, even though the two processes are related (Mannheim 1929: 32–3; 1933: 171–246). The concept of democratization is one of a number that sociologists have developed to refer to the process of relative social levelling that has taken place at a deep level in modern societies over several centuries. It was what Max Scheler had in mind when he described the twentieth century as the 'epoch of equalization' (quoted by Mannheim 1929: 251). It is well known that the power gradients between lord/peasant, aristocracy/bourgeoisie, capitalists/workers and between other groups have become less *over a long period*, even though they have far from disappeared entirely.

Alexis de Tocqueville noted in the early nineteenth century that permanent hierarchies of rank were gradually diminishing. He was one of the first to grasp an important consequence of this process: 'manners are softened as social conditions become more equal' (quoted in Mennell 1995: 10). Mennell (*ibid.*) also points out that Tocqueville reached the general insight that in such societies people would more readily identify with the sufferings of their fellow human beings. In his pre-1933 writings Karl Mannheim was also interested in the cognitive, cultural and social psychological consequences of the long-term process of democratization. He paid special attention to shifts in experienced *social distance* between groups (which he calls the process of 'de-distantiation') as societies gradually became less hierarchical (1933: 206ff.). He also developed in his later works the concept of 'fundamental democratization' as an instrument for investigating the political implications of the process (Mannheim 1940: 44ff.). For Mannheim, the countervailing forces running against democratization were dictatorship or monopolization of the various means of social power, both of which produced controlling élites (*ibid.*: 47).

Elias's concept of 'functional democratization' moves in a similar direction to that of Tocqueville's general insights and the early writings of Mannheim on social distance, although Elias pays much more attention than Tocqueville to simultaneous counter-trends and movements. Elias links the process of social equalization more closely to the increasingly multiple functions (affective as well as political and economic) that people perform *for* each other in modern societies. Elias's characterization of the concept is 'the narrowing of power differentials and development towards a less uneven distribution of power chances; it *permeates the whole gamut of social bonds*, although there are impulses simultaneously running counter to this trend' (1978a: 69, my emphasis). The absolute monarchs, he argues, increasingly had to take account of the people they ruled in order to preserve their position against their rivals, a process that increased social interdependence and went hand in hand with the growth of national markets. Gradually since then, the structure of human interdependence has become more and more complex as social functions of a political, economic and affective character have multiplied. It is this process that unintendedly integrates ever more tightly individuals and social groups which otherwise appear isolatedly to be pursuing only their own ends.[2]

According to Elias, the comprehensive trajectory of these developments indicates a long-term change in the overall distribution of power from greater to smaller power differentials. As more and more people were drawn into interdependencies, societies became increasingly 'polyarchic' (Elias 1984: 51). Many internal units developed, which made it more and more difficult to control from the centre. Put this way, this thesis can seem paradoxical and difficult to square with the known increase in the power of central government and the still sharp power differential between 'centres' and 'peripheries' (to use Shils's (1982) formulation) in modern societies. It is also hard to grasp if one approaches power differentials with a stark model of social domination and subordination in mind, rather than the more dynamic model of developing and shifting power *balances* employed by Elias.

Elias's point is that control from the centre becomes more difficult for rulers because they have to take account of other groups to a greater extent, thus contributing to the further *integration* of even mutually antagonistic strata and regions. It is the *overall* structure of interdependence that gradually becomes more polyarchic. For Elias, even groups that occupy a very superior power position are still interdependent with those whose power ratio is a good deal less. The attenuation of power differentials (though not their complete disappearance) between social groups also went hand in hand with an overall lessening – through various phases – of social distance between people. Put briefly, functional democratization refers to the long-term, unplanned process of the lessening of the power gradients and social distance between interdependent groups in societies that have become increasingly differentiated (Elias 1939/1978: 68ff.; 1939/1982: 302ff.; 1984: 48ff.; Mennell 1992: 124ff.).

These ideas have been developed further in the work of the Dutch sociologist Cas Wouters (1977, 1986, 1987, 1990) in the elaboration of the concept of *informalization*, which extends the work of Elias. This theory is of some significance for understanding and explaining certain recent developments in sociology.[3] It is important to stress that in my account below, for practical reasons I have had to present only its theoretical formulation. This presentation of the theoretical strand, which was developed in interplay with extensive empirical evidence unreported here, may have the misleading effect of seeming like the bald assertion of the existence of social processes that do not seem to be warranted by the nature of the evidence I present. I take it for granted in what follows that processes of functional democratization and informalization have been securely established empirically in relation to various periods in the development of other advanced European countries, including the Netherlands and Germany (Wouters, works cited above; Waldhoff 1995; and studies listed in part 2 of Kranendonk 1990). In my view, this impressive body of research provides the justification for seeking the further empirical instantiation of the theory for British social trends, in this case the link with sociological theoretical developments. In other words, this chapter is intended to be a contribution to the wider international network of research involved in testing and refining the theory.

Within the overall process of functional democratization there have occurred, according to Wouters, waves of informalization, for example during the 1890s, 1920s and the 1960s. In the spirit of Elias's insistence that functional democratization 'permeates the whole gamut of social bonds', Wouters argues that during these waves the dominant modes of social conduct, the power relationships between people and the social codes symbolizing them, have tended towards greater leniency, variety and differentiation. These are to be observed in a variety of areas, including the less formal regulation of the spoken and written language, clothing, music, dancing and hair styles. During a wave of informalization we can observe a two-sided trend of decreasing contrasts/increasing varieties of behaviour, corresponding to a further attenuation of the power differentials between people within the overall longer-term process of functional democratization. Put another way, as the chains of interdependency between classes and other groups become longer and more integrated, their modes of behaviour grow closer to each other. Outsider groups adopt ruling modes, established groups conceding and making more differentiations in theirs to compensate.

Concentrating in particular on the empirical study of the informalization wave that took place in the 1960s, which includes what is usually referred to as 'permissiveness', Wouters argues that a number of cultural and behavioural developments in this phase are explicable as an expression of strata undergoing emancipation (women, gays, workers, blacks, upwardly mobile people). As the balance of power tilts more in their favour it is possible to observe that the old code of behaviour associated with the previous generation (rigid, inflexible, formal codes of behaviour involving much prohibition, condemnation and suppression of desires) is, relatively speaking, relaxed. This is observed in a number of areas, including the relaxation of sexual taboos and various formal behaviour requirements. Negotiation rather than prohibition becomes more prominent in relations between parents and children and people begin to experiment with new forms of relationships ('open marriage', 'serial monogamy', communes, etc.) as they search for alternatives to the old code. This had demanded formal, life-long, monogamous marriage. In the course of this wave, many things that were once prohibited became permitted.

Psychologically speaking, an informalization phase brings to the surface more primal impulses, as people experiment with the boundaries of what is acceptable. This is because there is an intrapsychic counterpart to the diminishing of social differences which involves a shift in the balance between what is repressed and what is available to be released from repression in newly controlled ways. In some groups, Wouters suggests, there is

> the discovery and expression of hitherto concealed emotions as a prereq-
> uisite for knowing oneself ... [and] ... In some circles it sometimes
> looked as if hard battles were taking place in the competitive struggle for
> the reputation to present themselves as the people who had the best and
> most authentic knowledge of their inner selves.
>
> (Wouters 1986: 4)

In the 1960s–1970s wave of informalization, a prominent attitude amongst younger people and those caught up in the emancipatory movements of outsider groups was identification with the underdog, e.g. psychiatric patients (as in the anti-psychiatry movement), children, women, workers, squatters, down-and-outs, street people and the underprivileged nations and strata of the so-called Third World. Concomitantly with this went the denigration of the vitality of established groups which were dismissed as moribund. This was an attitude that showed little awareness, or perhaps even constituted an omnipotent denial, of the fact that these established groups, the groups of outsiders themselves, as well as those who championed them, were nevertheless all interdependent.

As the wave develops, a new group of 'established' begins to merge with the old 'established' group and, in a period of stablilization, a new hybrid behavioural code emerges. What were earlier informal modes of behaviour become formalized. There now develop acceptable forms of informality. There is generally an apparent 'return' to more formal lifestyles (as in the 1980s), but this is not simply a return to the old ways of the past. It represents a new generational establishment asserting its power and distinctiveness with a new hybrid code. (There will still be characteristic variations, usually fairly small, across class, status and other groups, but increasingly the new code imposes itself generally.) In the phase of *reformalization* the dominant identification is now with the established: there is a spread of what Wouters calls the 'upstairs perspective'. This is not so much a looking upwards, towards the top of the social hierarchy, as in the previous phases, but an expression of a new 'feeling for life'. Now identification with the established and its way of life is less of an emotional hurdle to leap because established and outsiders have drawn closer together in a new pattern of integration. In the present phase, rising strata orientate themselves towards this newer, formalized code of the established.

In this phase, it is plausible to suggest that, despite growing economic inequality, we witness not a return to hierarchy but arguably a further move in the direction of greater 'mutual identification' (Elias) between people. From the point of view of trying to assess the gains and losses of these changes, it could be argued that whilst the relaxation of taboos and prohibitions could be construed as a liberation from the restrictions of former days, for this to be possible people are probably now putting more pressure *on each other* than in the previous phase. This conclusion is far from uncontentious, although to take this matter further would be beyond my present scope. Whatever might be the answer to such questions, my argument is that it is plausible to expect to find mirrored in the sociological products of a phase, however obscurely, discontinuously or unevenly, the broad social psychological cast of the phase (particularly its changing behavioural codes) which can be empirically shown to be part of a shifting equilibrium of conflicting social forces. Let us now turn to the model.

The three phases of post-war sociology

In the following exposition I will weave together the theoretical developments in sociology with the extra-theoretical developments dealt with in the preceding two sections (i.e. institutionalization, functional democratization, informalization and inter-generational conflict), reflecting their intertwinement in a processual social reality.

In presenting the model of phases and the empirical materials, I have gone back only to 1945, which is admittedly a very recent date, chosen only for the sake of convenience and the manageability of the material, which is largely British, with some references to US developments where appropriate parallels can be drawn. The dates I have assigned are only approximate benchmarks added for the sake of our better orientation. The phases overlap with each other. It is these overlaps that enable us to understand some writers as 'precursors' of the main concerns of an impending phase or some paradigms as 'hangovers' from a previous one or particular moments as 'turning points' (Goudsblom 1989: 18).

I am aware that making this arbitrary cut-off point of the end of the Second World War obviously leaves out the phase preceding my first one, during which the Parsonian synthesis was gestated, as well as the phase prior to that and those earlier, when sociology was institutionalized very unevenly; and prior to that when no discipline of sociology as such existed, but only individual social scientists working largely in isolation and often for widely varying purposes and interests. Heilbron (1995: 2–8ff; 1991: 74) refers to this as the 'pre-disciplinary phase' of sociology and warns against projecting back into the work of forerunners assumptions derived from our experience of the institutionalized disciplines of today. The politico-military events of 1945 did not in themselves 'start off' the first phase that I present. Clearly the institutionalization of British sociology continued relatively autonomously throughout the war and after until the present day. This date is simply a symbolic marker to point up an important transitional period of continuity/discontinuity in British (and American) sociology during which the crucially important paradigm for the whole of the three phases (Parsonianism) can be seen with hindsight to be beginning to make itself felt.

(i) Monopoly phase: circa 1945–65

This phase has a particular character socially, psychologically and from the point of view of its sociological products. In British and American sociology approximately during these years there was the domination of the paradigm of structural functionalism deriving from Talcott Parsons and Robert K. Merton. Marxism, as a general theory of society, did exist but largely within socialist and communist parties. Relatively small paradigm communities embracing frameworks such as symbolic interactionism also existed within the institutions of sociology, but did not offer a total theory of society. And it is reasonable to assume that researchers working in a strict empirical mode on small-scale projects did not see themselves as researching wider social interconnections or testing hypotheses suggested by a general theory. (This does not mean, of course, that a general theory of society might not have been assumed but not made explicit.) At the LSE, Ginsberg and his pupils continued Hobhouse's evolutionism in a new form, perhaps as a 'hangover' from the preceding phase.

But by and large, structural functionalism *as a general theory of society* dominated in the academic establishments of Britain as an import from the United States.[4] Globally it was a period of American economic, military and cultural domination of Europe, as well as of the superpower confrontation between West and East – the cold war. During this period, Anglo-American sociology apparently came as close as it has ever come to achieving the status of a one-paradigm science (Friedrichs 1970: 23). At this stage of the institutionalization of British sociology, prior to the great expansion in the mid- to late 1960s, in the competition for the most convincing theory of society as a whole, the paradigm community of structural functionalists (though not extensively institutionally established) had no effective competitors. It was a situation of theoretical monopoly.

Functionalism, in its most sophisticated, Parsonian, form, stressed that society, as a social system of interrelated parts, survived because it evolved institutional structures to fulfil the basic needs of the system, its 'functional prerequisites'. In focusing on social order, integration and the stability of the system achieved via people internalizing commonly held values, functionalism had a reputation (though disputed by some advocates) for providing an essentially harmonious, stabilizing model of the whole society. One can surmise that at this stage of functional democratization and informalization in British society, even if not all sociologists embraced functionalism, many practitioners of sociology did find such a view of society emotionally satisfying. Why might this be so?

Britain was a society of clearer social boundaries than now, fewer behavioural contrasts and greater power and status differentials between groups. There was a strong tendency for lower strata to orientate themselves to the modes of conduct and lifestyle of the upper strata. It is a reasonable assumption, in the lack of secure empirical evidence to the contrary, that many sociologists had been recruited largely from upwardly mobile strata. Therefore structural functionalism probably felt comfortable because it seemed to articulate very closely the level of behavioural formality, formal self-regulation and social distance which they, as participants in that society, were routinely required to embrace through a strong super-ego formation.

This paradigm is aptly referred to by Anthony Giddens (following Atkinson 1971) as the 'orthodox consensus' (Giddens 1984: xv) and became the point of departure for a deluge of criticisms (summarized succinctly by Cohen 1968) in the next phase of the development of sociology. Socially, this latter (conflict) phase was one in which a wave of new social groups sought to emancipate themselves from the hegemony of established ones. Representatives of these groups not surprisingly expressed their new aspirations in theoretical terms directed towards the target of Parsons, because structural functionalism had by this stage developed a sufficiently broad following in the expanding institutional settings of sociology to provide the sociology establishment with one of its most prominent paradigmatic contours (amongst others). And it was a general theory of society with normative, social psychological and political implications that had to be reckoned with. Whatever its relative dominance in Britain in terms of numbers of adherents, the strident tone of the critiques of the Parsonian paradigm emanating from Britain (e.g. Atkinson 1971; Dawe 1970), or enthusiastically embraced from the United States (e.g. Gouldner 1970), suggests that something was also going on emotionally for his radical critics (more on this in the next section).

One important form of criticism came from the conflict perspective, which was to become a major theme in the sociology of the next phase, to which I have assigned that name. However, works by *precursors* of this perspective were published in Britain at the tail end of the monopoly phase. Some of these were indigenous products, but many were imported from the United States or Germany or were the work of refugees who had found a home here (e.g. Lockwood 1956; Dahrendorf 1959; Coser 1956; Mills 1956; Rex 1961). The content of their critiques of functionalism (i.e. essentially that it was conservative and depicted a misleadingly harmonious, consensual view of society) prefigured the social and theoretical tenor of the next phase.

(ii) Conflict phase: circa 1965–80[5]

This was a period of considerable ferment and conflict in sociology, during which rival paradigm groups, schools and factions competed fiercely to be heard in the sociological marketplace. They included adherents of structuralism, feminism, phenomenology, hermeneutics, ethnomethodology, Theorizing, existential sociology, symbolic interactionism, figurational sociology and varieties of neo-Marxism, including critical theory, Althusserian Marxism, Gramscian Marxism and other politically defined variants. Some groups identified themselves with various theoretical combinations and fusions, such as phenomenological Marxism, hermeneutic sociology or structuralist sociology. The functionalist paradigm continued, but its adherents, such as they were, were beleaguered during the 'war of the schools', in Bryant's phrase (1989a), which is another way of describing open theoretical competition within the expanding institutions of British sociology.

During the 1970s, at the height of this search for alternatives to the orthodox consensus, contesting paradigm groups flourished in British sociology and many manifestos appeared announcing the sundry 'new directions' for the reorientation of sociology championed by one or other of the competing groups (e.g. Filmer *et al.* 1972; Pelz 1974; Thorns 1976). It was a phase characterized by considerable diversity, strife and theoretical disarray, which one writer at the time described as 'sheer chaos, everything up for grabs' (Bernstein 1976: xii).[6]

In this phase, many sociologists expressed doubts about previously hallowed principles regarding knowledge, truth and the basics of social science and the possibility of a science of sociology was itself thrown into question from many perspectives.[7] The topics of cognitive, cultural and moral relativism were discussed with agonized thoroughness (Lukes 1977; Williams 1974–5; Finnegan & Horton 1973). And for many sociologists, their questionings and probings took them into the works of European philosophers such as Hegel, Heidegger, Husserl, Merleau-Ponty, Nietzsche, Sartre and many more, which imperceptibly became staples of the sociological theory diet. So pervasive was the influence of the later writings of Wittgenstein about social life being constituted by different language games (an argument used extensively against a positivistic sociology) that one commentator at the time, John Clammer (1976), felt justified in claiming that the influence had now constituted itself as a tendency, called 'Wittgensteinianism' (see also Mennell 1976).

One consequence of this influx of philosophical traditions was to change the nature of 'theory' in the discipline. As I have argued elsewhere (Kilminster 1992b: 139–41), in the present period, as the result of the legacy of the extensive self-reflection that went on in sociology in this phase and the philosophical style in which much of it was carried out, sociological theory has become a much more complex domain than it used to be. The traditional distinction between substantive theory and metatheory becomes more prominent in the (next) concentration phase to capture the two distinct kinds of theoretical activity now recognized as being practised on a large scale (Runciman 1989; Ritzer 1991).

As I remarked earlier, intense debate about the epistemological foundations of a discipline is often a symptom of its uncertain status, which is a point also made, of course, by Merton and Kuhn. It is less prominent in fields that rank highly in terms of either scientific success or general social status. In the case of sociology in the early part of the conflict phase the epistemological disarray was clearly related to the peculiarities of the sudden expansion and subsequent institutionalization of British sociology.[8] Its philosophical tenor is also indicative of the extent to which the lower ranking sociologists as a group deferred to philosophers, to whose higher status they aspired. It is interesting that in a phase where so much was being questioned, the autonomy of philosophy was still taken for granted and its establishment remained largely immune from external attack. At the same time, the epistemological tumult instantiates a general feature of the hegemony of views of society from the 'top down', such as structural functionalism. They often go hand in hand with claims to special scientific expertise by scientific establishments, i.e. with science closure, which is often justified epistemologically. Such a situation is always ripe for challenge by paradigm groups whose power ratio is less than that of such establishments.

However, more important from the point of view of my argument here is that the epistemological clamour was also symptomatic of theoreticians competing for the reputation to present themselves as the ones who had the most intimate knowledge of the most profound philosophical discussions of the bases of human knowledge. This was now in a situation where what had been in the monopoly phase regarded as safe and secure (positivism and empiricism as the philosophical underpinnings of a 'top down' sociology) was now open to questioning, *along with many other things in the wider society.*

This takes us to my main point. The explanation of the character of sociology in this phase is greatly strengthened if one grasps the connections between the shape of the phase as a whole and the functional democratization/informalization wave with which the sociological developments and the institutionalization of the discipline were intertwined. It is plausible to assume that many sociologists at this time would have participated in different degrees in the experiments with lifestyles and the pushing of the boundaries of social and sexual codes. If they were not directly part of the vanguard groups who set the style and goals of these experiments, they were interdependent with those who did and could not have been unaffected. Once the links to informalization are made, five features of sociological theory in this period are illuminated.

1. Many of the rival paradigms had a cognitive or social constructivist emphasis, that is, they concentrated on consciousness and the role of categories of the mind in shaping the world. This was true of all of the most influential schools: phenomenology, ethnomethodology and structuralism as well as fusions such as structuralist Marxism. Cognitivism and constructivism in various combinations formed a perspective that suited rising groups within the institutionalized settings of sociology because it fitted well both with beating off the challenge of other paradigm communities, as well as with challenging the orthodox consensus of the sociology establishment. Via a critique framed in this way (sometimes in various fusions with ideological or political critique) it is easier to challenge others' frameworks. One simply argues that, since all views of the world are interpretations or constructions, the viewpoint of the established is no more valid than any other, including that of the practitioners of the emancipatory movement or challenging paradigm group.

Outside sociology as such, the aspirations of emancipatory movements of outsiders can also be similarly effectively furthered by this same theoretical device, i.e. constructivism, because 'expressiveness' in general is implied in such a critique. In other words, the 'anything goes' rule (Feyerabend 1975: 28) has both cognitive and feeling aspects. A telling parallel is that in the controversy between nominalism and realism in the Church in the Middle Ages, nominalism – essentially a constructivist doctrine – was the theoretical weapon of the lower ranks of clergy, i.e. of *outsider* groups in an emancipatory phase, whereas realism was the doctrine of the theologians associated with the established Church (cited by Mannheim 1928: 203–4). There is a general sociological principle which emerges from these discussions: *constructivism has a strong affinity with outsider groups in an emancipatory phase and realism with establishments.*

2. Many paradigms competing in this phase placed a strong stress on everyday life and the skills of the ordinary, lay actor in giving their activities meaning.

The 'sociology of everyday life', as a major orientation, has its origins much earlier and in another country, in the work of Alfred Schutz, amongst others. But *in this phase* in Britain, it is congruent with the aspirations of the younger generations of sociologists who were its enthusiastic advocates. The whole thrust of ethnomethodology as a sociology of everyday life was to undermine the status of sociologists as specialists and to devalue the status of the authoritative knowledge claimed by the sociology establishment. The oft-invoked dictum that sociologists of the Parsonian paradigm regarded ordinary people as 'judgemental dopes' (Garfinkel) says it all. The sociology establishment was seen as patronizing and imperialistic. The epigraph printed on the title page of the first manifesto of the British ethnomethodologists (Filmer *et al.* 1972) was 'There's nowt so queer as folk (Lancashire saying)'.

The ethnomethodologists created a stir because what they were saying went to the heart of the claims to scientificity of the sociology establishment associated with the orthodox consensus (see in particular the shrill exchanges involving Garfinkel in the proceedings of Purdue Symposium on ethnomethodology in 1968 in Hill & Crittenden 1968). The ethnomethodologists said that ordinary people were also 'sociologists' and that, indeed, professional sociology had boot-legged into its so-called scientific concepts the everyday ways in which the sociologists themselves (as lay people) developed a sense of 'society'.

The parallel with the 'downstairs' perspective, i.e. the valorizing of the underdog and the denigration of established groups as moribund, suggests itself strongly here. The pervasive sensibility of the phase was nicely captured by a wall slogan at the University of Essex in 1969: 'Many are called. All are chosen.' This dimension of the informalization wave may also illuminate (though not entirely account for): (a) the extraordinary vitality of Marxism in this phase, which is a paradigm that preeminently views society from the point of view of the underprivileged; (b) the related predominance of 'Third Worldism'. This orientation seems to be phase-specific as the product of the intersection of global developments (see Chapter 6) with the developments within the advanced societies which I have subsumed under the headings of functional democratization and informalization. In this period, European colonial countries were giving up their colonies and the power balance was beginning to shift in favour of the former colonized. At the same time, the gap between the rich and poor nations, on the level of wealth, seemed particularly vast. (It arguably always had been considerable, relatively speaking.) This was at a time when, within the pacified social spaces in Western countries brought about by the military stand-off of the cold war, on the other hand, wealth creation and hence affluence were on the rise. As I explained in greater detail in Chapter 6, despite the wealth gap, the richer nations have in fact been compelled to show the poor ones greater respect. As social distance closed more between people *within* the advanced societies, corresponding with the rise of the 'underdog' perspective, a sensibility arose in which identification with the international underprivileged was also very strong, as a species of underdog identification. This expressed itself in the prominence of neo-Marxist theories of imperialism in the sociology of development in this phase.

3. Debates in this phase were often heated and frequently expressed in highly polarized either/or alternatives: Marxism *versus* sociology; positivism *versus*

hermeneutics; humanist *versus* structuralist Marxism; ethnomethodology *versus* orthodox sociology; feminist theory *versus* malestream sociology, and others. These conflicts were between paradigm communities nominally internal to the expanding institutions of sociology, but the boundaries of these institutions were not very firm (and remain so today, relatively speaking). Indeed, many of these combatants would probably have denied that they were 'insiders' to the institutions at all. Hence, one needs to look elsewhere to account for the passion of the academic encounters between paradigm groups and between them and representatives of the orthodox consensus.

The violence and the street demonstrations of the late 1960s and early 1970s are well known and have been well documented, as have been the occupations of the universities and the disruptions of teaching, which in some cases resulted in the closing down of some institutions (Cockburn & Blackburn 1969; Cohn-Bendit 1969; Blackburn 1972). In describing the social texture of this phase, insofar as it relates to the topic at hand, I think that the volatility of younger people *in a sociology context* at the time can be established with independent evidence. At the time, one prominent professor of sociology referred to 'present-day sociologists – whose camp resembles nothing more than a carnival of the (professional!) animals' (Fletcher 1976: ix). And the author of a conservative-minded study group report, highlighting what they saw as the widespread 'illiberalism' of the practices of Marxist radicals in this period, said:

> We ... argue that the hectoring and aggressive tone in which the 'radical option' is so frequently couched has its parallel in the ways in which its exponents often relate, both formally and informally, to their 'non-radical' colleagues.
>
> (Gould 1977: 11)

There is sufficient evidence in my view that there were, in sociological academic contexts, more displays of passionate irreverence than one would have encountered in the previous phase or in the one after. A plausible connection can be made again with an informalization wave, as part of the interwoven master processes outlined earlier. The same people involved in these academic conflicts were also involved in differing degrees with the experiments with lifestyles and the boundaries of what is permitted. More primal impulses are being brought to the surface and people are grappling with fear, jealousy and hate as they struggle to find new sexual and behavioural codes, and they are also struggling with guilt since, from positions of relative privilege and security, they feel compelled to identify with the underdog. These struggles generate high and sometimes extreme emotional intensity and ambivalence.

These emotions are coupled in any case with the rise of tensions across the social interdependencies as a whole, brought about by the complex processes of rising strata seeking emancipation in this phase, interlocked with growing global interdependencies. These processes seem to have generated individually fear images and aggressive and persecutory fantasies projected on to political and paradigmatic rivals or other imagined foes in government, bureaucracy and the establishment generally. Such fear images and fantasies are the psychological stock

in trade of people living in the complex tensions of highly differentiated and internally pacified nation-states, but during an informalization wave one can predict
their intensification.

That this process should be played out so vociferously in *sociology* is probably
because its practitioners are structurally more likely, in the nature of the subject-
matter of their discipline, to be able to understand, to rehearse and to reflect upon,
a variety of the behavioural and social alternatives being projected and experi-
mented with. In a wider sense, it is also a measure of the way in which a discipline
committed to understanding human social interdependencies, but still in the early
stages of its development to fuller autonomy and institutionalized detachment,
becomes a conduit for the many involvements generated by the conflicts
embedded in the social structure which it is struggling to comprehend.

Social networks run seamlessly through society and the institutions of sociology
(although boundaries will be variably permeable and constantly changing in this
respect). There is no sharp line of demarcation between what is inside and what is
outside sociology, particularly at its present stage of disciplinary institutionalization. If some of the tension generated by an informalization wave becomes
intertwined with or expressed in the normal cut and thrust of academic exchange
under conditions of free theoretical competition, small wonder it was often
conducted in this phase with a *particularly* high emotional charge. It is seldom, if
ever, encountered today, if the persistent lack of reports of such a thing is a good
indicator. At least in relation to sociology,[9] this emotional tone and its theoretical
consequences appear to be phase-specific to the structure of the conflict phase.

4.   The ways in which the Parsonian theory of socialization was attacked in
this period bear the marks of the aspirations and emotional struggles of its critics
within the social tensions characteristic of the phase.[10] Very dominant was the
idea that Parsons' theory implied an 'oversocialized' conception of people or
otherwise devalued the part played by active knowledgeable individuals in maintaining social order. To sociologists caught up in the particularly far-reaching
attempts to redefine in practice the codes of sexual and other behaviour
bequeathed by their parents, perhaps to an unprecedented degree compared with
other periods, it is not surprising that the issues of why we conform and why we
should conform to social norms should have come to prominence.

Dennis Wrong's seminal article from 1961, 'The Oversocialized Conception of
Man in Modern Sociology', was influenced by a group of neo-Freudian precursors
of the emotional concerns of this phase, Herbert Marcuse, Philip Rieff and
Norman O. Brown, writing in the late 1950s (Wrong 1975: 40). The article was
itself a precursor of the concerns of the conflict phase and its British reception
represents a 'turning point'. This article was translated into several languages; its
argument became a part of the conventional wisdom of sociology and the phrase
'oversocialized' became one of the most well known in the discipline. The author
even gave the article a new introduction when it was reprinted in 1975, so celebrated had it become. He had claimed, articulating the problem in a decisive
fashion, that Parsons' theory of socialization implied a model of human beings as
conforming and approval seeking, which left out of account the neurotic anxiety
with which the most conformist of people are wracked. Repression and sublima-
tion are the high price paid for civilization – 'civilization' in this case being, I would

argue, the specific level of behavioural formality, formal self-regulation and social distance pervading British and (in a slightly different way) American society and sociology in the monopoly phase.

From a different angle, but on a similar track, was the often expressed argument (e.g. by Garfinkel 1967; Dawe 1970; Cohen 1968) that the idea that social order was simply accomplished through people internalizing common values from a central pool of values was misleading. It wrongly implied that people did this learning in a passive and mechanical way, and effectively demoted human beings to the status of a mere reflex of the social system. (In his time, Durkheim's structural orientation faced this kind of objection too, but not in the many nuanced forms in which these objections were couched in this phase and not so vociferously nor in such a widespread fashion.) Younger sociologists, in a phase where the power differentials between the competing groups of which they are a part are decreasing, begin to feel empowered, so the last way in which they want to think of themselves is as a passive reflex of a normative system existing outside them. This particularly prominent critique of Parsons makes sense when one realizes that the boundaries of what is acceptable behaviour were becoming particularly problematic for many younger people generally at the time, for whom the sociological critics of Parsons became the unintended representatives. What people struggling with the problem of redefining the boundaries of acceptable behaviour want to hear and to believe is that they can actively *overcome the force of their socialization* and find a new balance of self-regulation.

5.   One important form of criticism of Parsons came from the conflict perspective, which was to become a major theme in the sociology of this phase. The impulse for moving in this theoretical direction may have been at least partly bound up with the previous considerations. If there was one thing that the generation involved in the social and relationship experiments and behavioural tendencies which I am arguing warrant conceptualization as an informalization process both experienced socially and felt internally as individuals, it was conflict. The appeal of Freud to so many people in this phase was that he seemed to provide a picture of human beings that adequately reflected their own internal struggles and ambivalence as a generation. The image of humankind in Freud was more congruent with the uneasy self-experience of the generation that was seeking to emancipate itself than the conforming/approval-seeking model associated – rightly or wrongly – with the paradigm of the sociology establishment. As Wrong said, quoting Norman O. Brown, 'man may properly be called . . . the "neurotic" or the "discontented" animal and repression may be seen as the main characteristic of human nature as we have known it in history' (Wrong 1961: 37). Like Marx, Freud has probably always appealed to younger generations, but my point is that what is distinctive is the way in which in this phase those ideas became intertwined both with academic discourse and the inner struggle for the self being acutely felt by a generation and acted upon in practical life.

At the same time, that two-sided movement (in academic discourse as well as within the self) was enmeshed with wider politico-military processes in a decisive way, making conditions conducive to the reception of conflict theories of various kinds particularly fertile. Conflict theory, as against the apparently consensual equilibriating model of society found in the dominant structural functionalist paradigm, seemed more obviously adequate than that paradigm to explain the political polarization, unrest and violence within the United States and Europe in the mid- to late 1960s (Friedrichs 1970). These conflicts were themselves partly an expression of the emancipatory movements of outsider groups, including a global dimension, which had raised the level of social tension and hence people's fear images. Couple this with psychological ambivalence felt by people who were also simultaneously participating in an informalizing phase (even though they themselves could not have put it that way) and the return to Freud for both social and self-understanding was highly likely.

Conflict versus consensus was therefore not surprisingly a dominant theme in this phase and the reconciliation of the two sides of antinomy was the beckoning theoretical prize. The debate about whether functionalism depicted a utopian society of complete integration, was conservative, could explain change, was scientific, and so on, raged between representatives of the orthodox consensus and the newer paradigms. These particular theoretical battles were fought more tenaciously than battles in the previous phase because, if the above analysis has any cogency, expressed in these 'academic' controversies was the whole basis in social existence of the interdependent paradigm groups themselves as each competed, via the championing of a paradigm, for the general sociological interpretation of that social existence. More was at stake, in other words, in this phase than in the previous one, in the winning of academic debating points. *It felt to the sociological combatants that what was at stake was life itself.*

The theoretical issues such as: could functionalism satisfactorily explain change? is it tautological? is it scientific? is it conservative? could probably not be definitively resolved anyway. But what is significant is that, with the exception of a few writers (Cohen 1968; Giddens 1977; Moore 1979) they were simply abandoned or forgotten when issues perceived as more generationally urgent – the relevance of sociology, theory and practice issues, ideology, attacking positivism and scientism, 'critical' theory, and so on – took centre stage. These then coloured far more of the theoretical products of the conflict phase. In the next (concentration) phase, functionalism re-emerges (Alexander 1987a; Holton & Turner 1986; Münch 1988) but in a new key, consonant with the social and sociological tenor of another figuration of theoretical and social forces, to which we will now turn.

(iii) Concentration phase: circa 1980 to the present (?)

A few introductory remarks are necessary before embarking upon this phase. It is inherently more difficult to discern the social psychological contours of the phase through which one is currently living and their consequences for the tenor of sociological theory, with the precision that the benefit of hindsight confers on the comprehension of the previous ones. It is even more difficult to discern in the scattered fragments of experience in the present their incipient coalescence into the outlines of the next phase that will succeed this one. I am convinced, however, that divining the character of the present social and sociological phase in a clear and detached manner will be greatly enhanced if we can see it as emerging from the previous one, both societally and intra-sociologically, and that this will help us in redefining the issue of theoretical progression in sociology and assessing the cognitive value of sociological effort in the present.

My aim in this chapter generally is to demonstrate the often underplayed sociological psychology of theoretical developments, but I would never claim that they are *reducible* to that aspect, important though it is. But elucidating the sociological psychology of paradigm change and sociological discussion generally should help us to discern the all-important *extent* to which theoretical developments say more about their practitioners' extra-sociological preoccupations than about their apparent sociological (cognitive) aims.

Focusing on, say, scientific networks, patronage or the structure of the academy itself (which would be alternative approaches to one adopted here) would probably produce the best results with regard to explaining scientific developments in more autonomous disciplines which are relatively more firmly institutionally insulated from the wider society. This is manifestly not the case with sociology, where the evidence suggests that what is most decisive in explaining paradigm conflict and theoretical change lies (for the present and the forseeable future, anyway) *outside* the sociology institutions themselves, which have somewhat permeable boundaries. Sociology institutions are far more susceptible than the natural science institutions to the shaping of their cognitive products by political, social psychological and other external influences, as I am endeavouring to demonstrate. Hence, *at this stage of the development of sociology*, a sociological psychology of the kind employed here seems most appropriate for discerning the relative cognitive merits of the products of sociological effort in the present period. It can potentially enable us to discern how far texts, theories, schools or approaches say more about the aspirations, fears, hopes and aims of their authors or adherents than about the changing social structures they are trying to grasp.

In order to bring out the complex social-psychological texture of the concentration phase more clearly, let me provide a further gloss on the three-phase model and the general strategy, drawing on the important work of Waldhoff (1995) (discussed by Wouters 1998). (Again, here I am only presenting the theoretical yield of Waldhoff's research, which is backed up with extensive empirical evidence drawn from the experience of Turkish immigrants in Germany.) During the earlier phase of social development, prior to the breaking through of the recent informalizing wave (in my model coinciding with the *monopoly phase* in sociology), identification with the established had the character, in Freudian terms, of an automatic personality structure, via a strong super-ego formation. The formality and social distance of the clearer hierarchical relations between people in this phase depended upon this structure. In their daily social encounters people were counting on a certain level of mutually expected self-restraint made possible by the robust and all-round character of the super-ego or conscience in this phase.

During an informalizing wave, Waldhoff affirms, there is a process of social de-hierarchization and differentiation and a general opening up of social and psychic dividing lines. There then ensues an *emancipation of emotions* and impulses hitherto repressed as part of a phase of emancipatory movements, rebellion against establishments and social experiment as people struggle to reject old behavioural and sexual codes and develop new ones. In the expanding networks of interdependencies, the social and psychical dividing lines are opening up, with a characteristic loosening of the martial and inexorable structure of self-controls typical of the earlier phase. That earlier phase is rife with fear images and persecutory fantasies directed at establishments. The emancipatory phase is one of intense social and psychic strife, to which corresponds the conflict phase in sociology.

The changes in behavioural codes, perspective, feeling for life, attitude and orientation begin to stabilize, relatively speaking, around a more *ego*-dominated mode of self-regulation. This corresponds with social groups becoming more and more integrated in what can be conceptualized as a far-reaching process of functional democratization with a global dimension. In this phase, the *balance* between super-ego and ego functions in the psyche consolidates *more towards the ego*, producing a different, more flexible, malleable pattern of controlling at the level of the individual. By the time the phase of reformalization has been reached (corresponding with the concentration phase in the development of sociology), a different pattern of self-regulation is already assumed at the level of interactions in the wider society. At this point, a type of person best survives who has a developed capacity for self-organization and self-orientation and can make connections of wider scope in society and adjust himself or herself in manifold ways to the increasing demands of the extending and integrating social interdependencies (nationally, regionally and globally).

This emerging pattern of affect management provides the psychological preconditions for a new sensibility which manifests itself in culture as new tastes in film, music, the arts and in leisure pursuits generally, as well as in the arena of sexuality. It appears at the level of *theoretical* elaboration as a higher general level of the capacity for conceptual synthesis, which I will illustrate shortly. This new pattern of self-regulation produces what is widely being called in the 1990s the age of 'reflexivity' or the 'risk' society, as well as the wider range of behavioural, particularly sexual, alternatives available in the present period, produced by the freer flowing and flexible connections between social groups and psychic functions. More people are now able to bring to the surface and control emotions and strange feelings previously repressed, because a different, more malleable pattern of self-regulation is demanded under contemporary conditions. (All this does of course put great demands on people, but the social and psychological costs of the current behavioural alternatives and choices are not well understood at present.)

At the level of theory, the many theories of 'postmodernity', 'reflexive modernization', 'autotelic self', 'risk society', etc. have an important part of their roots here, as do the characteristic current sociological preoccupations in this phase with constructivism and 'essentialism', particularly in the fields of sexuality and the sociology of scientific knowledge (but elsewhere too; see Speed 1991) (e.g. Watzlawick 1984; Gergen 1985; Burr 1995; Weekes 1991; Tester 1991; Craib 1997, and many more; I discussed this tendency in Chapter 1 as it manifested itself in the sociology of scientific knowledge). In this kind of work, 'essentialism' is located as something to combat at all costs because it suggests that a fixed personality stratum or predisposition exists in people, when identity *choice*, between many alternatives, particularly sexual, now seemingly presents itself. This is made possible by, and expresses, the emergent new psychic balance, through which people are now arguably more able to bring to the surface and *manage* repressed emotions and 'strange' feelings which, in former phases, when steeper social hierarchies and greater social distance existed, prevented people from even contemplating, let alone experiencing, the grey areas between (for example) the clear-cut either/or of male and female identities. The relentlessness of the constructivist attacks on essentialism points to the important symbolic function which they must perform for certain groups. Craib (1997) is right to associate constructivism, particularly in the field of sexuality, with manic defence in the psychoanalytic sense, but this process of denial needs to be more closely related to the shifting social pattern of self-control and affect management in the current period and the subsequent real problems of identity which people concretely face.

The previous remarks concentrated more on the changing psychic structure of the society associated with the third phase. I will now turn to the institutional aspects and flesh out the corresponding theoretical tendencies, weaving in the psychic level as appropriate. The paradigm conflicts of the conflict phase took place under conditions of more or less free competition within the expanding and consolidating institutionalization of the discipline. In these institutional settings, we could forecast that the competition between paradigm groups would take the following course, which the evidence seems to confirm. From their position of relative disadvantage, younger opposing paradigm groups, thrown together by the unprecedented expansion of sociology, challenged the sociology establishment, particularly the adherents of structural functionalism, which was perceived by the rising groups as a framework that was not consonant with their life experience and aspirations as a generation, within and part of the wider social and political polarizations. Structural functionalism was also American and hence associated with the international sociology establishment and American cultural hegemony – which partly explains why it became a prime target for rising outsider groups.

These confrontations developed into intense conflicts as paradigm groups challenged the authority of the sociological orthodoxy, which was not in fact a unified position and was probably more fragile than its American counterpart, even though it was perceived as monolithic. During the conflict phase, schools competed fiercely to be heard, often expressing their aims in terms of epistemological issues and the orthodoxy began more and more to concede theoretical ground to the overstatements of the challengers. For example, concessions were made on the important role of subjectivity or the knowledgeable actor, or on the idea that the hypothetico-deductive explanatory ideal was not cast in stone or that the discipline was not 'value free', that ethical questions were inscribed into research programmes, and much more. Since rival schools coexist in inescapable relationships of interdependency, eventually a less partisan kind of approach imposed itself to form the characteristic cast of the concentration phase. It arises from the structural features of competitive rivalry: one has to know one's enemy, win over others and form coalitions so as to compete for opportunities and resources. In a nutshell, the dominant paradigm group was compelled, by the nature of its intertwined conflicts with other groups, to take over concepts championed by them and to concede adaptations to its own, as the power gradient between the competing groups flattened out and alliances and mergers occurred.

Instead of claiming that they each possess the *only* valid paradigm, groups are now obliged to concede common ground between themselves as the competing groups become less polarized and more integrated. A process of greater 'mutual identification' (Elias, quoted by Mennell 1992: 138) between antagonists has, it could be argued, taken place, as the power gradient between them has somewhat flattened out. We have now come to a stage where *theoretical synthesis* is once again in the air and forms an increasingly discernible tendency (as I explained more fully at the beginning of Chapter 7). In this phase we also observe that the traces of group allegiance embedded in concepts have faded as the power gradient between the interdependent groups involved in elaborating the concepts has flattened out and group mergers have occurred, corresponding to the consolidation of a new generational sociological establishment.

A vocabulary of concepts has thus become the common property of all in the new establishment, paralleling the consolidation of new hybrid social and sexual codes in the wider society. New theoretical syntheses can now be seriously contemplated because the changing structure of the interdependent social existence of previously antagonistic sociological parties has developed into a new, integrated, more polyarchic pattern. It is this development that has 'neutralized' the conceptual apparatus, transformed its nature and made it generally available for synthesizing efforts, for example structuration theory.

A tangible manifestation of this trend is the appearance in the phase of a number of sociological dictionaries, encyclopaedias and lexicons designed to codify sociological concepts for *everyone* in the discipline (e.g. Hoult 1980; Mann 1983; Abercrombie *et al.* 1988; Jary & Jary 1991). As far as I have been able to ascertain, there were none of this kind published in the monopoly or conflict phases. These books are partly a response by publishers to increased student demand for this kind of reference work. At the same time, however, for it to be possible to include such a diverse range of concepts codified between the covers of a single volume, their paradigm origins forgotten or regarded as uncontentious, presupposes relative ideological peace. In these books, concepts and perspectives which people fought tooth and nail to establish as explanatory and important in the conflict phase, as part of the paradigm community to which they owed their allegiance, now appear side by side with concepts from the earlier functionalist 'orthodox consensus', whose representatives they once so fiercely fought (see Kilminster 1992b for an analysis of this development).

It is important to enter a qualification here. I am aware of the complex reality of counter-currents and relatively autonomous research enclaves within the differentiated world of institutionalized sociology. Groups of practitioners continue to research in, say, social stratification, unemployment, the sociology of religion or comparative and historical sociology, working with classical sociological concepts. Also, in the present phase, paradigm communities such as ethnomethodology (including conversation analysis), world-system theory, politicized variants of Marxism and feminism, the 'Strong Programme' in the sociology science and other fusions and hybrids, still exist in various forms within institutions, providing continuing and relatively autonomous research traditions. Some of these groups still to some degree compete with general sociology, even though many of their characteristic concepts and insights have *already* been absorbed into the general sociological pool of knowledge (something over which they as individuals or groups have little or no control). This absorption constitutes the common vocabulary which will provide the conceptual springboard to the next phase beyond the present one, in which it will be utilized by as yet unknown paradigm groups and research traditions who will learn it, employ it and further *transform* it, even though it was not of their direct creation in the first place.

Aware of this diversity, my argument is working at a different level of theoretical elaboration, whereby I am trying to locate the broad conceptual and social-psychological parameters of cognitive change in the sociological field and the conditions conducive to sociological synthesis and consensus or fragmentation. It is the broad trend that I am trying to discern, by looking at the meshing of societal, psychological and intra-sociological trends. Hence, on my model the social/theoretical trend towards synthesis is part of a two-sided movement. At the present time, I think that the evidence suggests that the longer-term *centripetal* tendency towards *synthesis* just has the upper hand over the *centrifugal* movement towards *fragmentation*. In the previous – conflict – phase the balance was tipped the other way. It could of course shift back again, initiating a new period of intense paradigm fragmentation. The interesting questions are: what intersection of social forces might precipitate such a process of fragmentation? What combination might strengthen the centripetal tendency?

A plausible case can be made out that it is possible to observe in the concentration phase attempts by new generational establishments within a now much more extensively institutionalized sociology, to stabilize their power advantage *in a sociologically distinctive fashion*. They are unlikely to do this either through a simple return to the 'orthodox consensus' or through the now socially incongruous advocacy of one single paradigm. Hence, the twin alternatives of *theoretical synthesis*[11] and *theoretical pluralism*[12] present themselves forcefully in this phase. Versions of both of these strategies can be assembled in such a way as to satisfy their practitioners of their newness and appropriateness to the current social condition. (Critical realism and post-empiricism are also important philosophical trends informing the work of many sociologists in this phase, although I cannot deal with them here. On these trends see Bryant 1989b and Kilminster 1992b.) The most prominent example in Britain of *theoretical synthesis* is the theory of structuration of Anthony Giddens (1984). I have dealt with this theory and its limitations extensively in Chapter 7, so it does not require further comment here.

The advocates of *theoretical pluralism*, as a sociological strategy, universalize the theoretical fragmentation specific to the conflict phase as being indicative of the *endemic* inconclusiveness of sociology. The discipline will, into the foreseeable future, so the argument runs, be condemned to a plethora of disputing schools and hence to a pluralism of perspectives, between which sensitive and respectful dialogue must occur. Here is a clear example:

> [T]he range of interests which can legitimately be taken in [sociology], the demands made of it, the host of problems which it has raised, are all too numerous to be dealt with by any one of the extant sociological approaches. No one of these can fulfil the requirements that may reasonably be made of sociology, and different approaches will inevitably develop as new demands are made of it. The subject is, in a word, pluralistic: at least for the present.
>
> (Anderson *et al.* 1985: 55)

These authors suggest that sociology is an 'argument subject', not a 'knowledge subject', so they advocate rejoicing in the diversity of theories, which is seen not as a symptom of crisis but an expression of the fact that disagreement in sociology will always be rife. This is because, they assert, 'there is very little common ground among the various sociological approaches' (p. 73). On this particular model of pluralism, sociology emerges as being more like philosophy, going round and round problems but never solving them. However, this programme not only implicitly pulls sociology back into philosophy, but also naively assumes that pluralism is endemic, when dialogue between perspectives may only be a strategy that suggests itself following a phase when centrifugal forces have dominated, producing theoretical fragmentation. It could be argued, on the other hand, that it would be precisely the domination of one, or perhaps the competition between two, major paradigms in sociology that would do most to aid the cumulative progress of sociological knowledge and reinforce the disclipline's institutional autonomy.

The current phase also provides the social-psychological and institutional conditions for sociological debates to begin to polarize around certain key anti-nomies, common to all debates and research programmes, changing in the process the *nature* of theoretical abstraction generally assumed in contemporary controversies. Theoretical elaboration at the most general level is 'abstract' today in a way different from the abstraction embodied in structural functionalism, for which it was so strenuously criticized. On the sociological question of how transformations in levels of abstraction occur, Mannheim was on the right track, it seems, when he said that 'the trend towards a higher stage of abstraction is a correlate of the amal-gamation of social groups' (1929: 271–2). Elias took this insight further when he pointed out that what we call high-level abstractions (e.g. the concept of time or the laws of geometry) are in fact examples of 'an extremely extensive synthesis' (1992: 133). An ascent to a higher level of synthesis is the social process whereby examples of a perceived social or natural regularity discovered in everday social practice come to be symbolically represented as 'special cases of a general regu-larity' (*ibid.*: 185). A 'higher' stage of abstraction is a further stage of synthesis, whereby the developing social reality successively creates conditions that give rise to the sedimentation of layers of experience and knowledge into concepts and the theories formed from their collocation.

In my model I have called the current phase the 'concentration' phase in the double sense of convergence and synthesis. Sociological discussions begin to converge around certain important but *transformed* dichotomies which are also 'synthetic' in the sense of layered. At a deep level, these oppositions (see Figure 2) come to permeate much research within the proliferating sociological specialisms (and within Marxism, which recapitulates the same pattern with a different, though occasionally similar, vocabulary).

These dualisms and the individual concepts that comprise them are, of course, neither new nor peculiar to the concentration phase. They existed prior to it and, indeed, have a very long-term genesis as symbols of a high level of synthesis already. My point is, however, that these dualisms confront us now as the self-evident parameters of sociological inquiry and steer discussion towards that predetermined conclusion. But they also represent the conceptual expression of a

structure	⇔	agency
cause	⇔	meaning
objectivism	⇔	subjectivism
realism	⇔	constructivism
macro	⇔	micro
system	⇔	lifeworld

Figure 2 Contemporary synthetic antinomies

new relative stabilization, a consolidation of new behavioural codes and psychic integration – they constitute the theoretical anatomy of a new level of social and cognitive synthesis. During the conflict phase, these pairings were inherited by sociologists, some from the structural functional orthodoxy and its critics and some from social philosophy influenced paradigm groups. Then one side – that which could best articulate the practical, emancipatory (extra-sociological) aims of the practitioners of the various paradigm groups – was exaggerated in an activistic direction, at the expense of its other side. This then informed part of the practical orientation of the various emancipatory groups in that phase or otherwise in paradigm rivalry.

In the course of this process of group conflict, as it entered a phase of greater levelling, *the conceptual extremities were sloughed off*, leaving us with the dualisms as tensions rather than an expression of mutually exclusive alternatives. The dualisms have been transformed into the putative endemic parameters of the social process and its analysis, through the sedimentation into them of new cognitive layers deriving from the trajectory of that relative social levelling process. In the new circumstances, transformed into 'dualities' (Giddens), they form part of the common vocabulary of a new generational sociology establishment. Interestingly, the higher level of synthesis permits the more *concrete* understanding of society and its problems than did the type of abstraction associated with the structural-functional and social system sociology of the monopoly phase.

Let me elaborate a little on the subject of conceptual synthesis in this context. Embedded with these oppositions are traces of the theoretical overstatements of some of the competing schools in the conflict phase as well as the concepts of the orthodox consensus which have continued ever since the monopoly phase, but in a new form. For example, taking the right-hand side of the pairings, it is possible to see condensed in *agency, meaning, subjectivism, constructivism, micro level and lifeworld*, traces of the various 'meaning sociologies', which were influenced by phenomenology and, in different ways, by symbolic interactionism. In the form of rival paradigm communities, these were in battle within institutionalized settings with the proponents of the orthodox consensus who constituted one of the main pillars of the sociology establishment. Traces of the latter paradigm can be detected in the other halves of the oppositions: *structure, cause, objectivism, realism, macro level and system*. The right-hand side (the former list) represents the residues of the emphasis of the radicals and activists who, through these concepts, expressed their conviction that there were no limits to change (politically, culturally and in terms of interpersonal behavioural codes) because all culture was constructed by active meaning-endowing actors and hence could be changed by them.[13] On the left-hand side (the latter list), this tendency represents the conceptual armoury of the more cautious groups and constitutes the realistic pole, emphasizing the limits to change within the realm of constraint.[14]

Central to the theory of informalization waves is that it is possible to recognize empirically a stage of 'reformalization' in which the new 'established' merges with old 'established' to develop a new hybrid code in a period of stabilization. Informal codes of behaviour become formalized and there is an apparent return to more formal lifestyles as the new establishment asserts its power and distinctiveness. There are new and acceptable forms of informality which are now taken for granted. This dominant trend does not represent, however, a return to old patterns of behaviour, but the grafting of new norms on to old and their adaptation, which are then carried forward in a new form. It also goes hand in hand with changes in what Wouters calls the 'general feeling for life ... and in dominant perspectives on past, present and future' (1986: 6).

At this later stage in the movement of the phase, the dominant identification is with the established, as against the underdog identification so characteristic of the previous phase. There is the spread of the 'upstairs' perspective. Again, this is not to be seen as simply the return to the more hierarchical social relations and social distance of the previous phase. It rather, arguably, represents a movement towards greater mutual identification between people, a new level of 'mutually expected self-restraint' (Goudsblom) which makes possible the manifold new forms of social behaviour, social movements and identity formation that we are witnessing today. Society and institutionalized sociology interpenetrate a great deal because the discipline is not, at this point in time, well insulated. It would be surprising if the character of sociology in the concentration phase did not also reflect in some (empirically ascertainable) measure the overall social and psychological tenor of the process of reformalization.

Before trying to make these connections more explicit, however, an important point needs to be made. A change in the nature of social conflict has occurred in the transition from the conflict to the concentration phases. In the conflict phase it could be said that antagonists had different interests but took for granted common ground between themselves and their paradigm opponents. In the concentration phase, a common interest between antagonists can no longer be assumed because it has been attenuated as the result of far-reaching functional democratization processes associated with globalization. Now, more ego-dominated, calculative, reflective and self-interested people are arguably coming to the fore, as the super-ego/ego balance of functions in their personalities shifts more towards greater ego integration.

In these circumstances, appeals to public issues and the common interest (so characteristic of the two previous phases) will fall on deaf ears. Socially, in the period corresponding to the conflict phase in sociology, people talked of the rights of minorities and made demands whereas, in the period corresponding to the concentration phase, people no longer ask *what is possible?* but rather *how high is the limit?* And correspondingly, demanding rights is superseded by conceding the centrality of duties, a perspective that corresponds to a different kind of (reflective) self-regulation at the level of the individual. Herein lie the social-psychological processes that also render plausible the 'postmodern' sensibility in sociology and adjacent fields. At the same time, they explain why the individualism associated with consumerism and economic liberalism has found in this phase so fertile a soil in which to grow and flourish. The next task is to correlate these developments as well as reformalization, with various trends in sociology.

1.   There has been a decline (even if not total fall) of Marxism, which now lives a low-profile and marginal existence within sociology, when it was once so strong and prevalent. Even in a far-reaching phase of reformalization, identity with the underdog does not disappear entirely. It is simply that in the new situation, when the power differentials between a great variety of groups have become less overall and the overt manifestations of the social force of the emancipatory movements has subsided, identification with the underdog takes on a more attenuated and less emotionally charged form. In my view, the decline of Marxism is explicable partly by this process, which also has a global dimension. Its decline is not simply the result of its being discredited by the domination of Western democracies by the political right. Both processes – the decline of sociological perspectives geared to the generalized point of view of the underprivileged and the success of the political right – are an expression of the same figurational shift towards reformalization, within the overall processes of extensive functional democratization and globalization.

2.   There has been a return to what can be called a more 'formalized' kind of sociology, in the double sense of professional behaviour and systematic, scientific orientation. It is literally true if one observes the way in which sociologists, men and women, dress (subdued and designer-conventional) and conduct themselves at professional conferences (very serious, briefcases, delivering formal papers), compared with the (comparatively speaking) greater informality and emotional volatility that pervaded people's conduct on similar 'formal' occasions such as seminars and lectures in the previous phase. The new attire and behaviour express the appropriate social and behavioural code through which to embrace (where this occurs) the relatively more formalized paradigms such as neo-Parsonianism, neo-functionalism, critical realism or neo-positivism, or otherwise professionally to practise, *in a common vocabulary*, a relatively less fragmented and overtly partisan sociology. (The success of critical realism is discussed further in Kilminster 1992b.)[15]

3.   In this phase paradigm conflict is not appropriate by virtue of the stage of development of inter-group conflict and the emerging pattern of extended social integration, so the characteristic concepts and orientations of those paradigm groups are now carried forward in a way acceptable to the sensibilities of the new established. There is now an 'acceptable face' to the perspective of the lay actor, the sociology of everyday life and constructivism, all so passionately advocated by specific groups in the earlier phase. In the form of the synthetic antinomies I tabulated earlier (Figure 2) they have been carried forward in a new form. They now form the more general theoretical issues of structure versus agency, micro versus macro, system versus lifeworld, etc. and the formal theoretical problem of how to reconcile them. In the previous phase, repeatedly one side of the antinomies was exaggerated at the expense of the other, since it formed the platform for critique in

paradigm strife or agitation in emancipatory movements. In other words, in the present phase, a higher level of theoretical synthesis is assumed in sociological reflections, where the extremities of argument have been whittled away by social processes. This new level of 'abstraction' (conceptual synthesis) is an expression of the higher level of social integration and theoretical synthesis which coincides with the social behavioural phase of reformalization. And the people who can handle its relatively non-partisan, unpolarized character are able to do so in virtue of a newly emergent balance of super-ego and ego functions at the level of the individual psyche. These trends *may* also indicate that people are now better able generally, than in the previous two phases, to perceive what they have in common with others – or, at least, better able to live with the reality of mutual antipathy.

Epilogue

The three-phase model has been provisionally advanced as a *preliminary* effort in the direction of a sociological approach to sociological knowledge itself, based on necessarily limited data. Rather than waiting until I had mustered fuller comparative evidence, which would have taken a very long time, I felt it was better to present now a provisional formulation of work in progress, as an invitation to others to follow. All I would claim is to have made some connections between seemingly diverse social, cultural and political trends and developments in sociology, particularly its theoretical endeavours, and that these discoveries bear on the issue of what has cognitive value in sociology in ways that are not, at the present stage of research and reflection, well understood.

9

CONCLUDING REMARKS

1.   A major theme of this study has been challenging the intellectual hegemony of the philosophers' establishment and continuing the process of redefining the problem of knowledge from the point of view of the profound revolution in knowledge that was inaugurated by the advent of sociology. However, the field of epistemology upon which many sociologists still uncritically draw, is still dominated by the formalistic argument about the 'genetic fallacy', as well as by a whole range of antinomies created by philosophers and perpetuated within the tradition, including:

> truth/falsity
> rational/irrational
> objective/subjective
> universal/particular
> quantitative/qualitative
> necessary/contingent
> transcendent/immanent
> form/content

It is my contention that we can no longer take these traditional antinomies for granted in the philosophical form in which we encounter them. Seeing the issue of valid knowledge through the philosophical spectacles that include those pairings (amongst others) imposes a rigid structure of 'timeless' validity which rules out in advance the social-psychological origins of theories from the assessment of their cognitive power. Models of what constitutes valid knowledge, which are of this static kind, have for a long time been championed and successfully disseminated as effectively absolute by philosophers. To sociologists who have deferred to philosophers on these matters, the status of the sociological knowledge produced by their own profession has seemed somewhat precarious. If it does not meet the absolutist standard, then they have feared that it must perforce be of low calibre. Not surprisingly, therefore, the issue that philosophers have garnered for themselves as that of 'validity', or 'justification' as it is sometimes called, is often suppressed in sociology. But few ask whether *any* theory could ever meet the stringent criteria and logical standards demanded by philosophers. These demands have fuelled the already profound status anxiety perennially felt by sociologists, driving them into one or other of a number of characteristic refuges: for example, redefining sociology as a type of cultural analysis; or a form of politics; or as a dialogic endeavour not committed to building up reliable knowledge. All of these manoeuvres provide a self-image for the practitioners of the discipline which partly serves to extricate them from the need to have to justify sociology as a science by criteria and standards that the discipline signally fails to meet and can never meet. (These self-definitions serve other purposes, too, in the present climate.)

2.   Exponents of the transcendental sociological approaches will have already implicitly rejected the socio-genetic alternative advocated in this study as a form of historicism, leading to self-referential cognitive circularity, relativism and irrationalism. However, the issue of validity is not as serious a difficulty as philosophers have made it out to be and is in any case in the process historically of being *reframed* sociologically. It is my contention that philosophers have a vested interest in rendering the issue of validity as intractable as possible and that sociologists have largely accepted this definition of the situation. The so-called pitfalls in the socio-genetic approach are, however, only apparent. They are largely the product of failing to view the issue dynamically and of the application of an ahistorical, absolutist epistemological standard based on the ideal of physics.

This study has made some preliminary moves in a certain socio-genetic research direction, although I am aware that that direction – which to some will smack of sociologism and developmentalism – is likely to put off a lot of people or demand of them sociological commitments which they are not prepared to make. The inquiry has abandoned the philosophical mode of thinking and all its traces in sociology for the uncharted waters of a work-in-progress dynamic sociological paradigm in which the issues previously raised by philosophers are in the course of being redefined and reframed. At this early stage, at any rate, when the shape and thread of the new direction – even after two centuries of sociological endeavour – is still only dimly perceived, the ultimate explanatory and liberatory potential embodied in the preliminary inquiries carried out here in its name, may not always be apparent.

Ultimately, what is at stake in the explorations that constitute Part II is a choice between two kinds of theories of society as a whole which have arisen in the wake of the sociological revolution: (a) variants of the analytic (transcendental) approach, through which concrete social relations are somewhat attenuated and which cannot account for its own possibility; (b) a workable synthesis of the real perspectives of society which more closely articulates the developing social relations of which it is a part. Structuration theory has emerged in this study as one of the furthest points that can be reached within the first model of sociology. However, it remains silent about the real figurational pattern of developing social antagonisms towards a greater levelling and its intra-psychic counterpart, which have made available, as a higher level of social and cognitive synthesis, the conceptual wherewithal which has made the creation of such a synthesis possible.

3.   Norbert Elias tried to capture the peculiar character of the development of knowledge by using the image of a spiral staircase:

> Under certain circumstances [people] can ... become aware of themselves as knowing that they are aware of themselves knowing. In other words, they are able to climb the spiral staircase of consciousness from

one floor with its specific view to a higher floor with its view and, looking down, to see themselves standing at the same time on other levels of the staircase. Moreover, the perspective characteristic of these other levels is assimilated into their own in one form or another, although its characteristics are not the same for people who take it for granted as for those who are able to view it with a certain detachment from a higher level of consciousness.

(Elias 1991b:103)

One could plausibly say that all theoretical endeavours (including structuration theory) in the (current) concentration phase presuppose that their practitioners, as members of society, are in the course of climbing the spiral staircase of consciousness. All of them have assimilated into their thinking many of the perspectives characteristic of the levels below, the most proximate of which are the two previous phases of the three-phase model I presented in Chapter 8. To extend Elias's insight, there is, though, a gradation of modes of assimilation here, representing different types of self-reflection.

First, there is the perspective of the relatively more involved mass of non-social scientists who absorb and carry forward, for example, hybrid social codes of behaviour, spontaneously and relatively unreflectively. Second, there is the perspective of theorists of society of the structurationist persuasion, and similar rationalistic approaches to a theory of the total society, such as rational choice theory or neo-Parsonianism, who assimilate the levels below in a more systematic fashion, with greater detachment. But they do so via a form of analytic synthesis which does not reflect fully upon, for example, the public code of behaviour and mode of self-restraint which is expressed in the model of the knowledgeable or rational actor assumed in the theories to be self-evident and cognitively salient.

Then, third, there is, beyond this, the more comprehensive cognitive accomplishment of the figurational approach, exemplified here, which achieves the assimilation of the lower levels in a relatively more detached fashion, inclusive of the two former perspectives, thus representing a higher level of synthesis. This approach scans the lower levels of the spiral staircase, i.e. glances down the sequence of phases, in a way that is *closer* to the actual texture of developing interdependencies, as *empirically* calibrated through changes in the whole gamut of social bonds. Because this paradigm is attempting more nearly to articulate the emergent dynamic structure of society as a whole on *all* dimensions of social bonding (in addition to the economic kind) and challenges the theorists *themselves* to achieve higher levels of self-distanciation, it represents a working synthesis at once more comprehensive and reality-adequate than the forms of rationalistic, analytic synthesis, the limits and hiatuses of which it can also explain. As such, it can potentially provide a more adequate form of social orientation (and simultaneously explain the sources of disorientation) in society.

4. The social processes (functional democratization, informalization, etc.) analysed in the three-phase model that I presented in Chapter 8 are so closely bound up with the developments in sociology that this fact also affects the *cognitive* status of the sociological theoretical products of the phases. *At the present stage of the institutionalization of sociology*, its permeable boundaries make it far more likely that

its practitioners' inquiries will be *more* informed by extra-sociological involvements than by institutionalized standards of fact orientation. Their inquiries will therefore tend *overall* (with some exceptions unevenly distributed) to tell us more about them than about the relatively autonomous 'objective' structures they are trying to grasp. Even as we state this, we are reframing the issue of the cognitive value of sociological products. The parameters of the inquiry have been transformed in such a way that central to the assessment of the cognitive weight of sociological theories becomes the judgement of the extent of involvements embedded within them – or, put in another fashion, the way in which their involvement/detachment balance is tilted.

This procedure contrasts with the application to sociological products of ahistorical logical or epistemological criteria derived uncritically from a model of science based on classical physics, which I alluded to earlier and outlined more fully at the beginning of Chapter 8. This standard emerges as simply inappropriate to the evaluation of work designed to explain the patterns observed in social interdependencies *sui generis*, from a perspective within and as part of those interdependencies themselves. It does not do justice to the ineliminable role of the observer in what is observed. To the extent that rival approaches fail to take this dimension into account at the core of their theory of knowledge, they represent a less inclusive and less adequate approach.

5.   The extension in recent years of the artificial field of 'social theory' does not help us very much to further the development of sociology as a science. Social theory treats the different schools of philosophy and sociology and their theoretical products as cognitively equipollent and hence as abstractly comparable, irrespective of their specific nature and origins. Social theory is a sustained attempt to avoid confronting some uncomfortable genetic questions which arise out of the current state of sociology. These are sidestepped through the rendering comparable of all theories and paradigms at a level of generality which shields its practitioners from the painful task of having to reject and abandon as inappropriate or as of low cognitive weight, possibly whole swathes of social philosophizing and other forms of proto- and para-sociology.

The advocates of social theory claim that the 'field' embraces, amongst other things, a range of reflections about the nature of action applicable to all the social sciences. This pursuit performs the important additional function for the sociology profession of enabling its members to retreat from the implications of the fact that the master social science, which subsumes those very questions as part of its theoretical level, is *sociology itself*. This conclusion presents itself convincingly from an investigation of the development of sociology, but it is one that I suspect sociologists shun for fear of being accused of sociological imperialism, nineteenth-century Comteanism, illiberalism, intolerance or worse. In my view, however – and I have tried to show it in a preliminary fashion in this study – is that all the evidence points to some form of *sociologism* as the compelling epistemological outcome of the rise of sociology. The sense of historical responsibility associated with this conclusion has to be embraced in all its implications, not suppressed.

6.   The enterprise of social theory bears the marks not only of philosophizing (which I explained in Chapter 7) but also of the institutionalization of sociology in recent times. To repeat an important point which I also made there, this

creates the echoing intellectual milieu which enables its exponents to discover convergences between the schools that they find ready to hand and side by side in curricula, journals, conference papers, databases and publications. But this procedure takes for granted the specificity of these intellectual frameworks and how they came to achieve their salience, which the three-phase model that I elaborated in Chapter 8 is designed to illuminate. The process of institutionalization itself plays a part in juxtaposing the approaches and making them available for scrutiny. It cannot be taken for granted. This is why we need a theory of scientific development that is linked closely to a theory of social development to help us to discriminate effectively between the theories and approaches we find in this complex world of institutionalized intellectual activity. We need to be able to control for the status and origin of concepts. We also need to be able to ascertain whether any one theory or concept amongst the mass of theoretical discussions available to us, is an advance over a previous stage of more or less adequate elaboration. Only with such a benchmark can we reliably judge which of the contemporary theories and concepts that we find available and disseminated are:

(i)   rehashes of what were dead-ends even at a previous stage;
(ii) based on philosophical abstractions;
(iii) reworkings of theoretical ground already gained in the past; or
(iv) genuine innovations in theoretical sociology.

Theories and concepts within all four of these categories may be institutionally consolidated, mixed up together and available for scrutiny, so need to be differentiated. The various exponents of social theory who attempt to build rational, analytic sociological syntheses as part of that enterprise, Giddens being the most prominent British example, fuse many concepts and insights at a certain level of heuristic generality, but pay the high price of over-abstraction. What is the cognitive value of the rational synthesis if it contains concepts or assumptions *themselves* of dubious cognitive value or sociological relevance? What image of humans is implied in such attenuated syntheses? How much do they contribute to our orientation? Why not, alternatively, strive towards a workable synthesis which more or less closely articulates the actually existing perspectives that go to make up the total society, its genesis and demonstrable tendencies? And couple this approach with controlling for involvements, metaphysics, politics, economism and individualism? Then, armed with this, note all theories embodying partial perspectives or angles on the world or theoretical lapses into those fallacies and traps, and try to perceive the thread of development or progression?

Because of what Baldamus (1992) rightly identified as 'the slow rate of obsolescence' of cognitive achievements in sociology, most of our effort effectively reworks ground already gained, with true innovations (as opposed to spurious claims to novelty) being actually at a premium. The socio-genetic approach exemplified by this study could in principle provide criteria for *rejecting or disregarding* theories under categories i and ii, i.e. rehashes of dead-ends and philosophizing, as simply unserviceable. Most sociologists would, I suspect, find the prospect of having to do this daunting and uncomfortable because of its implications for their self-image and career and their relations with other academic establishments.

Hence, we see in the current phase, to paraphrase Elias (1987b), the retreat of the theoretical sociologists into the elaborate edifice of equivocation that is social theory, which brushes the emotionally challenging issues such as these under the carpet.

7.   Ultimately, if sociology is to fufil its promise and develop into a fully scientific disclipline committed to cumulative empirical inquiry, then its practitioners will have to learn to live with errors, false starts and a lot of gaps in their knowledge. To achieve this kind of research ethos, which presupposes that sociologists, when acting as scientists, are *entirely* interested in understanding society as such, there would need to be a much firmer and more stable institutionalization of sociology than we have at present, organized around a central paradigm embodying scientific standards of detachment and empirical investigation. The present underdeveloped, pre-scientific state of sociology is one in which the normal condition of the discipline is that many sociologists take it for granted that it is legitimate to disguise their politics as sociological research. Indeed, for some, so dominant are their involvements of this kind that the problematics being discussed here, which already embody a considerable degree of detachment, are not taken seriously and, in some cases, are barely comprehensible.

The social conditions that would make for the greater institutional autonomy of sociology – and hence institutionalized standards of neutrality and fact orientation which would minimize the intrusion of extra-scientific evaluations and tilt the involvement/detachment balance more towards the latter pole – have not yet fully matured. And we have to face the fact that they may never do so. Whether the institutionalization of such standards occurs in sociology, or how far it can go, depends, amongst other things, on the 'safety–danger balance' (Elias 1987a: lxxi) characteristic of the society concerned (including regional and global dimensions) which shapes the level of social fears. This, in turn, affects the overall involvement/detachment balance possible in the standard of knowledge. All of this is ultimately out of the control of the individual sociologist, although collectively it might be possible to affect or augment such a movement.

Hence, what can be done at this point – and this realization emerges from the inquiries in this book – is to apply to the products of sociology the criteria of cognitive evaluation and the standard of detachment, which would be widely taken for granted if the discipline had achieved a higher degree of self-perpetuating, institutional autonomy. In applying these criteria and the standard of detachment, we *anticipate* their future stronger institutionalization and, hopefully, help to bring it about, although in the present their consistent application is by no means an effortless matter and the outcome by no means certain.

8. Contrary to a commonly expressed view, I think that the belief that the golden age of sociology has come and passed, is fallacious. And phrases such as '*late* modernity' and '*late* capitalism', which are often employed in diagnoses of that kind, seem to me to be, like the thesis itself, highly misleading products of a drastic foreshortening of perspective, implicitly informed by wish fulfilment. Sociology proper is still in its very early stages, struggling to maintain a weak and unstable institutional toehold. One implication of my analysis of globalization in Chapter 6 is that *the great age of sociology may be yet to come*. As the European Union potentially becomes more integrated and national boundaries become blurred, nations merge

and new hegemonic groups come to dominate in complex, new, larger regional units, perhaps one consequence might be that a revitalized sociology will come to flourish as social scientists compete to grasp the resultant integration crises. How firm will be its institutionalization and what will be its central paradigm(s), who can say? But if the development of individual European nation-states is anything to go by, the consolidation of this new regional social formation (and maybe others elsewhere) will take a very long time, if indeed it occurs – perhaps several hundred years. Possibly the greatest age of sociology will therefore be under way by about the year 2600 – maybe later. I hope that in a modest way this study anticipates that time.

NOTES

1 SOCIOLOGISTS AND PHILOSOPHY

1 Earlier formulations of the argument presented here were given at sociology seminars in various British universities in the late 1980s, as well as at the joint meeting of the Theory Groups of the British and German Sociological Associations on the theme of 'Social Structure and Culture' held at the University of Bremen in June 1987. The present chapter grew out of that lecture (Kilminster 1989a). Further elaborations of the thesis, as well as more empirical examples, are to be found in Kilminster (1993) in relation to the work of Karl Mannheim and Norbert Elias and in Kilminster & Wouters (1995) in respect of Elias's relationship with neo-Kantianism.

2 See Talcott Parsons (1951: 327ff). It has been pointed out that Parsons' four primary sub-divisions of the cultural system (cognitive, moral-evaluative, expressive, symbolic) follows the actual order of listing of items contained in Edward Tylor's often cited anthropologist's definition of culture of 1891, though rephrased (Schneider 1973: 120). Parsons was well aware of the nature of much modern philosophy, although he does not question its autonomy, as such. For him it is a belief system combining 'non-empirical' reference and 'existential' significance and of relevance to the system of action. For belief systems of this kind which are below a certain level of explicitness and logical articulation Parsons reserved the term 'proto-philosophy' (1951: 331 and 359ff). See also Boas (1948).

3 Lawrence C. Becker (1977) defends a definition of philosophy which contains this idea of philosophy as an activity: 'The nature of philosophy as an ongoing enterprise – as a way of life rather than a set of doctrines – is also suggested by the definition. Its ultimate allegiances appear clearly as discursive truth reached by reasoned argument, and its character as a way of life (it follows) must be disciplined, intellectual, and comprised of conduct consistent with what is known by reason' (1977: 251). See also Scharfstein (1980: 384ff). This conception of philosophy was also embraced by Karl Jaspers (see preface to Schilpp 1957: xi). It is satirized by Hankinson (1985).

4 This straightforward fact is expressed with characteristic philosophical obscurity by Roy Bhaskar (1979: 64) as he struggles to justify the autonomy of philosophy: 'the syncategorematic (or, as it were, only proxy-referential) character of the nevertheless irreducible discourse of philosophy . . . has to be contrasted with the directly referential character of social scientific discourse.'

5 The sociological account of the origins of sociology in the text follows a number of standard accounts but draws especially on Elias (1984).

6 The compatibility of the views of Marx and Durkheim about the inherent sociality of individuals, against the assumption of isolated individuals made by contract theories of society, and by utilitarians, is noted also by Frisby & Sayer (1986: 93ff).

7 As, for example, in the following statement by Marx: 'By social we understand the co-operation of several individuals, no matter under what condition, in what manner and to what end. It follows from this that a certain mode of production, or industrial stage, is

always combined with a certain mode of co-operation, or social stage, and this mode of co-operation is itself a productive force' (Marx & Engels 1845a: 41).

8 I realize that the three social scientists mentioned were simultaneously fighting battles on other fronts, both theoretical and political, and that Durkheim and Weber worked in university institutions in conditions very different from those of the exiled Marx living in London and supporting himself through journalism and gifts from Engels. They worked in different countries at different times and these countries each embraced different paths of development. Clearly, too, the transformation of Marx's ideas into forms of Marxism was presupposed as a critical point of departure by Weber and Durkheim. But for the sake of the argument in the text I have concentrated on the relatively autonomous issue of breaking with philosophy, and moving towards sociology, which they all share.

9 I make no claim that this table is exhaustive. It is, rather, a preliminary summary of an emerging pattern, and has a marked European focus. One significant absence is the work of Peirce, James, Dewey and the North American tradition of pragmatism, with its latter-day representatives such as Richard Rorty and sociological offshoots in Mead and his followers. Many of its founding writers also tried to move beyond the dualistic, ego-centred and rationalistic European philosophical tradition, towards a social action-based epistemology – albeit still firmly within philosophy. Others, later on, however, have even questioned the autonomy of philosophy itself (e.g. Rorty 1979 and 1982). Advanced discussions of the pragmatist tradition and its relevance for sociology are to be found in Joas (1993; 1996). Whilst there is a little psychological and psychoanalytic literature on philosophy and individual philosophers (e.g. 1953; Erikson 1958; Glover 1966; Hanly & Lazerowitz 1970; Feuer 1970; Scharfstein 1980), sociological studies of the origins of philosophy as a discipline and its development into a profession are almost non-existent. One notable exception is the work of Collins (1987). Sociologists generally appear to have taken its existence for granted. Perhaps the study of the origins and nature of philosophy is not a subject that has had a strong emotional significance or urgency for them. Much more research needs to be done into the institutionalization of philosophy, the formation of schools, professionalization and the changing relations between scientific establishments and the philosopher's establishment. And the psychological research needs to be integrated into a general sociological framework. This chapter is partly intended as a contribution to the 'sociology of philosophy' (a term first coined by Leclerq 1955; see also Feuer 1958) and as the outlines of a research programme to be taken up by others.

10 These pairs of Kantian concepts underlie, for example, the critiques of Karl Mannheim's sociology of knowledge in the early 1930s by the philosophers Ernst Grünwald (1934a and 1934b) and Alexander von Schelting (1936).

11 The influence of the logical empiricists on the sociology of science is explained by Dolby (1972).

12 See the 'Introduction' to Benton (1977) and Becker (1977).

13 These oppositions have been developed by transcendental philosophers of various schools. See for example Schutz & Luckmann (1974: 262, 289, 304, 311, 326); Luckmann (1983: 22ff); and Heidegger (1927: 31ff).

14 See Hegel (1807: preface; 1830b: introduction); Rose (1981: 103); Kilminster (1975 and 1979: chs 2 and 5); Marcuse (1941: 389ff; 1936).

15 Some exceptions are Benton (1977: 4ff) on the factual/conceptual and 'first-'/'second'-order distinctions; Mannheim (1929: 262ff) on genesis/validity; and Elias (1982: 32) on the historical/systematic distinction.

16 For reasons of space I have given less attention to the fate of the philosophies of existence and 'fundamental ontology' of the twentieth century in the light of the rise of sociology within the social processes outlined. Briefly, I think that fundamental ontology in the field of society (for example, in the works of Heidegger) constitutes a blurred way of talking about the routine subject-matter of the sociological tradition: the 'social' as a structured range of impersonal social regularities *sui generis*. The furthest sociological

point possible within fundamental ontology is the vague statement that the 'mode of being' of humankind is always being-with-others, or a similar hyphenated formulation which tries to capture social interdependencies in a non-individualistic way (see Kilminster 1988). A promising alternative to the philosophical speculations about modes of being, and one that has the advantage of rendering the problem area amenable to empirical test, is the theory of scientific differentiation and levels of integration developed by Elias (1987a). See Benthem van den Bergh (1986) and Wassall (1990) for further reflections on this model compared with the work undertaken within other paradigms.

17 I have explored the tensions in Marx's thought at much greater length in Kilminster (1979: part 1).

18 The dualistic nature of Marx's theory of base and superstructure was pointed out by Karl Mannheim in his essay 'The Problem of a Sociology of Knowledge' (1925: 142–4 and 162–3; and more recently by Heideggerians – see Axelos (1976: 145ff). See also Tillich (1933: 116), Elias (1971: 135ff.) and Chapter 3 of this study.

19 There have been some instances when an institutionally strong discipline of sociology in a particular country has achieved a sufficiently high prestige ranking, relative to others, to enable certain philosophers, in specific circumstances, to shelter under *its* wing. Julien Freund (1978: 184) cites (with disapproval) the case of the Frankfurt School in exile in the United States in the 1940s as an example: 'even if this school contributed to the progress of sociological research, especially during its American period (that is, in exile), it still misled scientific sociology into an impasse. Its members took advantage of sociology's prestige to put across a primarily philosophical message.' A similar point about the Frankfurt School was made by Shils (1982: 303ff.).

20 The distinction between 'first-' and 'second'-order questions is also found, in a slightly different form, for example, in Schutz (1932).

21 On the tendency of imperialism by 'tool-providing' fields in the sciences, see Ravetz (1973: 88ff.).

22 The work of Roy Bhaskar (1979) on the 'critical realist' theory of science, so influential in Britain in the present period, also exemplifies this transcendental tendency. It relies for its basic cogency on a transcendental argument. His fundamental allegiance is announced early in the book: 'If philosophy is to be possible . . . then it must follow the Kantian road' (p. 6). For a further discussion of the success of critical realism see Kilminster (1992b).

23 The philosopher A.R. Manser (1973) finds parallels between Marx and Wittgenstein who both, in their different ways, declared the 'end of philosophy'. But instead of moving in a sociological direction from this comparison, however, he falls back on the stock philosophers' device referred to in the text: 'the two programmes for the end of philosophy thus themselves give rise to a further philosophical problem, that of deciding between them' (*ibid.*, p.13). See Chapter 2 of this study for further discussion of the 'end of philosophy' thesis in Left and Right Hegelianism.

2 THE HEGELIAN APOGEE

1 In this chapter I have drawn at various points on arguments I first presented in Kilminster (1983), but have considerably extended and deepened the discussion of the sociological implications of Hegelian philosophy only sketched there.

2 See Chapter 3 for a further discussion of this issue.

3 Complementary to Rose's interpretation of Durkheim is that of Nye & Ashworth (1971: 133–48) which sees Durkheim as on the threshold of Hegelian dialectics, i.e. less straightforwardly Kantian than at first might appear. See also La Capra (1972) on this issue and my remarks on Durkheim in Chapter 1. It is a drawback generally of classifying all the classical sociologists (except Marx) in a blanket fashion as Kantian, that it does not always leave room for appreciating the tensions and ambiguities within their works with respect to Kantian concepts and assumptions and the extent to which they

struggled to transcend them, some more successfully than others. Nor should it detract from the possibility of detecting in their successive efforts a trend towards a greater clarification of the issue for subsequent sociologists perhaps to take the matter further. The Hegelian view seems to condemn the rest of us non-Hegelians tragically to making standard Kantian moves in perpetuity, so long as the realm of 'unfreedom' is said to circumscribe all our efforts.

4 In her interpretation of Georg Lukács, Rose has mainly drawn on *History and Class Consciousness*, leaving out of her account Lukács's important essay 'Moses Hess and the Problems of Idealist Dialectics' of 1926 in which he explicitly distances himself from the Fichteanism attributed to him by Rose. There is extensive discussion of the epistemological problems associated with Lukács' conception of the imputed class consciousness of the proletariat in Kilminster (1979: part 2).

5 Edgar Wind (1967: 54) writes: 'Among Renaissance theologians it was almost a commonplace to say that the highest mysteries transcend the understanding and must be apprehended through a state of darkness in which the distinctions of logic vanish.'

3 MARX'S THEORY OF KNOWLEDGE AS A PARTIAL BREAKTHROUGH

1 In this chapter I have drawn on Kilminster (1982a), which was a lecture written for a philosophical audience. In the present chapter, however, I have concentrated more on the sociological implications of the philosophical aspects of Marx's theory of truth in the context of a broader argument about the historical relationship between sociology and philosophy.

2 Theory, meaning a set of principles of an art or technical subject as distinct from its practice, was first used in that sense in English in 1613. The opposition was used to refer to abstract knowledge opposed to practice in 1624. The use of the word 'theory' to refer to a mental scheme or conception of something to be done, dates from 1597. The adjective 'practical' was opposed to theoretical, speculative or ideal from 1617 onwards (*Shorter Oxford Dictionary*).

3 Alfred Schmidt's neat formulation of Marx's theoretical strategy mentioned in the text, though essentially accurate, does not, like Marx's remarks on the transcendence of idealism and materialism via the category of practice, separate the epistemological and ontological dimensions in the two doctrines. My text at this point is thus ambiguous in this respect. In Marx, however, the same ambiguity may be a product of his attempting to recast the debate in a way that moves away from the older philosophical materialism towards a theory of social mediations in which extra-human nature is independent of human beings but not a final ontological level. On this point, see Schmidt (1971: 113ff. and ch. 1), Bernstein (1971: 42ff.) and Kitching (1988: 26ff.).

4 The apparent similarity between Marx's theory of truth and the way in which pragmatist philosophers in the North American tradition have related the 'truth' value of knowledge to social problem solving, can be raised here, although I cannot take the matter very far. Much more research is needed in this area. Various writers have noticed this affinity, if not compatibility between them (see Bloch 1971; Moore 1971; Livergood 1967; Kolakowski 1971; Goff 1980). Gavin Kitching (1988: 2–3) even claims to offer an interpretation of Marx that relies on 'a strongly pragmatist reading of Wittgenstein', which suggests even further compatibilities. Hans Joas (1996: 94ff.) is by implication more sceptical because his prior interest in the creative dimension of action leads him to assimilate Marx's conception of action to a 'production model'. Hence, he does not notice affinities with pragmatism in Marx's (admittedly unsystematic) remarks on a sociological theory of knowledge and science. There is also a parallel between the pragmatists' insistence on the truth value of knowledge being related to its discovered usefulness in cumulative phases of human action and the neo-Marxist view of 'proving the truth' of theory in a process of action, which I summarized in the text. Unlike the pragmatist theories, the latter was developed entirely in the context of political action.

The crucial difference seems to be that in Marx the dialectical (Hegelian) tendency in his work means that practical (political) activity, rightly or wrongly, is seen as the *realization* of 'universal' potentialities inherent in social development, something specifically eschewed as metaphysical by most of the pragmatist philosophers. Much of what Marx wrote on action was in the form of unpublished and often ambiguous notes and drafts, which makes systematic comparisons with the work of pragmatist philosophers inherently difficult. For example, we will never know exactly what he meant by an ambiguous sentence in the second thesis on Feuerbach which seems crucial for an understanding of Marx's theory of knowledge: 'Man must prove the truth, i.e. the reality and power, the this-sidedness *(Diesseitigkeit)* of his thinking in practice.' This could be, and has been, interpreted in many different ways. I have discussed at length the problems of interpretation involved here and in the *Theses* in general, in Kilminster (1979: 15–22).

5 For a defence of Bruno Bauer against Marx and Engels, see Kilminster (1979: ch. 2).

6 Close to what Marx probably had in mind by the phrase is Gramsci's statement: 'The identity of theory and practice is a critical act, through which practice is demonstrated rational and necessary and theory realistic and rational' (Gramsci 1971: 365). It is probable from the context and what is known about Gramsci's thought, that he is here talking simultaneously about the practical realization of both knowledge *and* ethics. The polar opposite of Marx's concept is surely Salvador Dali's definition of surrealist painting as 'paranoiac-critical activity'. This is defined as: 'Spontaneous method of "*irrational knowledge*", based on the critical and systematic objectification of delirious associations and interpretations' (from Dali's *Philosophic Provocations* of 1934, extracted in Chipp 1968: 415–16, emphasis in original).

7 I am reminded here of F.H. Bradley's apocryphal dictum that 'What *might* be, if it *must* be, assuredly *is*'.

8 Reinhold Neibuhr eloquently captured the basic dilemma of social action in his *Prayer* of 1934: 'O God, give us serenity to accept what cannot be changed, courage to change what should be changed, and wisdom to distinguish the one from the other' (cited in Berki 1981: iv). My conviction is that, properly done, sociology is uniquely placed to make a contribution to the latter task ('wisdom'). Indeed, it is part of sociology's vocation and historic responsibility to take on this traditional philosophical task, but in a new key.

9 Another, more remote factor is that, as philosophy, the work of these two writers – and that of many others in Western Marxism – is saturated with the European tradition of philosophical rationalism, particularly the philosophies of Kant and Hegel, which have left behind in social science and European culture in general, modes of thinking profoundly prone to idealization. Any writer evaluating social and political realities largely through philosophical spectacles (and this will include all of the most prominent exponents of 'postmodernism') will be likely to reproduce this tendency and its characteristic obfuscating level of abstraction.

10 This may involve, as we saw in the text, the postulating of the 'ideal speech situation'. It may also take the form of 'discourse ethics' (Habermas); 'a priori regulative principles' (Apel); an appeal to 'being-with-the-other' as a 'pre-social' moral awareness (Bauman 1989: 174, quoting Lévinas); or other attempts to base a 'centred' universal morality on a 'transcendental foundation beyond reason' (Heller 1996: 116) or on the dialectics of 'thinking the Absolute' (Adorno, Rose – see Chapter 2). All of these approaches insist on maintaining an abstract utopian 'moment' or 'horizon' in all sociological inquiry and political thinking. All exhibit a fundamentally philosophical, conceptual structure, based on a distinction between the particular and the universal, or some variant. And all of them ultimately depend upon forms of transcendental argumentation. Variants on this style of thinking are very pervasive. One of the negative psychological consequences associated with this kind of thinking in politics and ethics is that it is a philosophy that exhorts us to derive our whole life's meaning from working towards the realization of some state of perfection that we *know* is intrinsically unachievable, e.g. the ideal speech situation or other utopian state of affairs. The appar-

ently positive overtones of the employment of absolutist yardsticks of this kind are illusory. What follows from their use is that, like a housewife or a child who can never live up to internalized images of the 'perfect' wife or child, if we pursue such idealized goals we are condemned to frustration. We can never fully give ourselves credit for our achievements, we can never feel fully satisfied, because we know that against the perfect, but forever unattainable ideal, our efforts will *always* fall short. As Durkheim put it: 'To pursue a goal which is by definition unattainable is to condemn oneself to a state of perpetual unhappiness' (Durkheim 1897: 248). For a further discussion of this issue see Kilminster (1982b).

4 THE LIMITS OF TRANSCENDENTAL SOCIOLOGY

1 This chapter and the excursus draw on arguments originally presented in a different form in Kilminster (1989b and 1992c).
2 Münch wrongly interprets Elias's theory of civilizing processes as a monocausal one focusing solely on the monopolization of force. In doing so, he ignores the specific role of the monopolization of taxation in the theory. Nor does he take account of Elias's extensive remarks in numerous places about the monopolization of the means of production and of orientation as separately identifiable sources of power; as well as his emphasis on the way in which any individual or group withholding what others need, i.e. monopolizing it, is a source of power (Elias 1978a: ch. 5; Mennell 1992: 264). Münch's analysis also leaves out of account the importance of Elias's notion of the sequential order of intertwining cumulative changes in a structured process (Elias 1977b and 1987b).
3 The remarks here and in the excursus about the development of British sociology in recent years should be read in conjunction with the three-phase model which I present in Chapter 8, particularly the conflict phase.
4 In view of the utter centrality of Kantian themes to the structure of Parsons' theory of society, it is baffling that in a recent book devoted entirely to expounding Parsons' ideas (Holmwood 1996) neither Kant nor neo-Kantianism is mentioned anywhere and do not even appear in the index!
5 The occurrence of the word 'function' in Elias's work does not make him a functionalist in the traditional sense. For Elias, individuals and groups in networks of interdependence perform various functions *for* each other. Similarly, rules or codes – say, etiquette – can perform the function for nobles of showing their social superiority over bourgeois groups. Whereas, for functionalists, the function *of* social elements is to ensure the adaptive survival of the social system as a whole. For a helpful discussion of this difference, see Goudsblom (1977a: 175–80).
6 This aspect of Elias's work is not well understood. See Arnason (1987) for an analysis of this issue and a critique of Elias in terms of what Arnason regards as Elias's reduction of the phenomenon of culture to a reflex of power. This is a point made in a slightly different way by Mouzelis (1995: ch. 4). In Elias's terms, however, this criticism falls back into the culture/structure dualism and has failed fully to grasp the role of what I have called in the text 'figurational compulsion', in the maintenance of the specific orderedness of society, even during revolutions, rebellions, riots and wars.

5 THE STRUCTURE OF STRUCTURALISM

1 Kate Soper (1986: 122) shows how, in the context of French intellectual and political culture, anti-humanism was a strong reaction to any kind of loyalty to the unique individual, who possesses consciousness, will and reason and who is opposed to irrationality in the name of progress – an attachment that was seen as purely sentimental. She also shows how many of the anti-humanist arguments still tacitly depended on 'humanist' assumptions.

2 In an interview in 1972, Lévi-Strauss admitted: 'I am by temperament somewhat of a misanthrope . . . there is nothing I dread more than a too-close relationship with my fellow men' (quoted by Pace 1983: 39).

3 Lévi-Strauss rather predictably described himself and his own writings thus: 'I don't have the feeling that I write my books. I have the feeling that my books get written through me' (1979: 3). Compared with this, Foucault was much more playful and ironic about the structuralist paradox of individuality. Beginning his inaugural lecture at the Collège de France in 1970, he said: 'I wish I could have slipped unnoticed into this lecture that I am supposed to be giving today . . . I wish there had been a nameless voice speaking before me, for a long time, so that when my turn came I had only to take up what it was saying, continue the sentence, lodge myself in its gaps, without anyone noticing' (quoted by Sheridan 1982: 121).

4 See Axelos (1976: 145ff) who discloses the metaphysical dualism at the heart of Marx's theory of base and superstructure in a critique that is comparable with one that might have been mounted by a structuralist, but is in fact undertaken from a point of view heavily indebted to Heidegger.

5 See Lévi-Strauss 1968: 475. Bauman rightly concludes that, sociologically speaking, the generative rules can surely only be deemed to be invariant as the result of the crystallization of human culture over many generations. As such, the only sense in which they can be regarded as *necessary*, that is as the *only* 'imaginable' rules that can generate practical and cognitive order, is that from the individual's point of view they may *appear* to possess a 'transcendental law-like necessity' (1973a: 69–77). However, in Lévi-Strauss invariant means something closer to universal than it does for Foucault. For Foucault, the generative rules of a discourse or of the relations between discursive practices within an epistème are only transcendentally necessary, i.e. invariant, for as long as the arrangement of knowledge effected by the epistème continues. A new epistème ushers in a new historical apriori. The change from one epistème to another is said to occur in a saltatory fashion, precipitated unpredictably by 'some event' which causes the epistemological arrangements 'to crumble' (Foucault 1966: 387). Foucault goes no further than those vague phrases to explain the change from one epistème to another. He advances no diachronic theory of structured social change that might explain the *succession* of discontinuous epistèmes, so cannot deal theoretically with the reality of historical continuities.

6 A number of writers have wrongly equated the concept of structure in structuralism with the idea of an essence behind the appearances (see e.g. Giddens 1976: 119, and 1979: 60; Godelier 1967: 91; Bottomore & Nisbet 1979: 593). This error misses the fundamental point that it was precisely a rejection of versions of this dualism that constituted the structuralists' whole philosophical point of departure.

7 Shalvey (1979: 158–60) says that Lévi-Strauss is ambiguous about the irreducibility of culture to nature and argues that the reductionist tendency in his work converges more and more with socio-biology. On the other hand, Bénoist (1978: 210–11) argues that the abolition of the traditional form/content distinction in structuralism (he quotes Lvi-Strauss himself on this point) leads in the opposite direction, away from reductionism (and positivism). It enables the analyst to uncode the different structuring principles in a *local* way, in a process of the continuous remodelling of different, incongruent but overlapping areas of inquiry, without assuming reduction to a single ordering principle. (On this point see also Bauman 1973b: 74; Kilminster & Varcoe 1992: 211.)

8 See Layder (1994: 106–13) for a clear and helpful summary, from a sociological point of view, of the limitations, gaps and swings of emphasis in Foucault's work. But Layder does not trace the vagueness nor any of the other drawbacks in Foucault's work, back to its philosophical character in the context of French political and cultural life.

6 GLOBALIZATION AS AN EMERGENT CONCEPT

This chapter is a revised version of Kilminster (1997).

1 Within the Marxist tradition there are, of course, various theories of imperialism and dependency and many controversies between them. Not all Marxists, for example, would regard Wallerstein's work as faithful to the spirit and letter of Marx. But for the limited purposes of this chapter, I did not think it necessary to digress into the shades of difference between the Marxist variants nor the many positions taken in the debates between them, which often have political undertones. My interest is in Marx himself, as a pioneer. For a comprehensive review of the Marxist literature on imperialism see Brewer (1980).

2 Interestingly, Wallerstein has expressed similar sentiments in responding to what he saw as the false and tendentious contrast by Roy Boyne of his economistic theory with one that emphasizes culture: 'Emphasizing "culture" in order to counterbalance the emphases others have put on the "economy" or the "polity" does not at all solve the problem; it in fact just makes it worse. We must surmount the terminology altogether' (Wallerstein 1990: 65).

3 My treatment of Herder's ideas on nations and internationalism is only the tip of the iceberg of insights to be found in his works (see Barnard 1965; Mueller-Vollmer 1987). He had much to say on art, philosophy, language, creativity, metaphysics and much else, and has sometimes been dubbed the 'German Rousseau'. Other commentators have also found in his works discussions of issues that have a contemporary resonance. For example, Richard S. Leventhal (1987: 187–9) has convincingly shown that Herder anticipated the current scepticism about 'foundationalism', as well as discoursed at length on what we would today call reflexivity and the institutional embeddedness of power/knowledge; Michael Morton (1987: 171) has shown how Herder developed a theory of symbolism comparable with contemporary 'semiotics', a word that Herder also used; and Hans Joas (1996: 75–85) has found in Herder an unsurpassed discussion of the expressive character of human action.

4 The subject of Marx's critique of Hegel is much more complicated than I have been able to report it in the text. As I have argued at length elsewhere (Kilminster 1979: part 1) Marx's inversion of Hegel's dialectic makes no sense because Hegel's dialectic was never on its head. Nor is there in Hegel an assumed spirit-force driving history forward to self-knowledge. Nor does Hegel's philosophy of history necessarily imply an end-state of human perfection, but rather, as Gillespie has rightly said, 'a circular process that continually finds and continually loses its perfection' (1984: 115). The explanation for why Marx insists on a crudely teleological, dualistic and spiritual reading of Hegel lies in Marx's prior moral–political commitment to the communist movement. His critique of Hegel was one that produced a theoretical result which enabled him to maximize his chances of success in the competition between groups of socialists for the prize of the most complete 'scientific' theory of socialism.

5 The place in his writings where Marx grapples with the conceptual expression of these heady matters is in his unpublished drafts on the dialectical method, a neglected and often misunderstood aspect of Marx's work (Marx 1857a). Here Marx takes seriously Hegel's depiction of history as the filling out of many 'determinations' of concrete universals, even agreeing with Hegel that the historical movement of categories from abstraction to concrete fullness is a real sequence. But he disagrees with the conclusion that Hegel allegedly drew from those sequences, i.e. that their driving force is pure absolute thinking communing with itself via the categories (Marx 1873: 19–20). (See note 4 above.)

6 There is a common explanation of the declining likelihood that the powerful, richer Western states in particular will resort to military violence against weaker states, which goes as follows. It is held to have less to do with growing 'respect' for poorer nations and more to do with the fact that it is becoming increasingly difficult to mobilize popular support for war in post-industrial countries. This political explanation has been argued, for example, by Martin Shaw (1991). But we need to look more closely into the socio-logical preconditions that lie behind this trend. Why have people's attitudes changed in such a way that it has become more and more difficult, politically, to convince public

opinion towards accepting the need to go to war? The far-reaching democratization and informalization processes that have taken place in the advanced societies, mentioned in the text, have, amongst other things, brought about greater mutual identification and mutually expected self-restraint between people. This has arguably created greater respect for others in general, including peoples of other nations, one manifestation of which is a widespread anti-war sensibility. The existence of this then makes it difficult for politicians to mobilize support for going to war.

7 The concept of functional democratization is being used here in the specific sociological sense developed by Norbert Elias. It refers to the long-term, unplanned process of the lessening of the power gradients and social distance between interdependent groups in differentiated societies. This has gradually come about because groups have become more interdependent in virtue of the extensive specialized functions that they perform for each other. I have discussed this concept in detail in Chapter 8 (pp. 149–51). See also Mennell (1992: 124ff.)

8 For example, David Loye (1991: 12–13) lists as symptoms of the breakdown of systems which can lead to 'social chaos', a wide range of trends, events and processes which are of different kinds, working at different levels, which he, along with others who invoke systems theory, calls 'crises and discontinuities'. These are described as being of a financial, food, political and military nature and all said to be 'driven' by changes in technology, ecological problems, the gap between rich and poor countries, the degradation of fertile land and population pressures. However, it is unclear how these items are related to changes in the real relations between groups within nations, or in the relations between nations. The analysis is further vitiated by the alarmist language which makes it less than successful as a contribution to our orientation in the present period: food crises are said to be 'ravaging' Africa; there is ecological 'devastation'; there is the 'desertification' of productive land; all brought about by what Loye obscurely describes as 'the churning of history' (ibid.).

7 STRUCTURATION THEORY AS A WORLD-VIEW

1 This chapter is a shortened and slightly revised version of an article by the author with the same title which originally appeared in Bryant and Jary (1991).

2 Sanderson (1987) refers to many other prominent professed eclectics in sociology, including Ralf Dahrendorf, Arthur Stinchcombe, Jack Goody and Jonathan Turner. In this connection, eclecticism is seen as something *positive*, a respectable alternative to the grand theories which have fallen out of favour. In Marxism, however, the words 'eclecticism' and 'eclectic' are used as terms of abuse or ridicule to describe non-Marxist theoretical efforts. See, for example, the evaluation of Habermas's early writings in Therborn (1971). The *negative* sense of the word continues an early nineteenth-century meaning also found in Marx. The term 'eclecticism', referring to arbitrary borrowing, had become a pejorative term at the turn of the eighteenth century in philosophy and in painting. Romantics contrasted the stylistic borrowings of eclectics and plagiarists with the exalted power of imagination associated with genius (see Wittkower 1965).

3 Popper wrote, with obvious allusions to Mannheim:

> [Holists] insist that the specialist's study of 'petty details' must be complemented by an 'integrating' or 'synthetic' method which aims at reconstructing 'the whole process'. . . . But this holistic method necessarily remains a mere programme. Not one example of a scientific description of a whole, concrete situation is ever cited. And it cannot be cited, since in every such case it would always be easy to point out aspects which have been neglected.
>
> (Popper 1961: 79)

4 Giddens (1982a) acknowledges the stature of Comte's early work *Cours de philosophie posi-tive*, but suggests that Comte's later *Religion of Humanity* constituted something of a decline from the 'cool rationalism' of the early work because of its 'passionate advo-cacy'. But as a whole, he claims, Comte's work is of little relevance to sociology today. It is noticeable, however, how much of the raffish detail of Comte's controversial life (for example, his relationship with a prostitute, his violent rages and bouts of madness) Giddens irrelevantly parades in the course of his exposition and discussion of Comte's work. Presumably this has been done to discredit Comte's ideas by association. For contrasting assessments see Elias (1978a: ch. 1), Dunning (1977) and Heilbron (1995).

5 The vision of capitalism as relentlessly pervading more and more spheres of society, as creating monopolies and spreading across the globe to form a world market, is most forcefully expressed by Marx in the *Communist Manifesto*, the content of which in this respect is heavily indebted to the French political economist Constantin Pecquer (Evans 1951).

6 The hodiecentric tendency in Giddens' work is apparent particularly in the stated ratio-nale behind the collection *Profiles and Critiques* (Giddens 1982a: preface and ch. 15) and in his *Nation State and Violence* (1985: chs 1 and 11).

7 The classical statement by Max Weber is:

> 'Economically conditioned' power is not, of course, identical with 'power' as such. On the contrary, the emergence of economic power may be the conse-quence of power existing on other grounds. Man does not strive for power only in order to enrich himself economically.
>
> (from *Economy and Society*, 1922, in Gerth and Mills 1970: 180)

8 I am not suggesting that Giddens is denying that people have emotions, but rather that the study of their social regulation is excluded from structuration theory by its very nature. In a word, the theory is rationalistic. This is an issue about which Giddens is clearly aware, but he does not follow it through in the theory. In discussing the writings of Herbert Marcuse, he rightly points out the differing appropriations of Freud by Marcuse and Habermas:

> the conception of an ideal speech situation [in Habermas], interesting as it may be in its own right, remains on a peculiarly cognitive level. What of affect, of sexuality, love, hate and death? Whereas Marcuse's formulation of critical theory is founded upon an abiding concern with these phenomena, Habermas's account provides little way of coping with them conceptually.
>
> (Giddens 1982a: 158)

This judgement about Habermas by Giddens is effectively an auto-critique.

8 SOCIOLOGY SINCE 1945: SOCIO-GENETIC AND PSYCHOGENETIC ASPECTS

1 The founding of *New Left Review* and the expansion of the New Left, which brought Marxism into the culture of the universities, were developments independent of the institutionalization of sociology. The New Left came to gain prominence both within sociology and cultural studies in the late 1970s and 1980s. The character of these tendencies was not unconnected with the processes of functional democratization and informalization spelled out later in the text.

2 The historical process of centre–local interaction and the growth of national markets associated with capitalism have of course been extensively researched and theorized by numerous comparative and historical sociologists and I realize that there is a huge literature on the subject (some recent examples include Bendix 1978; Skocpol 1979; Mann 1986; Anderson 1974a and 1974b, and many more). My main purpose is

the further testing and elucidation, in relation to the case of British sociology since 1945, of certain concepts developed by Elias and others within the figurational paradigm community. The important task of integrating Elias's theory of state formation, upon which his remarks about the origins of sociology referred to in the text depend, with the findings of recent comparative sociologists such as these, is necessarily beyond my scope here (on these issues, see Kuzmics 1997).

3 Although it was not his primary focus, in the course of his inquiries Wouters also perceived the connection between the informalization wave and developments in sociology which I have tried to establish systematically in the text. He comments in passing, citing Goudsblom (1977a), that 'Among sociologists, this kind of informalizing process manifested itself in an increase in "sociological reflection" and in the "sociology of sociology"' (Wouters 1986: 4–5). Interestingly, at least three books were published in 1970 which included the reflexive phrase 'sociology of sociology' in their titles (Friedrichs 1970; Reynolds & Reynolds 1970; Halmos 1970) and constitute an interesting cluster. The main titles of the last two volumes were *The Sociology of Sociology*, and the Reynolds & Reynolds book was allusively sub-titled *Analysis and Criticism of the Thought, Research, and Ethical Folkways of Sociology and Its Practitioners*. Friedrichs (1970: xx) insisted on the more circumspect title of *A Sociology of Sociology*.

4 I am not claiming that in the monopoly phase all sociologists in Britain embraced structural functionalism. This is particularly not the case in the early part of the phase, when in any case the key works of the American representatives of the tradition had only just been published in the United States. In the late 1940s, following the Labour Party's victory in the 1945 General Election and the building of the welfare state, many groups of sociologists were orientated towards forms of empirical research designed to reveal the extent of social inequalities. This orientation was quite compatible with seeking to embrace the behavioural norms and social codes of the established. It is reasonable to assume that these researchers *both* orientated themselves to the formal, distancing modes of conduct of upper strata *and* identified with the underprivileged. This would probably have expressed itself as a paternalistic stance towards the disadvantaged, whereby these sociologists probably perceived themselves as members of politically responsible élites. This argument is consistent with my general point in the text that in the monopoly phase, although other kinds of sociology were also present within institutionalized sociology, structural functionalism *as a general theory of society* effectively had no rivals. Its equilibrating, consensual tenor went hand in hand with the dominant identification with the established and the mode of individual self-regulation that was involved. This would be particularly so towards the end of the phase and overlapping with the early part of the conflict phase, as functionalism began more and more to fill the institutional space available during the expansion of sociology. At that stage there were fewer competing paradigm groups and the open competition of the conflict phase as such was only nascent.

5 In an earlier formulation of the three phases (Kilminster 1991a) I called this phase the competitive phase.

6 Today, sociologists are divided in their views about this extraordinary period in the development of British sociology. For example, John Hall (1986a) is particularly scathing about the work done in metatheory at this time, dismissing much of it as 'idealist' and as constituting a wrong turn, or a diversion, in the development of sociology from the path of the classics of Marx, Weber and Durkheim. A similar scepticism has been expressed by Skocpol (1986) and Mouzelis (1991) on slightly different grounds, whereas Outhwaite takes a more charitable view, regarding the 'great outpouring of theoretical and programmatic works' (1989: 3) in this period as symptomatic of a healthy and fundamental rethinking of the model of scientific activity generally accepted and followed by sociologists. Giddens (1984) is in broad agreement with that judgement and openly acknowledges what he has learned from that outpouring. The highly critical, dismissive assessments are arguably unsociological, simply rejecting out

of hand, based on unstated value assumptions, something that needs to be explained, understood and assimilated.

7   More common in sociology than in other social sciences are metatheoretical works and other reflections which are trying to subvert the status of sociology as a science or even to deny its very possibility. That such critiques should be so enthusiastically constructed at all by practitioners *within* an institutionalized discipline, apparently oblivious to the incongruity of doing so, is perhaps a measure of its equivocal status at this stage. Over the three phases such critiques have come from a variety of sources, such as Marxism, ethnomethodology and its offshoot Theorizing, feminism, postmodernism and Wittgensteinian philosophy. They were more common during the conflict phase.

8   Epistemological controversies have of course raged in the social sciences in other periods and in other national societies, for example in Germany in the early years of this century and during the Weimar period and during the French Third Republic, when the Durkheimian school was centrally involved (see Shils 1982: ch. 11; Heilbron 1991; Clark 1968; Schiera 1991).

9   There is evidence that in addition to sociology, at least the philosophy of science, anthropology, psychology and political science also went through similar episodes of theoretical tumult in this phase (see, respectively, Feyerabend 1975: 17; Goldschmidt 1966: vii; Henriques *et al.* 1984: 3–4; Almond 1990: 7, 14–15.) More research needs to be carried out both on these disciplines and on others in order to establish how far this trend was a transdisciplinary one. My hunch would be that how far the questionings and controversy went would have depended on the social weight and status of the discipline and the strength of its institutional boundaries.

10 Today, some Parsonians have reassessed the deluge of criticisms which rained down on his work and found many of them to be misguided, invalid or based on misunderstandings of what Parsons was trying to do (see, for example, Münch 1987 and 1988; and the discussion in Chapter 4 of this volume). During the conflict phase, his work was demonized by a younger generation of critics who, via what Gouldner perceptively called a 'newly emerging structure of sentiments' (Gouldner 1970: 7) projected on to Parsons and his followers the source of all they perceived as being wrong with the American dream, Western capitalism and the sociology establishment.

11 Exponents of various forms of *synthesis* in the present phase, in addition to Giddens, include: Collins (1993); Alexander (1987a); Münch (1987, 1988); Coleman (1990); Luhmann (1986); Elias (1939); and, from earlier days, Lenski (1966) and Parsons (1937). Bryant & Jary (1991: 30) refer to the 'renewed prominence for synthesis and pluralism as two sides of a *continuing* dialectic in social theory' and cite in this connection Feyerabend (1981), Bernstein (1983) and Jary (1981, 1989). On the important difference between synthesis and eclecticism, see Sanderson (1987) and Chapter 7 of this volume.

12 Various forms of theoretical *pluralism* are common in the present phase. As Joas (1996: 254) writes: 'Diagnoses of contemporary society may be right to dispute the plausibility of life being increasingly reduced to *one* form of action, arguing instead for a plurality of types of action and for tension or compromise between them.' Alexander (1987b), for example, advocates the working out of disagreements through institutionalized dialogue between paradigms or theories. In a similar vein, it would be possible to list many books that teach sociology as a 'multi-perspective', i.e. pluralistic, social science (Haralambos & Holborn 1995; Cuff *et al.* 1990). In the recently developed methodological strategy of empirical 'adjudicationism' (Wright 1985; Pawson 1989) empirical tests are devised to compare the relative support for competing theories against each other, through maximizing what they have in common. But it should be noted that this strategy assumes and relies upon there being a plurality of rival theories, something that is taken for granted. This methodological programme appears to be a measure designed to legitimate the professional activity of sociology as a science in the post-fragmentation phase. It is noticeable, too, how writers trying to assess the implications for sociology of the controversial current debates about postmodernism and

postmodernity have also been driven inexorably towards a viewpoint of theoretical pluralism and dialogue (Bauman 1992; Boyne & Rattansi 1990; Seidman 1992). Their position, too, is implicated in the centrifugal movement.

13 The idea that culture is constructed by meaning-endowing actors could be read not only in an activistic, leftist fashion as a doctrine informing the changing of the world (which I mentioned in the text) but also in a conservative way. The idea of meaning as vital for human communities can lead to the position in which the authentic, no matter how puzzling or strange, is respected – and that would include tradition. This argument is to be found, for example, in Shils (1981) and in a different form in the rationalism of Winch (1958), Dray (1957) and Louch (1966). (See discussion in Fay 1997: 95.) My argument is that whilst that is so, the conservative tendency was not very prominent in the conflict phase. The traces of the ideas of agency, constructivism, meaning, everyday lifeworld and subjectivism *and the particular connotations they have in sociology today* owe their origins *more* to the activistic strand than to the conservative one, even though the conception of meaning as such is not exclusive to it.

14 Alan Dawe's (1970) conception of the history of sociology as constituting permutations of a basic 'two sociologies' structure, that of social system and social action, is a symptomatic embodiment of the dominant theoretical polarization which imposed itself with such force in the conflict phase. One of the sociologies was said to evince a pessimistic view of humans as passive and was concerned with social order (effectively this referred to Parsons), and the other an optimistic view of humans as active and was concerned with social control, i.e. with people wresting control of social institutions which are their own products. The latter conception partly derived from the young Marx and chimed in with the activistic thrust of many of the schools in this period as well as the aspirations of the emancipatory movements. It also embraced a leftist interpretation of the meaning-endowing capacities of humans (see the previous note). Later, as the theoretical disputes of the conflict phase began to assume a less strident and potentially more conciliatory form, he conceded (Dawe 1979) that the two sociologies were *both* fundamentally sociologies of action, each embracing different *moral* solutions to the problematic of human agency as such.

15 It is sometimes argued that the most cogent explanation for the change in the character of sociology and sociologists in the 1980s is a political one, i.e. their response to the higher education funding policies of the Thatcherite conservative governments. It is this that is sometimes said to explain the recent trends in sociology towards a narrowing of scope, policy relevance, the reprofessionalization of the discipline, decline of Marxism and the prominence of methodology and critical realism. The political successes of these governments, in the sense of their persistent re-election and the social consequences of their policies, are intertwined with the phase of reformalization. I think it would be a mistake, however, to see any one element, say, the Tory policies, in this complex and changing matrix as the one-way 'cause' of another. As I argued in the text, as a result of the far-reaching processes of informalization and globalization, it is plausible that in the present phase more ego-dominated, calculative, reflective and self-interested people are increasingly coming to the fore in Western societies, as the super-ego/ego balance of functions in their personalities shifts more towards greater ego integration. It is *this* development that goes a long way towards explaining why in this phase the individualism associated with consumerism and the economic liberalism of Thatcherism found so fertile a soil in which to grow and flourish in the first place. Moreover, all the theoretical developments also have an *immanent* origin as solutions to problems bequeathed by the previous stage and are transformations of theories and concepts made possible by a higher level of social and theoretical synthesis. Although not unaffected by knowledge-transcendent developments of a political or economic kind, they are not directly caused by, let alone *reducible* to, them.

BIBLIOGRAPHY

Abercrombie, Nicholas, Hill, Stephen, & Turner, Bryan S. (1988) *The Penguin Dictionary of Sociology*, 2nd edn, London: Penguin Books.

Abrams, Philip (1981) 'The Collapse of British Sociology?' in Philip Abrams, Rosemary Deem, Janet Finch & Paul Rock (eds) *Practice and Progress: British Sociology 1950–1980*, London: George Allen & Unwin.

——, Deem, Rosemary, Finch, Janet & Rock, Paul (eds) (1981) *Practice and Progress: British Sociology 1950–1980*, London: George Allen & Unwin.

Adorno, Theodor W. (1973) *Negative Dialectics*, trans. E.B. Ashton, London: Routledge & Kegan Paul.

Albrow, Martin (1992a) 'Globalization', in Tom Bottomore & William Outhwaite (eds) *The Blackwell Dictionary of Twentieth Century Social Thought*, Oxford: Basil Blackwell.

—— (1992b) 'Interpreting the Emergence of the Concept of Globalization', paper presented to the Research Committee for the History of Sociology, ISA, Budapest, 9 April.

—— (1996) *The Global Age: State and Society Beyond Modernity*, Cambridge: Polity Press.

—— & King, Elizabeth (eds) (1990) *Globalization*, London: Sage.

Alexander, Jeffrey C. (1983) *Theoretical Logic in Sociology, Volume 4, The Modern Reconstruction of Classical Thought: Talcott Parsons*, Berkeley: University of California Press.

—— (1987a) *Sociological Theory Since 1945*, London: Hutchinson.

—— (1987b) 'The Centrality of the Classics' in Anthony Giddens & Jonathan Turner (eds) *Social Theory Today*, Oxford: Polity Press.

——, Giesen, Bernhard, Münch, Richard & Smelser, Neil J. (eds) (1987) *The Micro–Macro Link*, London: University of California Press.

Almond, Gabriel (1990) *A Discipline Divided: Schools and Sects in Political Science*, London: Sage.

Althusser, Louis (1969) *For Marx*, London: New Left Books.

Anderson, Perry (1974a) *Passages from Antiquity to Feudalism*, London: New Left Review Editions.

—— (1974b) *Lineages of the Absolutist State*, London: New Left Review Editions.

Anderson, R.J., Hughes, J.A. & Sharrock, W.W. (1985) *The Sociology Game: An Introduction to Sociological Reasoning*, London: Longman.

—— (eds) (1987) *Classic Disputes in Sociology*, London: Allen & Unwin.

Apel, Karl-Otto (1980) *Towards a Transformation of Philosophy*, trans. Glyn Adey and David Frisby, London: Routledge & Kegan Paul.

Archer, Margaret (1982) 'Morphogenesis Versus Structuration: On Combining Structure and Action', *British Journal of Sociology* 33(4), December.

—— (1988) *Culture and Agency: The Place of Culture in Social Theory*, Cambridge: Cambridge University Press.

Arnason, Johann (1987) 'Figurational Sociology as a Counter-Paradigm', *Theory, Culture and Society* 4(2–3), June: 429–56.

Aron, Raymond (1957) *German Sociology*, London: Heinemann.

Arrighi, Giovanni (1978) *The Geometry of Imperialism*, London: New Left Books.

Atkinson, Dick (1971) *Orthodox Consensus and Radical Alternative: A Study in Sociological Theory*, London: Heinemann Educational Books.

Attewell, Paul (1974) 'Ethnomethodology Since Garfinkel', *Theory and Society* 1: 179–210.

Axelos, Kostas (1976) *Alienation, Praxis and Techne in the Thought of Karl Marx*, London: University of Texas Press.

Bachelard, Gaston (1972) *L'Engagement rationaliste*, Paris: Presses Universitaires de France.

Badcock, Christopher R. (1975) *Lévi-Strauss' Structuralism and Sociological Theory*, London: Hutchinson.

Baldamus, W. (1976) *The Structure of Sociological Inference*, London: Martin Robertson.

—— (1977) 'Ludwig Fleck and the Development of the Sociology of Science', in Peter Gleichmann, Johan Goudsblom & Hermann Korte (eds) *Human Figurations: Essays for Norbert Elias*, Amsterdam: Sociologisch Tijdschrift.

—— (1992) 'A Critical Exploration of Habermas', *History of the Human Sciences* 5(2), May.

Banks, Olive (1968) *The Sociology of Education*, London: B.T. Batsford (rpt 1970).

Barnard, F.M. (1965) *Herder's Social and Political Thought: From Enlightenment to Nationalism*, Oxford: Clarendon Press.

Bauman, Zygmunt (1973a) *Culture as Praxis*, London: Routledge & Kegan Paul.

—— (1973b) 'The Structuralist Promise', *British Journal of Sociology* 24(3): 67–83.

—— (1976a) *Socialism: The Active Utopia*, London: George Allen & Unwin.

—— (1976b) *Towards a Critical Sociology: An Essay on Commonsense and Emancipation*, London: Routledge & Kegan Paul.

—— (1989) *Modernity and the Holocaust*, Cambridge: Polity Press.

—— (1992) *Intimations of Postmodernity*, London: Routledge.

Baumer, Franklin L. (1977) *Modern European Thought: Continuity and Change in Ideas, 1600–1950*, London: Macmillan.

Baynes, Kenneth, Bohman, James & McCarthy, Thomas (eds) (1987) *After Philosophy: End or Transformation?* London: MIT Press.

Becker, Henk & Bryant, Christopher (eds) (1989) *What Has Sociology Achieved?*, London: Macmillan.

Becker, Lawrence C. (1977) 'A Definition of Philosophy', *Metaphilosophy* 8(2–3): 249–52.

Bendix, Reinhard (1978) *Kings and People: Power and the Mandate to Rule*, Berkeley: University of California Press.

Bénoist, Jean-Marie (1970) 'The End of Structuralism', *Twentieth Century Studies*, February: 30–54.

—— (1978) *The Structural Revolution*, New York: St Martin's Press.

Benthem van den Bergh, Godfried van (1986) 'The Improvement of Human Means of Orientation: Towards Synthesis in the Social Sciences', in Raymond Apthorpe & Andreás Kráhl (eds) *Development Studies: Critique and Renewal*, Leiden: E.J. Brill: 109–36.

—— (1992) *The Nuclear Revolution and the End of the Cold War: Forced Restraint*, London: Macmillan.

Benton, Ted (1984) *The Rise and Fall of Structural Marxism: Althusser and his Influence*, London: Macmillan.

—— (1977) *Philosophical Foundations of the Three Sociologies*, London: Routledge & Kegan Paul.

Berger, Peter & Luckmann, Thomas (1967) *The Social Construction of Reality*, London: Allen Lane, The Penguin Press.

——— and Pullberg, Stanley (1965) 'Reification and the Sociological Critique of Consciousness', *History and Theory* IV: 2.

Bergesen, Albert (1990) 'Turning World-System Theory on Its Head', *Theory, Culture and Society*, 7(2–3), June: 67–81.

Berki, R.N. (1981) *On Political Realism*, London: J.M. Dent.

Bernstein, Richard J. (1971) *Praxis and Action: Contemporary Philosophies of Action*, Philadelphia: University of Pennsylvania Press.

——— (1976) *The Restructuring of Social and Political Theory*, London: Methuen.

——— (1983) *Beyond Objectivism and Relativism*, Oxford: Blackwell.

Bhaskar, Roy (1978) *A Realist Theory of Science*, 2nd edn, Hemel Hempstead: The Harvester Press.

——— (1979) *The Possibility of Naturalism: A Philosophical Critique of the Contemporary Human Sciences*, Brighton: The Harvester Press.

——— (1986) *Scientific Realism and Human Emancipation*, London: Verso.

Bieri, Peter, Horstmann, Rolf & Kürger, Lorenz (eds) (1979) *Transcendental Arguments and Science*, Dordrecht: D. Reidel.

Blackburn, Robin (ed.) (1972) *Ideology in Social Science: Readings in Critical Social Theory*, London: Fontana/Collins.

Bleicher, Josef (1980) *Contemporary Hermeneutics: Hermeneutics as Method, Philosophy and Critique*, London: Routledge & Kegan Paul.

Bloch, Ernst (1971) *On Karl Marx*, New York: Herder & Herder.

Blum, Alan (1974) *Theorizing*, London: Heinemann.

Blumer, Herbert (1969) *Symbolic Interactionism: Perspective and Method*, Englewood Cliffs, NJ: Prentice Hall.

Boas, G. (1948) 'The Role of Protophilosophies in Intellectual History', *Journal of Philosophy*, 45: 673–84.

Bogner, Artur (1987) 'Elias and the Frankfurt School', *Theory, Culture and Society* 4(2–3), June: 249–85.

Bottomore, Tom & Nisbet, Robert (1979) 'Structuralism', in Tom Bottomore & Robert Nisbet (eds) *A History of Sociological Analysis*, London: Heinemann.

——— & Rubel, M. (eds) (1967) *Karl Marx: Selected Writings in Sociology and Social Philosophy*, Harmondsworth: Penguin.

Bouchard, Donald F. (ed.) (1977) *Language, Counter-Memory, Practice: Selected Essays and Interviews by Michel Foucault*, Ithaca, NY: Cornell University Press.

Bourdieu, Pièrre (1967) 'Sociology and Philosophy in France since 1945: Death and Resurrection of a Philosophy without a Subject', *Social Research* 34: 162–212.

——— (1968) 'Structuralism and Theory of Sociological Knowledge', *Social Research* 35, Winter: 681–706.

——— (1983) 'The Philosophical Institution', in Alan Montefiore (ed.) *Philosophy in France Today*, Cambridge: Cambridge University Press.

——— (1984) *Distinction: A Social Critique of the Judgement of Taste*, trans. Richard Nice, London: Routledge.

——— (1990) *In Other Words: Essays Towards a Reflexive Sociology*, Oxford: Polity Press.

———, Chamboredon, Jean-Claude & Passeron, Jean-Claude (1991) *The Craft of Sociology: Epistemological Preliminaries*, Berlin and New York: Walter de Gruyter.

Boyne, Roy (1995) 'Structuralism', in Bryan Turner (ed.) *The Blackwell Companion to Social Theory*, Oxford: Basil Blackwell.

——— & Rattansi, Ali (eds) (1990) *Postmodernism and Society*, London: Routledge.

Bramsted, E.K. & Melhuish, K.J. (eds) (1978) *Western Liberalism: A History in Documents from Locke to Croce*, London: Longman.

Brewer, Anthony (1980) *Marxist Theories of Imperialism: A Critical Survey*, London: Routledge & Kegan Paul.

Brinkerhoff, David B. and White, Lynn K. (1991) *Sociology*, 3rd edn, St Paul, MN: West.

Brown, Richard (1987) 'Norbert Elias in Leicester: Some Recollections', *Theory, Culture and Society*, 4(2–3), June: 533–9.

Bryant, Christopher (1989a) 'Tales of Innocence and Experience: Developments in Sociological Theory Since 1950' in Henk Becker & Christopher Bryant (eds) *What Has Sociology Achieved?*, London: Macmillan.

—— (1989b) 'Towards Post-empiricist Sociological Theorising', *The British Journal of Sociology* 40(2), June: 319–27.

—— (1992) 'Sociology Without Philosophy? The Case of Giddens' Structuration Theory', *Sociological Theory* 10(1), Spring: 137–49.

—— (1995) *Practical Sociology: Post-empiricism and the Reconstruction of Theory and Application*, Oxford: Polity Press.

—— & Jary, David (eds) (1991) *Giddens' Theory of Structuration: A Critical Appreciation*, London: Routledge.

Buchdahl, Gerd (1961) *The Image of Newton and Locke in the Age of Reason*, London: Sheed & Ward.

Burkitt, Ian (1991) *Social Selves: Theories of the Social Formation of Personality*, London: Sage.

—— (1993) 'Overcoming Metaphysics: Elias and Foucault on Power and Freedom', *Philosophy of the Social Sciences* 23(1): 50–72.

Burr, Vivien (1995) *An Introduction to Social Constructionism*, London: Routledge.

Chiari, Joseph (1975) *Twentieth Century French Thought: From Bergson to Lévi-Strauss*, London: Paul Elek.

Chipp, Herschel B. (1968) *Theories of Modern Art: A Source Book for Artists and Critics*, Berkeley: University of California Press.

Chirot, Daniel (1977) *Social Change in the Twentieth Century*, New York: Harcourt Brace Jovanovich.

Clammer, John (1976) 'Wittgensteinianism and the Social Sciences', *Sociological Analysis and Theory* 6(3): 241–55.

Clark, Terry N. (1968) 'Émile Durkheim and the Institutionalization of Sociology in the French University System', *European Journal of Sociology* IX: 37–71.

—— (ed.) (1969) *Gabriel Tarde: On Communication and Social Influence: Selected Papers*, Chicago and London: University of Chicago Press.

Clarke, Simon (1981) *The Foundations of Structuralism: A Critique of Lévi-Strauss and the Structuralist Movement*, Brighton: The Harvester Press.

Cockburn, Alexander & Blackburn, Robin (eds) (1969) *Student Power: Problems, Diagnosis, Action*, Harmondsworth: Penguin.

Cohen, Jerry M. (1972) 'Philosophy in the Academy', *Radical Philosophy*, issue 2, Summer: 7–9.

Cohen, Percy (1968) *Modern Social Theory*, London: Heinemann.

Cohn-Bendit, Daniel (1969) *Obsolete Communism: The Left-Wing Alternative*, trans. Arnold Pomerans, London: Penguin.

Coleman, James S. (1990) *Foundations of Social Theory*, London: Belknap Press.

Collingwood, R.G. (1946) *The Idea of History*, Oxford: Oxford University Press, 1973.

Collins, Randall (1987) 'Micro–macro Theory of Intellectual Creativity: The Case of German Idealistic Philosophy', *Sociological Theory* 5(1), Spring: 47–69.

—— (1993) *Four Sociological Traditions*, Oxford: Oxford University Press.

Comte, Auguste (1830–42) *Cours de philosophie positive*, trans. Harriet Martineau, 3 vols, London: G. Bell, 1913.

Coser, Lewis A. (1956) *The Functions of Social Conflict*, New York: Free Press.

Coward, Rosalind & Ellis, John (1977) *Language and Materialism: Developments in Semiology and the Theory of the Subject*, London: Routledge & Kegan Paul.

Craib, Ian (1976) *Existentialism and Sociology: A Study of Jean-Paul Sartre*, Cambridge: Cambridge University Press.

—— (1989) *Psychoanalysis and Social Theory: The Limits of Sociology*, London and New York: Harvester Wheatsheaf.

—— (1992) *Anthony Giddens*, London: Routledge.

—— (1997) 'Social Constructionism as a Social Psychosis', *Sociology* 31(1): 1–15.

Crook, Stephen (1991) *Modernist Radicalism and Its Aftermath*, London and New York: Routledge.

Cuff, E.C., Sharrock, W.W. & Francis, D.W. (1990) *Perspectives in Sociology*, London: Unwin Hyman.

Cumming, Robert Denoon (1979) *Starting Point: An Introduction to the Dialectic of Existence*, Chicago: University of Chicago Press.

Dahrendorf, Ralf (1959) *Class and Class Conflict in Industrial Society*, London: Routledge & Kegan Paul (rpt 1972).

—— (1968) *Essays in the Theory of Society*, London: Routledge & Kegan Paul.

Dawe, Alan (1970) 'The Two Sociologies', *British Journal of Sociology* XXI(2): 207–18.

—— (1979) 'Theories of Social Action', in Tom Bottomore & Robert Nisbet (eds) *A History of Sociological Thought*, London: Heinemann.

DeGeorge, Richard & DeGeorge, Fernande (eds) (1972) *The Structuralists: From Marx to Lévi-Strauss*, New York: Anchor Books.

Descombes, Vincent (1980) *Modern French Philosophy*, trans. L. Scott-Fox and J.M. Harding, Cambridge: Cambridge University Press.

Dobson, Kevin (1979) 'Persons and People: Conceptualizing Individuality and Collectivity through Evelyn Waugh's *The Ordeal of Gilbert Pinfold*', *Leeds Occasional Papers in Sociology* No. 9, June.

Dolby, R.G.A. (1972) 'The Sociology of Knowledge in Natural Science', in Barry Barnes (ed.) *Sociology of Science*, London: Penguin.

Dray, William H. (1957) *Laws and Explanation in History*, Oxford: Oxford University Press.

—— (1964) *Philosophy of History*, Englewood Cliffs, NJ: Prentice Hall.

Dunning, Eric (1977) 'In Defense of Developmental Sociology: A Critique of Popper's *Poverty of Historicism* with Special Reference to the Theory of Auguste Comte', *Amsterdams Sociologisch Tijdschrift* 4(3): 327–48.

—— & Rojek, Chris (1993) *Sport and Leisure in the Civilizing Process*, London: Routledge.

Durkheim, Émile (1893) *The Division of Labour in Society*, trans. W.D. Halls, London: Macmillan, 1984.

—— (1897) *Suicide: A Study in Sociology*, trans. John A. Spaulding and George Simpson, ed. George Simpson, London: Routledge (rpt 1970).

—— (1915) *The Elementary Forms of the Religious Life*, trans. Joseph Ward Swain, London: George Allen & Unwin, 1968.

—— (1924) *Sociology and Philosophy*, trans. D.F. Pocock, New York: The Free Press, 1974.

Edwards, E.G. (1982) *Higher Education For All*, London: Spokesman Press.

Eldridge, John (1980) *Recent British Sociology*, London: Macmillan.

Elias, Norbert (1929) 'Contributions to Discussion on Karl Mannheim, Die Bedeutung der Konkurrenz im Gebeite des Geistigen', in *Verhandlungen des Sechsten Deutschen Soziologentages von 17 zu 19 September 1928 in Zürich*, Tübingen: J.C.B. Mohr.

—— (1939) *The Civilizing Process*, 2 vols: *The History of Manners* (1978) and *State Formation and Civilization* (1982), trans. Edmund Jephcott, Oxford: Basil Blackwell [also in 1 vol. (1994)].

—— (1968) 'Introduction' to the 2nd edn of *The Civilizing Process, Vol. I: The History of Manners*, Oxford: Basil Blackwell (1978).

—— (1969) 'Sociology and Psychiatry', in S.H. Foulkes & G. Stewart Prince (eds) *Psychiatry in a Changing Society*, London: Tavistock.

—— (1970) 'Processes of State Formation and Nation-Building', in *Transactions of the Seventh World Congress of Sociology*, Varna, vol. III, Sofia: International Sociological Association, 1972: 274–84.

—— (1971) 'The Sociology of Knowledge: New Perspectives', *Sociology* V, 2 and 3: 149–68, 355–70.

—— (1972) 'Theory of Science and History of Science: Comments on a Recent Discussion', *Economy and Society* I(2): 117–33.

—— (1974) 'The Sciences: Towards a Theory', in Richard Whitley (ed.) *Social Processes of Scientific Development*, London: Routledge.

—— (1977a) 'Adorno-Rede: Respekt und Kritik', in Norbert Elias & Wolf Lepenies (eds) *Zwei Reden anläßlich der Verleihung des Theodor W. Adorno-Preises*, Frankfurt am Main: Suhrkamp Verlag.

—— (1977b) 'Zur Grundlegung einer Theorie sozialer Prozess', *Zeitschrift für Soziologie* 6(2), April: 127–49.

—— (1978a) *What is Sociology?*, London: Hutchinson.

—— (1978b) 'Zum Begriff des Alltags', *Kölner Zeitschrift für Soziologie und Sozialpsychologie*, 30 (Sonderheft): 22–9.

—— (1982) 'Scientific Establishments', in Norbert Elias, Herminio Martins & Richard Whitley (eds) *Scientific Establishments and Hierarchies*, Dordrecht and London: Reidel.

—— (1983) *The Court Society*, Oxford: Basil Blackwell.

—— (1984) 'On the Sociogenesis of Sociology', *Sociologisch Tijdschrift* 11(1), May: 14–52.

—— (1985) *The Loneliness of the Dying*, Oxford: Basil Blackwell.

—— (1987a) *Involvement and Detachment*, Oxford: Basil Blackwell.

—— (1987b) 'The Retreat of the Sociologists into the Present', *Theory, Culture and Society* 4(2–3), June: 223–47.

—— (1991a) *The Symbol Theory*, ed. Richard Kilminster, London: Sage.

—— (1991b) *The Society of Individuals*, Oxford: Basil Blackwell.

—— (1992) *Time: An Essay*, Oxford: Basil Blackwell.

—— (1994) *Reflections on a Life*, trans. Edmund Jephcott, Cambridge: Polity Press.

—— (1996) *The Germans: Power Struggles and the Development of Habitus in the Nineteenth and Twentieth Centuries*, ed. Michael Schröter, trans. Eric Dunning and Stephen Mennell, Cambridge: Polity Press.

—— & Dunning, Eric (1986) *Quest for Excitement: Sport and Leisure in the Civilizing Process*, Oxford: Basil Blackwell.

Erikson, Erik H. (1958) *Young Man Luther*, New York: W.W. Norton.

—— (1968) *Identity: Youth and Crisis*, London: Faber & Faber (1983).

Evans, David (1951) *Social Romanticism in France 1830–1848*, Oxford: Oxford University Press.

Fay, Brian (1975) *Social Theory and Political Practice*, London: Allen & Unwin.

—— (1997) *Contemporary Philosophy of Social Science: A Multicultural Approach*, Oxford: Basil Blackwell.

Featherstone, Mike (ed.) (1990) *Global Culture: Nationalism, Globalization and Modernity*, London: Sage.

Ferrante, Joan (1992) *Sociology: A Global Perspective*, Belmont: Wadsworth.

Feuer, Lewis (1958) 'The Sociology of Philosophic Ideas', *Pacific Sociological Review* I(2): 77–80.

—— (1970) 'Lawless Sensations and Categorial Defenses: The Unconscious Sources of Kant's Philosophy', in Charles Hanly and Morris Lazerowitz (eds) *Psychoanalysis and Philosophy*, New York: International Universities Press.

Feyerabend, Paul (1975) *Against Method: Outline of an Anarchistic Theory of Knowledge*, London: Verso.

—— (1981) *Realism, Rationalism and Scientific Method*, Cambridge: Cambridge University Press.

Filmer, Paul, Phillipson, M. & Silverman, D. (eds) (1972) *New Directions in Sociological Theory*, London: Collier-Macmillan.

Finnegan, R. & Horton, R. (eds) (1973) *Modes of Thought: Essays on Thinking in Western and Non-Western Societies*, London: Faber & Faber.

Fletcher, Ronald (1976) 'Introduction', in Kenneth Thompson, *Auguste Comte: The Foundation of Sociology*, London: Thomas Nelson.

Foucault, Michel (1966) *The Order of Things: An Archaeology of the Human Sciences*, London: Tavistock (1974).

—— (1969) *The Archaeology of Knowledge*, trans. A.M. Sheridan Smith, London: Tavistock (1974).

—— (1970) 'Preface', *The Order of Things*, English edn, London: Tavistock (1974).

—— (1971) 'Nietzsche, Genealogy and History', in Donald F. Bouchard (1977) *Language, Counter-memory, Practice: Selected Essays and Interviews by Michel Foucault*, Ithaca, NY: Cornell University Press.

—— (1975) *Discipline and Punish: The Birth of the Clinic*, trans. Alan Sheridan, Harmondsworth: Penguin (1979).

—— (1976) *The History of Sexuality: Vol. I: An Introduction*, trans. Robert Hurley, Harmondsworth: Penguin (1981).

Freeden, Michael (1978) *The New Liberalism: An Ideology of Social Reform*, Oxford: Clarendon Press.

Freud, Sigmund (1933) *New Introductory Lectures on Psychoanalysis*, London: Hogarth Press (1957).

Freund, Julien (1978) 'German Sociology in the Time of Max Weber', in Tom Bottomore and Robert Nisbet (eds) *A History of Sociological Analysis*, London: Heinemann.

Friedrichs, Robert W. (1970) *A Sociology of Sociology*, New York: Collier-Macmillan.

Frisby, David (1992) *The Alienated Mind: The Sociology of Knowledge in Germany 1918–1933*, 2nd edn, London: Routledge.

—— & Sayer, Derek (1986) *Society*, London: Tavistock.

Gadamer, Hans-Georg (1960) *Truth and Method*, London: Sheed & Ward (1975).

Gardner, Howard (1981) *The Quest for Mind: Piaget, Lévi-Strauss, and the Structuralist Movement*, 2nd edn, Chicago and London: University of Chicago Press.

Garfinkel, Harold (1967) *Studies in Ethnomethodology*, Englewood Cliffs, NJ: Prentice Hall.

Garrett, William R. (1992) 'Thinking Religion in the Global Circumstance: A Critique of Roland Robertson's Globalization Theory', *Journal for the Scientific Study of Religion* 31(3): 296–332.

Gay, Peter (1973) *The Enlightenment: An Interpretation, Vol. 2: The Science of Freedom*, London: Wildwood House.

Gehlke, Charles E. (1915) *Émile Durkheim's Contributions to Sociological Theory*, New York: Columbia University Press.

Gellner, Ernest (1964) *Thought and Change*, London: Weidenfeld & Nicolson.

Gergen, Kenneth (1985) 'The Social Constructionist Movement in Modern Psychology', *American Psychologist* 40: 266–75.

Gerth, Hans & Mills, C. Wright (eds) (1970) *From Max Weber: Essays in Sociology*, London: Routledge & Kegan Paul.

Giddens, Anthony (1965) 'Georg Simmel (1858–1917)', in Timothy Raison (ed.) (1969) *The Founding Fathers of Social Science*, Harmondsworth: Penguin.

—— (1971) *Capitalism and Modern Social Theory: An Analysis of the Writings of Marx, Durkheim and Max Weber*, Cambridge: Cambridge University Press.

—— (1973) *The Class Structure of the Advanced Societies*, London: Hutchinson.

—— (1974) (ed.) *Positivism and Sociology*, London: Heinemann.

—— (1976) *New Rules of Sociological Method: A Positive Critique of Interpretative Sociologies*, London: Hutchinson.

—— (1977) *Studies in Social and Political Theory*, London: Hutchinson.

—— (1979) *Central Problems in Social Theory*, London: Macmillan.

—— (1981) *A Contemporary Critique of Historical Materialism*, London: Macmillan.

—— (1982a) *Profiles and Critiques in Social Theory*, London: Macmillan.

——(1982b) *Sociology: A Brief but Critical Introduction*, London: Macmillan.

—— (1982c) 'Historical Materialism Today: An Interview', *Theory, Culture and Society* I(2), September: 63–77.

—— (1982d) 'On the Relation of Sociology to Philosophy', in Paul Secord (ed.) *Explaining Human Behaviour: Consciousness, Human Action and Social Structure*, London: Sage.

—— (1982e) 'Power, the Dialectic of Control and Class Structuration', in Anthony Giddens & Gavin Mackenzie (eds) *Social Class and the Division of Labour: Essays in honour of Ilya Neustadt*, Cambridge: Cambridge University Press.

—— (1984) *The Constitution of Society*, Cambridge: Polity Press.

—— (1985) *The Nation State and Violence*, Cambridge: Polity Press.

—— (1990) *The Consequences of Modernity*, Cambridge: Polity Press.

—— (1991) *Modernity and Self-Identity: Self and Society in the Late Modern Age*, Cambridge: Polity.

—— (1997) *Sociology*, 3rd edn, Oxford: Polity Press.

—— & Turner, Jonathan (eds) (1987) *Social Theory Today*, Oxford: Polity Press.

Gillespie, Michael Allen (1984) *Hegel, Heidegger and the Ground of History*, Chicago and London: University of Chicago Press.

Gleichmann, Peter, Goudsblom, Johan & Korte, Hermann (eds) (1977) *Human Figurations: Essays for Norbert Elias*, Amsterdam: Sociologisch Tijdschrift.

Glover, Edward (1966) 'Metapsychology of Metaphysics', *Psychoanalytical Quarterly* 35.

Glucksmann, Miriam (1974) *Structuralist Analysis in Contemporary Social Thought: A Comparison of the Theories of Claude Lévi-Strauss and Louis Althusser*, London: Routledge & Kegan Paul.

Godelier, Maurice (1967) 'System, Structure and Contradiction in *Capital*', in John Savile & Ralph Miliband (eds) *The Socialist Register*, London: Merlin Press.

Goff, Tom W. (1980) *Marx and Mead: Contributions to a Sociology of Knowledge*, London: Routledge & Kegan Paul.

Goldschmidt, Walter (1966) *Comparative Functionalism: An Essay in Anthropological Theory*, Berkeley and Los Angeles, CA: University of California Press.

Gordon, Colin (ed.) (1977) *Power/Knowledge: Selected Interviews and Other Writings 1972–1977 by Michel Foucault*, Brighton: Harvester Press (1980).

Goudsblom, Johan (1977a) *Sociology in the Balance*, Oxford: Basil Blackwell.

—— (1977b) 'Responses to Norbert Elias's Work in England, Germany, the Netherlands and France', in Peter Gleichmann, Johan Goudsblom & Hermann Korte (eds) *Human Figurations: Essays for Norbert Elias*, Amsterdam: Sociologisch Tijdschrift.

—— (1987) 'The Sociology of Norbert Elias: Its Resonance and Significance', *Theory, Culture and Society* 4(2–3), June: 323–37.

—— (1989) 'Human History and Long-Term Social Processes', in Johan Goudsblom, E.L. Jones & Stephen Mennell (eds) *Human History and Social Process*, Exeter: University of Exeter Press.

—— (1990) 'The Humanities and the Social Sciences', in E. Zürcher & T. Langendorff (eds) *The Humanities in the Nineties: A View from the Netherlands*, Amsterdam: Swets & Zeitlinger.

——, Jones, E.L. & Mennell, Stephen (eds) (1989) *Human History and Social Process*, Exeter: University of Exeter Press.

Gould, Julius (1977) *The Attack on Higher Education: Marxist and Radical Penetration: Report of a Study Group of the Institute for the Study of Conflict*, London: Institute for the Study of Conflict.

Gouldner, Alvin (1970) *The Coming Crisis of Western Sociology*, London: Heinemann.

Gramsci, Antonio (1971) *Selections from the Prison Notebooks of Antonio Gramsci*, ed. and trans. Quintin Hoare & Geoffrey Nowell Smith, London: Lawrence & Wishart.

Grünwald, Ernst (1934a) 'The Sociology of Knowledge and Epistemology', trans. Rainer Koehne, in James Curtis & John W. Petras (eds) *The Sociology of Knowledge: A Reader*, London: Gerald Duckworth (1970).

—— (1934b) 'Systematic Analyses', trans. Rainer Koehne, in James Curtis & John W. Petras (eds) *The Sociology of Knowledge: A Reader*, London: Gerald Duckworth (1970).

Habermas, Jürgen (1970a) 'On Systematically Distorted Communication', *Inquiry* 13: 205–18.

—— (1970b) 'Toward a Theory of Communicative Competence', in Hans Peter Drietzel (ed.) *Recent Sociology No. 2*, New York: Macmillan.

—— (1972) *Knowledge and Human Interests*, London: Heinemann.

—— (1974) *Theory and Practice*, trans. John Viertel, London: Heinemann.

—— (1987) *Theory of Communicative Action*, 2 vols, London: Heinemann.

Hall, John (1986a) 'Theory', in M. Haralambos (ed.) *Developments in Sociology: An Annual Review*, Ormskirk: Causeway Press.

—— (1986b) *Powers and Liberties*, London: Penguin.

Halmos, Paul (ed.) (1970) *The Sociology of Sociology*, The Sociological Review Monograph Number 16, Keele: University of Keele.

Halsey, A.H., Floud, J. & Anderson, C.A. (eds) (1961) *Education, Economy and Society*, Glencoe, IL: Free Press.

Hankinson, Jim (1985) *Bluff Your Way in Philosophy*, London: The Bluffers Guides.

Hanly, Charles & Lazerowitz, Morris (eds) (1970) *Psychoanalysis and Philosophy*, New York: International Universities Press.

Hannerz, Ulf (1990) 'Cosmopolitans and Locals in World Culture', *Theory, Culture and Society* 7(2–3), June: 237–51.

Haralambos, Michael & Holborn, Martin (1995) *Sociology: Themes and Perspectives*, 4th edn, London: HarperCollins.

Harris, H.S. (1972) *Hegel's Development: Towards the Sunlight 1770–1801*, Oxford: Oxford University Press.

Hartmann, Klaus (1966) 'On Taking the Transcendental Turn', *Review of Metaphysics* 20(2): 223–49.

Hawthorn, Geoffrey (1976) *Enlightenment and Despair: A History of Sociology*, Cambridge: Cambridge University Press.

Hegel, Georg W.F. (1796) 'Earliest System-Programme of German Idealism', in H.S. Harris (1972) *Hegel's Development: Towards the Sunlight 1770–1801*, Oxford: Oxford University Press.

—— (1798) 'Frankfurt Sketch on Faith and Being', in H.S. Harris (1972) *Hegel's Development: Towards the Sunlight 1770–1801*, Oxford: Oxford University Press.

—— (1807) *The Phenomenology of Mind*, trans. J.B. Baillie, London: George Allen & Unwin (1966).

—— (1812) *The Science of Logic*, trans. A.V. Miller, London: George Allen & Unwin (1969).

—— (1820) 'Preface', *The Philosophy of Right*, trans. T.M. Knox, Oxford: Oxford University Press (1971).

—— (1822) 'Reason and Religious Truth', foreword to H.Fr.W. Hinrich, *Die Religion im inneren Verhältnisse zum Wissenschaft*, trans. A.V. Miller, in Frederick G. Weiss (ed.) (1974) *Beyond Epistemology: New Studies in the Philosophy of Hegel*, The Hague: Martinus Nijhoff.

—— (1830a) *The Logic* [first part of *The Encyclopaedia of the Philosophical Sciences*], trans. William Wallace, 2nd edn, London: Oxford University Press (1892, rpt 1972).

—— (1830b) *The Philosophy of History*, trans. J. Sibree, New York: Dover (1956).

Heidegger, Martin (1927) *Being and Time*, trans. John Macquarrie & Edward Robinson, Oxford: Basil Blackwell (1973).

Heilbron, Johan (1984) 'Interview with Norbert Elias' (manuscript).

—— (1991) 'The Tripartite Division of French Social Science: A Long-Term Perspective', in Peter Wagner, Björn Wittrock & Richard Whitley (eds) *Discourses on Society: The Shaping of the Social Science Disciplines*, Dordrecht: Kluwer Academic.

—— (1995) *The Rise of Social Theory*, Cambridge: Polity Press.

Heinemann, F.H. (1953) *Existentialism and the Modern Predicament*, London: Adam & Charles Black.

Hekman, Susan (1986) *Hermeneutics and the Sociology of Knowledge*, Notre Dame: University of Notre Dame Press.

Heller, Agnes (1996) 'Omnivorous Modernity', in Richard Kilminster & Ian Varcoe (eds) *Culture, Modernity and Revolution: Essays in Honour of Zygmunt Bauman*, London: Routledge.

Hempel, Carl G. (1966) *Philosophy of Natural Science*, Englewood Cliffs, NJ: Prentice Hall.

Henriques, Julian, Holloway, Wendy, Urwin, Cathy, Venn, Couze & Walkerdine, Valerie (1984) *Changing the Subject: Psychology, Social Regulation and Subjectivity*, London and New York: Methuen.

Hesse, Mary (1980) *Revolutions and Reconstructions in the Philosophy of Science*, Brighton: Harvester Press.

Hill, Richard J. & Crittenden, Kathleen S. (eds) (1968) *Proceedings of the Purdue Symposium on Ethnomethodology*, Lafayette, Indiana: Institute for the Study of Social Change, Purdue University.

Hirst, Paul (1982) 'The Social Theory of Anthony Giddens: A New Syncretism?', *Theory, Culture and Society* 1(2), Autumn: 78–82.

Hoffman, Kurt (1957) 'The Basic Concepts of Jaspers' Philosophy', in Paul Arthur Schilpp (ed.) *The Philosophy of Karl Jaspers*, La Salle, IL: Open Court.

Hoffman, Louise E. (1982) 'From Instinct to Identity: Implications of Changing Psychoanalytic Concepts of Social Life from Freud to Erikson', *Journal of the History of the Behavioral Sciences* 18: 130–46.

Holmwood, John (1996) *Founding Sociology? Talcott Parsons and the Idea of General Theory*, London and New York: Longman.

Holton, R.J. & Turner, Bryan (1986) *Talcott Parsons on Economy and Society*, London: Routledge.

Honigsheim, Paul (1923) 'Die soziologische Bedeutung des Nominalismus', in M. Pályi (ed.) *Hauptprobleme der Soziologie*, vol. II, Munich and Leipzig: Duncker & Humblot.

Horkheimer, Max & Adorno, Theodor (1944) *The Dialectic of Enlightenment*, New York: Herder & Herder (1972).

Hoult, Thomas F. (ed.) (1980) *Dictionary of Modern Sociology*, Totowa, NJ: Littlefield Adams.

Hoy, David Couzens (ed.) (1986) *Foucault: A Critical Reader*, Oxford: Basil Blackwell.

Husserl, Edmund (1931) *Cartesian Meditations*, trans. Dorion Cairns, The Hague: Martinus Nijhoff (1977).

—— (1938) *The Crisis of European Sciences and Transcendental Phenomenology*, trans. David Carr, Evanston, IL: Northwestern University Press (1970).

Iggers, Georg (1968) *The German Conception of History: The National Tradition of Historical Thought from Herder to the Present*, Middletown, CT: Wesleyan University Press.

Jary, David (1981) 'The "New Realism" in Sociological Theory', in P. Abrams & P. Laithwaite (eds) *Development and Diversity: British Sociology 1950–80*, vol. 2, London: British Sociological Association.

—— (1989) 'Beyond Objectivity and Relativism: Paul Feyerabend's Two "Argumentative Chains"', *Poznan Studies in the Philosophy of Science and Humanities* 20: 1–13.

—— & Jary, Julia (eds) (1991) *Collins Dictionary of Sociology*, London: HarperCollins.

Joas, Hans (1991) 'Between Power Politics and Pacifist Utopia: Peace and War in Sociological Theory', *Current Sociology* 9(1), Spring: 47–66.

—— (1992) 'Pragmatism', in Tom Bottomore & William Outhwaite (eds) *The Blackwell Dictionary of Twentieth Century Social Thought*, Oxford: Basil Blackwell.

—— (1993) *Pragmatism and Social Theory*, Chicago: University of Chicago Press.

—— (1996) *The Creativity of Action*, Cambridge: Polity Press.

Johnson, Terry, Dandeker, Christopher, & Ashworth, Clive (1984) *The Structure of Social Theory*, London: Macmillan.

Kaufmann, Walter (1966) *Hegel: A Reinterpretation*, New York: Anchor Books.

Keat, Russell & Urry, John (1975) *Social Theory as Science*, London: Routledge & Kegan Paul.

Kecskemeti, Paul (1953) 'Introduction', in Karl Mannheim, *Essays on Sociology and Social Psychology*, London: Routledge & Kegan Paul.

Kerbo, Harold R. (1989) *Sociology: Social Structure and Social Conflict*, New York: Macmillan.

Kettler, David, Meja, Volker & Stehr, Nico (1984) *Karl Mannheim*, London: Tavistock.

—— (1993) 'Their "Own Peculiar Way": Karl Mannheim and the Rise of Women', *International Sociology* 8(1) March: 5–55.

Kilminster, Richard (1975) 'On the Structure of Critical Thinking', *Leeds Occasional Papers in Sociology* no. 2, Department of Sociology, University of Leeds.

—— (1979) *Praxis and Method: A Sociological Dialogue with Lukács, Gramsci and the Early Frankfurt School*, London: Routledge & Kegan Paul.

—— (1982a) 'Theory and Practice in Marx and Marxism', in G.H.R. Parkinson (ed.) *Marx and Marxisms*, Cambridge: Cambridge University Press.

—— (1982b) 'Zur Utopiediskussion aus soziologischer Sicht', in Wilhelm Voßkamp (ed.) *Utopieforschung: Interdisziplinäre Studien zur neuzeitlichen Utopia*, Band 1, Stuttgart: J.B. Metzler Verlag.

—— (1983) 'From the Standpoint of Eternity', *Theory, Culture and Society* 2(1): 118–33.

—— (1988) 'Review of *Hermeneutics and the Sociology of Knowledge* by Susan Hekman', *Contemporary Sociology* 17(3), May: 377–80.

—— (1989a) 'Sociology and the Professional Culture of Philosophers', in Hans Haferkamp (ed.) *Social Structure and Culture*, Berlin and New York: Walter de Gruyter.

—— (1989b) 'The Limits of Transcendental Sociology', *Theory, Culture and Society* 6(4): 655–63.

—— (1991a) 'Structuration Theory as a World-View', in Christopher Bryant & David Jary (eds) *Giddens' Theory of Structuration: A Critical Appreciation*, London: Routledge.

—— (1991b) 'Editor's Introduction', in Norbert Elias, *The Symbol Theory*, London: Sage.

—— (1991c) 'Evaluating Elias', *Theory, Culture and Society* 8(2), May: 165–76.

—— (1992a) 'Alienation', in Tom Bottomore & William Outhwaite (eds) *The Blackwell Dictionary of Twentieth Century Social Thought*, Oxford: Basil Blackwell.

—— (1992b) 'Theory', in Mike Haralambos (ed.) *Developments in Sociology*, Ormskirk: Causeway Press.

——(1992c) 'Phenomenology', in Tom Bottomore & William Outhwaite (eds) *The Blackwell Dictionary of Twentieth Century Social Thought*, Oxford: Basil Blackwell.

——(1992d) 'Praxis', in Tom Bottomore & William Outhwaite (eds) *The Blackwell Dictionary of Twentieth Century Social Thought*, Oxford: Basil Blackwell.

—— (1993) 'Norbert Elias and Karl Mannheim: Closeness and Distance', *Theory, Culture and Society* 10(3): 81–114.

—— (1994) '*The Symbol Theory* as a Research Programme', paper presented to the Ad Hoc Sessions on Figurational Sociology, XIII ISA World Congress of Sociology, Bielefeld, 18–23 July.

—— (1997) 'Globalization as an Emergent Concept', in Alan Scott (ed.) *The Limits of Globalization: Cases and Arguments*, London: Routledge.

—— & Varcoe, Ian (1992) 'Sociology, Postmodernity and Exile: An Interview with Zygmunt Bauman', in Z. Bauman, *Intimations of Postmodernity*, London: Routledge.

—— (1996a) *Culture, Modernity and Revolution: Essays in Honour of Zygmunt Bauman*, London: Routledge.

—— (1996b) 'Introduction: Intellectual Migration and Sociological Insight', in Richard Kilminster & Ian Varcoe (eds) *Culture, Modernity and Revolution: Essays in Honour of Zygmunt Bauman*, London: Routledge.

—— (1996c) 'Culture and Power in the Writings of Zygmunt Bauman', in Richard Kilminster & Ian Varcoe (eds) *Culture, Modernity and Revolution: Essays in Honour of Zygmunt Bauman*, London: Routledge.

—— & Wouters, Cas (1995) 'From Philosophy to Sociology: Elias and the Neo-Kantians: A Response to Benjo Maso', *Theory, Culture and Society* 12(3), August: 81–120.

Kitching, Gavin (1988) *Karl Marx and the Philosophy of Praxis*, London: Routledge.

Knorr-Cetina, Karin D. (1983) 'Towards a Constructivist Interpretation of Science', in Karin D. Knorr-Cetina & Michael Mulkay (eds) *Science Observed: Perspectives on the Social Study of Science*, London: Sage.

Kohn, Hans (1971) 'Nationalism and Internationalism', in Warren Wagar (ed.) *History and the Idea of Mankind*, Albuquerque: University of New Mexico Press.

Kolakowski, Leszek (1971) 'Karl Marx and the Classical Definition of Truth', in *Marxism and Beyond*, London: Paladin.

—— (1972) *Positivist Philosophy: From Hume to the Vienna Circle*, trans. Norbert Guterman, Harmondsworth: Penguin.

Korte, Hermann (1988) *Über Norbert Elias*, Frankfurt: Suhrkamp Verlag.

Kranendonk, Willem H. (1990) *Society as Process: A Bibliography of Figurational Sociology in the Netherlands (up to 1989): Sociogenetic and Psychogenetic Studies*, Amsterdam: Publikatiereeks Sociologisch Instituut, Universiteit van Amsterdam.

Kuhn, Thomas (1962) *The Structure of Scientific Revolutions*, 2nd edn, London: Chicago University Press (1970).

Kurzweil, Edith (1980) *The Age of Structuralism: Lévi-Strauss to Foucault*, New York: Columbia University Press.

Kuzmics, Helmut (1997) 'State Formation, Economic Development and Civilization in North-Western and Central Europe: A Comparison of Long-Term Civilizing Processes in Austria and England', *Geschichte und Gegenwart* 2: 16 Jahrgang, May.

La Capra, Dominick (1972) *Émile Durkheim, Sociologist and Philosopher*, Ithaca, NY: Cornell University Press.

Lachs, John (1967) *Marxist Philosophy: A Bibliographical Guide*, Chapel Hill: University of North Carolina Press.

Lakatos, Imre (1976) *Proofs and Refutations*, Cambridge: Cambridge University Press.

Lane, Michael (ed.) (1970) *Introduction to Structuralism*, New York: Basic Books.

Lassman, Peter, Velody, Irving & Martins, Herminio (eds) (1989) *Max Weber's 'Science as a Vocation'*, London: Unwin Hyman.

Latour, Bruno & Woolgar, Steve (1979) *Laboratory Life: The Social Construction of Scientific Knowledge*, London: Sage.

Law, John (ed.) (1986) *Power, Action and Belief: A New Sociology of Knowledge?*, Sociological Review Monograph 32, London: Routledge.

Layder, Derek (1994) *Understanding Social Theory*, London: Sage.

Leach, Edmund (1970) *Lévi-Strauss*, London: Fontana/Collins.

Leclerq, Jacques (1955) 'La Sociologie de la Philosophie', *Bulletin de l'Institut de Recherches Economiques et Sociales* 21(7): 677–92.

Lenin, Vladimir I. (1913) 'The Three Sources and Three Component Parts of Marxism', in Karl Marx & Frederick Engels, *Selected Works in One Volume*, London: Lawrence & Wishart (1973).

Lenski, Gerhard (1966) *Power and Privilege: A Theory of Social Stratification*, New York: McGraw-Hill.

—— & Lenski, Jean (1987) *Human Societies: An Introduction to Macro-sociology*, New York: McGraw-Hill.

Leventhal, Richard S. (1987) 'Critique of Subjectivity: Herder's Foundation of the Human Sciences', in Kurt Mueller-Vollmer (ed.) *Herder Today*, Berlin and New York: Walter de Gruyter.

Lévi-Strauss, Claude (1955) *Tristes tropiques*, trans. John & Doreen Weightman, New York: Atheneum (1978).

—— (1958) *Structural Anthropology*, trans. Claire Jacobson and Brooke Grundfest Schoepf, Harmondsworth: Penguin (1977).

—— (1962) *The Savage Mind*, London: Weidenfeld & Nicolson (1976).

—— (1966a) *The Elementary Structures of Kinship*, trans. J. Bell, J. von Sturmer & Rodney Needham, London: Eyre & Spottiswoode (1969).

—— (1966b) *From Honey to Ashes: Introduction to a Science of Mythology: 2*, trans. John & Doreen Weightman, New York: Harper & Row (1973).

—— (1968) *The Origin of Table Manners: Introduction to a Science of Mythology: 3*, trans. John & Doreen Weightman, New York: Harper & Row (1978).

—— (1969) *The Raw and the Cooked: Introduction to a Science of Mythology: 1*, trans. John & Doreen Weightman, New York: Harper & Row (1975).

—— (1979) *Myth and Meaning*, New York: Schocken Books.

Livergood, Norman (1967) *Activity in Marx's Philosophy*, The Hague: Martinus Nijhoff.

Lobkowicz, Nicholas (1967) *Theory and Practice: History of a Concept from Aristotle to Marx*, Indiana: Notre Dame University Press.

Lockwood, David (1956) 'Some Remarks on the Social System', *British Journal of Sociology* 7: 134–43.

Lodge, David (1989) *Nice Work*, Harmondsworth: Penguin.

Louch, A.R. (1966) *Explanation and Human Action*, Oxford: Basil Blackwell.

Löwith, Karl (1932) *Max Weber and Karl Marx*, trans. Hans Fantel, ed. Tom Bottomore & William Outhwaite, London: George Allen & Unwin (1982).

—— (1941) *From Hegel to Nietzsche*, London: Constable (1964).

Loye, David (1991) 'Chaos and Transformation: Implications of Nonequilibrium Theory for Social Science and Society', in Ervin Laszlo (ed.) *The New Evolutionary Paradigm*, New York: Gordon & Breach Science Publishers.

Luckmann, Thomas (ed.) (1978) *Phenomenology and Sociology*, Harmondsworth: Penguin.

—— (1983) *Lifeworld and Social Realities*, London: Heinemann.

Luhmann, Niklas (1986) *Ecological Communication*, trans. J. Bednarz, Cambridge: Polity Press.

Lukács, Georg (1923) *History and Class Consciousness: Studies in Marxist Dialectics*, trans. Rodney Livingstone, London: Merlin Press (1971).

—— (1926), 'Moses Hess and the Problem of Idealist Dialectics', in Rodney Livingstone (ed.) (1972) *Georg Lukács, Political Writings 1919–1929*, London: New Left Books.

Lukes, Steven (1975) *Émile Durkheim: His Life and Work: A Historical and Critical Study*, Harmondsworth: Penguin.

—— (1977) *Essays in Social Theory*, London: Macmillan.

—— (ed.) (1992) *Power*, Oxford: Basil Blackwell.

Lyotard, Jean-François (1979) *The Postmodern Condition: A Report on Knowledge*, trans. Geoffrey Bennington & Brian Massumi, Manchester: Manchester University Press (1984).

McHugh, Peter, Raffel, Stanley, Foss, Daniel C. & Blum, Alan (1974) *On The Beginning of Social Enquiry*, London: Routledge.

McLellan, David (ed.) (1971) *Karl Marx: Early Texts*, Oxford: Basil Blackwell.

McMullin, Ernan (1970) 'The History and Philosophy of Science', *Minnesota Studies in the Philosophy of Science, vol. V*, Minneapolis: Minnesota University Press.

Mann, Michael (ed.) (1983) *The Macmillan Student Encyclopaedia of Sociology*, London: Macmillan (rpt 1989).

—— (1986) *The Sources of Social Power*, Cambridge: Cambridge University Press.

Mannheim, Karl (1922) 'The Structural Analysis of Epistemology', in *Essays on Sociology and Social Psychology*, London: Routledge & Kegan Paul (1953).

—— (1925) 'The Problem of a Sociology of Knowledge', in *Essays on the Sociology of Knowledge*, Routledge & Kegan Paul (1972).

—— (1927) 'Conservative Thought', in *Essays on Sociology and Social Psychology*, London: Routledge & Kegan Paul (1953).

—— (1928) 'Competition as a Cultural Phenomenon', in *Essays on the Sociology of Knowledge*, London: Routledge & Kegan Paul (1972).

—— (1929) *Ideology and Utopia*, trans. Edward A. Shils & Louis Wirth, London: Routledge & Kegan Paul (1968).

—— (1932–3) 'Towards a Sociology of the Mind', in *Essays on the Sociology of Culture*, London: Routledge & Kegan Paul (1956).

—— (1933) 'The Democratization of Culture', in *Essays on the Sociology of Culture*, London: Routledge & Kegan Paul (1956).

—— (1934) 'German Sociology (1918–1933)', in *Essays on Sociology and Social Psychology*, London: Routledge & Kegan Paul (1953).

—— (1940) *Man and Society in an Age of Reconstruction*, London: Routledge & Kegan Paul.

—— (1946) 'Foreword', in Viola Klein, *The Feminine Character: History of an Ideology*, London: Kegan Paul, Trench, Trübner & Co.

—— (1953) *Essays on Sociology and Social Psychology*, London: Routledge & Kegan Paul.

—— (1972) *Essays on the Sociology of Knowledge*, London: Routledge & Kegan Paul (5th imp., 1972).

—— & Stewart, W.A.C. (1935) *An Introduction to the Sociology of Education*, London: Routledge & Kegan Paul (1962).

Manser, A.R. (1973) 'The End of Philosophy: Marx and Wittgenstein', Inaugural Lecture, University of Southampton.

Marcuse, Herbert (1936) 'The Concept of Essence', in *Negations*, trans. Jeremy J. Shapiro, London: Allen Lane, Penguin (1968).

—— (1941) *Reason and Revolution: Hegel and the Rise of Social Theory*, London: Routledge & Kegan Paul (1968).

Marshall, T.H. (1982) 'Foreword', in Anthony Giddens & Gavin Mackenzie (eds) *Social Class and the Division of Labour: Essays in Honour of Ilya Neustadt*, Cambridge: Cambridge University Press.

Martins, Herminio (1974) 'Time and Theory in Sociology', in John Rex (ed.) *Approaches to Sociology: An Introduction to Major Trends in British Sociology*, London: Routledge & Kegan Paul.

Marx, Karl (1843) 'Contribution to the Critique of Hegel's *Philosophy of Right*', in David McLellan (ed.) (1971) *Karl Marx: Early Texts*, Oxford: Basil Blackwell.

—— (1844) *Economic and Philosophic Manuscripts*, trans. Martin Milligan, Moscow: Progress (1967).

—— (1845) *Theses on Feuerbach*, in *Selected Works in One Volume*, London: Lawrence & Wishart (1971).

—— (1857a) 'Introduction', in Maurice Dobb (ed.) (1971) *A Contribution to the Critique of Political Economy*, London: Lawrence & Wishart.

—— (1857b) *Grundrisse: Foundations of the Critique of Political Economy (Rough Draft)*, trans. Martin Nicolaus, Harmondsworth: Penguin (1973).

—— (1859) 'Preface to *A Contribution to the Critique of Political Economy*', in Karl Marx & Frederick Engels (1974) *Selected Works in One Volume*, London: Lawrence & Wishart.

—— (1867) *Capital*, vol. I, Moscow: Foreign Languages Publishing House (1954).

—— (1873) 'Afterword', in *Capital*, 2nd German edn, London: Lawrence & Wishart (1970).

—— (1885) *Capital*, vol. II, Moscow: Foreign Languages Publishing House (1957).

—— (1894) *Capital*, vol. III, Moscow: Foreign Languages Publishing House (1962).

—— & Engels, Frederick (1845a) *The German Ideology*, London: Lawrence & Wishart.

—— & Engels, Frederick (1845b) *The Holy Family*, trans. R. Dixon, Moscow: Progress (1956).

—— & Engels, Frederick (1975) *Selected Correspondence*, Moscow: Progress.

Mendelsohn, Everett, Weingart, Peter & Whitley, Richard (eds) (1977) *The Social Production of Scientific Knowledge*, Dordrecht: D. Reidel.

Mennell, Stephen (1976) 'Ethnomethodology and the New *Methodenstreit*', in David C. Thorns (ed.) *New Directions in Sociology*, Newton Abbot: David & Charles.

—— (1977) '"Individual" action and its "social" consequences in the work of Norbert Elias', in Peter Gleichmann, Johan Goudsblom & Hermann Korte, *Human Figurations: Essays for Norbert Elias*, Amsterdam: Sociologisch Tijdschrift.

—— (1990) 'The Globalization of Human Society as a Very Long-term Social Process: Elias's Theory', *Theory, Culture and Society* 7(2–3), June: 359–71.

—— (1992) *Norbert Elias: An Introduction*, Oxford: Basil Blackwell.

—— (1995) *Civilization and Decivilization, Civil Society and Violence*, Inaugural Lecture, University College Dublin.

Merleau-Ponty, Maurice (1945) *Phenomenology of Perception*, trans. Colin Smith, London: Routledge & Kegan Paul (1962).

—— (1960) 'The Philosopher and Sociology', in Thomas Luckmann (ed.) (1978) *Phenomenology and Sociology*, Harmondsworth: Penguin.

Merton, Robert K. (1968a) *Social Theory and Social Structure*, London: Collier–Macmillan.

—— (1968b) 'On the History and Systematics of Sociological Theory', in *Social Theory and Social Structure*, London: Collier–Macmillan.

—— (1981) 'Foreword: Remarks on Theoretical Pluralism', in Robert K. Merton and Peter M. Blau (eds) *Continuities in Structural Inquiry*, Beverley Hills: Sage.

Meyer, Alfred (1954) *Marxism: The Unity of Theory and Practice*, Cambridge, MA: Harvard University Press.

Mills, C. Wright (1956) *The Power Elite*, Oxford: Oxford University Press (rpt 1968).

Mitchell, G.D. (1970) 'Sociology – An Historical Phenomenon', in Paul Halmos (ed.) *The Sociology of Sociology*, The Sociological Review Monograph Number 16, Keele: University of Keele.

Mokrzycki, Edmund (1989) 'The Problem of Going *To*: Between Epistemology and the Sociology of Knowledge', *Social Epistemology* 3(3): 205–16.

Montefiore, Alan (ed.) (1983) *Philosophy in France Today*, Cambridge: Cambridge University Press.

Moore, Stanley (1971) 'Marx and the Origin of Dialectical Materialism', *Inquiry* 14(4), Winter: 420–9.

Moore, Wilbert E. (1966) 'Global Sociology: The World as a Singular System', *American Journal of Sociology* 71: 475–82.

—— (1979) 'Functionalism', in Tom Bottomore & Robert Nisbet (eds) *A History of Sociological Analysis*, London: Heinemann.

Morawski, Stefan (1998) 'Bauman's Ways of Seeing the World', *Theory, Culture and Society* 15(1), February.

Morton, Michael (1987) 'Changing the Subject: Herder and the Reorientation of Philosophy', in Kurt Mueller-Vollmer (ed.) *Herder Today*, Berlin and New York: Walter de Gruyter.

Mouzelis, Nicos P. (1991) *Back to Sociological Theory: The Construction of Social Orders*, London: Macmillan.

—— (1995) *Sociological Theory: What Went Wrong? Diagnosis and Remedies*, London and New York: Routledge.

Mueller, Gustav E. (1958) 'The Hegel Legend of "Thesis–Antithesis–Synthesis"', *Journal of the History of Ideas* 19: 411–18.

—— (1983) *Dialectic: A Way Into and Within Philosophy*, London: University Press of America.

Mueller-Vollmer, Kurt (ed.) (1987) *Herder Today*, Berlin and New York: Walter de Gruyter.

Münch, Richard (1987) *Theory of Action: Towards a New Synthesis Going Beyond Parsons*, London and New York: Routledge.

—— (1988) *Understanding Modernity: Toward a New Perspective Going Beyond Durkheim and Weber*, London and New York: Routledge.

Neustadt, Ilya (1965) *Teaching Sociology: An Inaugural Lecture*, Leicester: Leicester University Press.

Nizan, Paul (1971) *The Watchdogs: Philosophers and the Established Order*, trans. Paul Fittingoff, New York and London: Monthly Review Press.

Nye, D.A. & Ashworth, C.E. (1971) 'Émile Durkheim: Was He a Nominalist or a Realist?', *British Journal of Sociology* 22: 133–48.

O'Malley, Joseph J. (1977) 'Marx, Marxism and Method', in Shlomo Avineri (ed.) *Varieties of Marxism*, The Hague: Martinus Nijhoff.

Oommen, T.K. (1991) 'Internationalization of Sociology: A View from Developing Countries', *Current Sociology* 39(1), Spring: 67–84.

Outhwaite, William (1985) 'Hans-Georg Gadamer', in Quentin Skinner (ed.) *The Return of Grand Theory in the Human Sciences*, Cambridge: Cambridge University Press.

—— (1987) *New Philosophies of Social Science: Realism, Hermeneutics and Critical Theory*, London: Macmillan.

—— (1989) 'Theory', in Mike Haralambos (ed.) *Developments in Sociology: An Annual Review*, Ormskirk: Causeway Press.

Pace, David (1983) *Claude Lévi-Strauss: The Bearer of Ashes*, London: Routledge & Kegan Paul.

Parsons, Talcott (1937) *The Structure of Social Action*, New York: The Free Press of Glencoe.

—— (1938) 'The Role of Theory in Social Research', in Peter Hamilton (ed.) (1985) *Readings from Talcott Parsons*, London: Tavistock.

—— (1951) *The Social System*, New York: The Free Press of Glencoe.

—— (1962) 'Individual Autonomy and Social Pressure: An Answer to Dennis H. Wrong', *Psychoanalysis and Psychoanalytic Review* 49: 70–80.

Pawson, Ray (1989) *A Measure for Measures: A Manifesto for Empirical Sociology*, London: Routledge.

Pelz, Werner (1974) *The Scope of Understanding in Sociology: Towards a More Radical Reorientation in the Social Humanistic Sciences*, London: Routledge.

Piaget, Jean (1971) *Structuralism*, trans. and ed. Chaninah Maschler, London: Routledge & Kegan Paul.

Popper, Karl (1961) *The Poverty of Historicism*, London: Routledge & Kegan Paul.

Poster, Mark (1975) *Existential Marxism in Postwar France: From Sartre to Althusser*, Princeton, NJ: Princeton University Press.

Ragin, Charles & Chirot, Daniel (1985) 'The World System of Immanuel Wallerstein: Sociology and Politics as History', in Theda Skocpol (ed.) *Vision and Method in Historical Sociology*, Cambridge: Cambridge University Press.

Ravetz, Jerome (1973) *Scientific Knowledge and its Social Problems*, Harmondsworth: Penguin.

Rée, Jonathan (1997) 'Selflessness' [review article about Emmanuel Levinas], *London Review of Books* 19(9), 8 May: 16–19.

Remmling, Gunter W. (1967) *Road to Suspicion: A Study of Modern Mentality and the Sociology of Knowledge*, Englewood Cliffs, NJ: Prentice Hall.

Reé, John (1961) *Key Problems in Sociological Theory*, London: Routledge & Kegan Paul.

Reynolds, Larry T. & Janice M. Reynolds (eds) (1970) *The Sociology of Sociology: Analysis and Criticism of the Thought, Research, and Ethical Folkways of Sociology and Its Practitioners*, New York: David McKay.

Ritzer, George (1991) *Metatheorizing in Sociology*, Lexington, MA: Lexington Books.

Robertson, Roland (1990) 'Mapping the Global Condition: Globalization as the Central Concept', *Theory, Culture and Society* 7(2–3): 1–14.

—— (1992) '"Civilization" and the Civilizing Process: Elias, Globalization and Analytic Synthesis', *Theory, Culture and Society* 9(1), February: 211–27.

—— & Chirico, Joann (1985) 'Humanity, Globalization and Worldwide Religious Resurgence: A Theoretical Exploration', *Sociological Analysis* 46: 219–42.

—— & Lechner, Frank (1985) 'Modernization, Globalization and the Problem of Culture in World-Systems Theory', *Theory, Culture and Society* 2(3): 103–17.

Robey, David (ed.) (1973) *Structuralism: An Introduction*, Oxford: Clarendon Press.

Rorty, Richard (1979) 'Transcendental Arguments, Self-Reference, and Pragmatism', in Peter Bieri, Rolf-Peter Horstmann & Lorenz Krüger (eds) *Transcendental Arguments and Science*, Dordrecht: D. Reidel.

—— (1982) 'Philosophy in America Today', in *Consequences of Pragmatism*, Brighton: Harvester.

Rose, Gillian (1981) *Hegel Contra Sociology*, London: Athlone Press.

—— (1984) *The Dialectic of Nihilism: Post-Structuralism and the Law*, Oxford: Basil Blackwell.

Rossi, Ino (ed.) (1982a) *Structural Sociology*, New York: Columbia University Press.

—— (1982b) 'Relational Structuralism as an Alternative to the Structural and Interpretative Paradigms of Empiricist Orientation', in *Structural Sociology*, New York: Columbia University Press.

Rotenstreich, Nathan (1965) *Basic Problems of Marx's Philosophy*, New York: Bobbs-Merrill.

—— (1972) *Philosophy: The Concept and its Manifestations*, Dordrecht: D. Reidel.

—— (1977) *Theory and Practice: An Essay in Human Intentionalities*, The Hague: Martinus Nijhoff.

Runciman, W.G. (1989) *A Treatise on Social Theory, Vol. II: Substantive Social Theory*, Cambridge: Cambridge University Press.

Sanderson, Stephen K. (1987) 'Eclecticism and its Alternatives', in John Wilson (ed.), *Current Perspectives in Social Theory: A Research Annual*, vol. 8, London: Jai Press.

Sandywell, Barry, Silverman, David, Roche, Maurice, Filmer, Paul & Phillipson, Michael (eds) (1975) *Problems of Reflexivity and Dialectics in Sociological Inquiry: Language Theorizing Difference*, London: Routledge & Kegan Paul.

Sartre, Jean-Paul (1936) *The Transcendence of the Ego*, trans. Forrest Williams & Robert Kirkpatrick, New York: Noonday Press (1957).

Scharfstein, Ben-Ami (1980) *The Philosophers: Their Lives and the Nature of their Thought*, Oxford: Basil Blackwell.

Schelting, Alexander von (1936) 'Review of *Ideology and Utopia*', *American Sociological Review*, 1(4): 664–74.

Schiera, Pierangelo (1991) ' "Science and Politics" as a Political Factor: German and Italian Social Sciences in the Nineteenth Century', in Peter Wagner, Björn Wittrock & Richard Whitley (eds) *Discourses on Society: The Shaping of the Social Science Disciplines*, Dordrecht: Kluwer Academic.

Schilpp, Peter Arthur (ed.) (1957) *The Philosophy of Karl Jaspers*, La Salle, IL: Open Court.

Schmidt, Alfred (1971) *The Concept of Nature in Marx*, trans. Ben Fowkes, London: New Left Books.

Schneider, Louis (1973) 'The Idea of Culture in the Social Sciences: Critical and Supplementary Observations', in Louis Schneider & Charles M. Bonjean (eds) *The Idea of Culture in the Social Sciences*, Cambridge: Cambridge University Press.

Schutz, Alfred (1932) *The Phenomenology of the Social World*, trans. George Walsh & Frederick Lehnert, London: Heinemann (1972).

—— (1940) 'Phenomenology and the Social Sciences', in Marvin Farber (ed.) *Philosophical Essays in Memory of Edmund Husserl*, London: Greenwood Press (rpt 1968).

—— & Luckmann, Thomas (1974) *The Structures of the Lifeworld*, trans. Richard M. Zaner & H.Tristram Engelhardt Jr, London: Heinemann.

Scott, Alan (ed.) (1997) *The Limits of Globalization*, London: Routledge.

Seidman, Steven (1983) *Liberalism and the Origins of European Social Theory*, Oxford: Basil Blackwell.

—— (1992) 'Postmodern Social Theory as Narrative with a Moral Intent', in Steven Seidman & David Wagner (eds) *Postmodernism and Social Theory: The Debate over General Theory*, Oxford: Basil Blackwell.

Shalvey, Thomas (1979) *Claude Lévi-Strauss: Social Psychotherapy and the Collective Unconscious*, Brighton: The Harvester Press.

Shaw, Martin (1991) *Post-Military Society: Militarism, Demilitarism, Demilitarization and War at the End of the Twentieth Century*, Cambridge: Polity Press.

Sheridan, Alan (1982) *Michel Foucault: The Will to Truth*, London: Tavistock.

Shils, Edward A. (1970) 'Tradition, Ecology and Institution in the History of Sociology', *Daedalus*, 99 (iv), Fall: 760–825 [also in Shils (1982)].

—— (1981) *Tradition*, Chicago and London: University of Chicago Press.

—— (1982) *The Constitution of Society*, Chicago and London: University of Chicago Press.

Simonds, A.P. (1978) *Karl Mannheim's Sociology of Knowledge*, Oxford: Clarendon Press.

Sklair, Leslie (1991) *Sociology of the Global System*, Hemel Hempstead: Harvester Wheatsheaf.

Skocpol, Theda (1979) *States and Social Revolutions*, Cambridge: Cambridge University Press.

—— (1986) 'The Dead End of Metatheory', *Contemporary Sociology* 16: 10–12.

Smart, Barry (1985) *Michel Foucault*, London: Tavistock.

Soper, Kate (1986) *Humanism and Anti-humanism*, London: Hutchinson.

Speed, Bebe (1991) 'Reality Exists, O.K.? An Argument Against Constructivism and Social Constructionism', *Journal of Family Therapy* 13(4): 395–409.

Spiegel-Rösing, Ina & da Solla Price, Derek (eds) (1977) *Science, Technology and Society: A Cross-Disciplinary Perspective*, London and California: Sage.

Steiner, George (1978) *Heidegger*, London: Fontana/Collins.

Stepelevich, Lawrence S. (ed.) (1983) *The Young Hegelians: An Anthology*, Cambridge: Cambridge University Press.

Strange, Susan (1989) 'Toward a Theory of Transnational Empire', in Ernst-Otto Czempiel & James N. Rosenau (eds) *Global Changes and Theoretical Challenges*, Lexington: Lexington Books.

Swaan, Abram de (1995) 'Widening Circles of Social Identification: Emotional Concerns in Sociogenetic Perspective', *Theory, Culture and Society* 12(2): 25–39.

—— (1997) 'Widening Circles of Disidentification: On the Psycho- and Sociogenesis of the Hatred of Distant Strangers – Reflections on Rwanda', *Theory, Culture and Society* 14(2): 105–22.

Tarde, Gabriel (1898) 'La Sociologie', in Terry N. Clark (ed.) (1969) *Gabriel Tarde: On Communication and Social Influence, Selected Papers*, Chicago and London: University of Chicago Press.

Tester, Keith (1991) *Animals and Society: The Humanity of Animal Rights*, London: Routledge.

Therborn, Göran (1971) 'Habermas: A New Eclectic', *New Left Review* 67: 69–85.

Thomas, J.R.R. (1985) 'Ideology and Elective Affinity', *Sociology* 19(1), February: 39–54.

Thompson, Kenneth (1976) *Auguste Comte: The Foundation of Sociology*, London: Thomas Nelson.

Thorns, David C. (ed.) (1976) *New Directions in Sociology*, Newton Abbot: David & Charles.

Tillich, Paul (1933) *The Socialist Decision*, trans. Franklin Sherman, New York: Harper & Row (1977).

Tiryakian, Edward A. (1986) 'Sociology's Great Leap Forward: The Challenge of Internationalization', *International Sociology* 1(2), June: 155–71 [also in Albrow & King (1990)].

Tudor, Andrew (1982) *Beyond Empiricism: Philosophy of Science in Sociology*, London: Routledge & Kegan Paul.

Turgot, Anne Robert Jacques (1750) 'A Philosophical Review of the Successive Advances of the Human Mind', in Ronald Meek (ed.) (1973) *Turgot on Progress, Sociology and Economics*, Cambridge: Cambridge University Press.

Turner, Jonathan, H. (1987) 'Analytical Theorizing', in Anthony Giddens & Jonathan Turner (eds) *Social Theory Today*, Oxford: Polity Press.

Vaughan, Michalina (1978) 'The Intellectuals', in Salvador Giner & Margaret Archer (eds) *Contemporary Europe: Social Structures and Cultural Patterns*, London: Routledge & Kegan Paul.

——, Kolinsky, Martin & Sheriff, Peta (1980) *Social Change in France*, Oxford: Martin Robertson.

Wagar, Warren (1971) 'The Western Tradition', in Warren Wagar (ed.) *History and the Idea of Mankind*, Albuquerque: University of New Mexico Press.

Waldhoff, Hans-Peter (1995) *Fremde und Zivilisierung. Wissensoziologische Studien bei der Verarbeiten von Gefühlen der Fremdheit. Probleme der modernen Peripheri-Zentrums-Migration am türkisch-deutschen Beispiel*, Frankfurt am Main: Suhrkamp Verlag.

Wallerstein, Immanuel (1979) *The Capitalist World Economy*, Cambridge: Cambridge University Press.

—— (1990) 'Culture as the Ideological Battleground of the Modern World System', *Theory, Culture and Society* 7(2–3): 31–55.

—— (1991) *Geopolitics and Geoculture: Essays on the Changing World-system*, Cambridge: Cambridge University Press.

Walzer, Michael (1986) 'The Politics of Michel Foucault', in David Couzens Hoy (ed.) *Foucault: A Critical Reader*, Oxford: Basil Blackwell.

Wardell, Mark L. & Turner, Stephen P. (1986) *Sociological Theory in Transition*, London: Allen & Unwin.

Wassall, Terence (1990) 'The Development of Scientific Knowledge in Relation to the Development of Societies: A Problem in the Contemporary Sociology of Science', unpublished PhD thesis, University of Leeds.

Watzlawick, Paul (1976) *How Real is Real?*, New York: Vintage Books.

—— (ed.) (1984) *The Invented Reality*, New York: W.W. Norton.

Weber, Max (1904) '"Objectivity" in Social Science and Social Policy', in *The Methodology of the Social Sciences*, trans. Edward A. Shils & Henry A. Finch, New York: The Free Press (1949).

—— (1918) 'Politics as a Vocation', in H.H. Gerth & C. Wright Mills (eds) *From Max Weber: Essays in Sociology*, London: Routledge & Kegan Paul (1970).

—— (1922) *Economy and Society*, vol. 1, New York: Bedminster Press (1968).

Weekes, Jeffrey (1991) *Against Nature: Essays on History, Sexuality and Identity*, London: Rivers Oram Press.

Wetter, Gustav (1958) *Dialectical Materialism: A Historical and Systematic Survey of Philosophy in the Soviet Union*, London: Routledge & Kegan Paul.

Williams, Bernard (1974–5) 'The Truth in Relativism', *Proceedings of the Aristotelian Society* lxxv, Cambridge: Cambridge University Press (1981) [also in his *Moral Luck*].

Williams, Raymond (1973) 'Base and Superstructure in Marxist Cultural Theory', *New Left Review* 82, November/December: 3–16.

—— (1976) *Keywords: A Vocabulary of Culture and Society*, London: Fontana/Croom Helm.

Winch, Peter (1958) *The Idea of a Social Science*, London: Routledge & Kegan Paul.

Wind, Edgar (1967) *Pagan Mysteries in the Renaissance*, Harmondsworth: Penguin.

Wisdom, J.O. (1953) *The Unconscious Origin of Berkeley's Philosophy*, London: The Hogarth Press.

Wittkower, Rudolf (1965) 'Imitation, Eclecticism and Genius', in Earl R. Wasserman (ed.) *Aspects of the 18th Century*, London and Baltimore: Johns Hopkins University Press.

Woldring, Henk (1986) *Karl Mannheim: The Development of his Thought*, Assen and Maastricht: Van Gorcum.

Wolff, Janet (1981) *The Social Production of Art*, London: Macmillan.

Wolff, Kurt (1959) 'The Sociology of Knowledge and Sociological Theory', in Llewellyn Gross (ed.) *Symposium on Sociological Theory*, New York: Harper & Row.

Wouters, Cas (1977) 'Informalization and the Civilizing Process', in Peter Gleichmann, Johan Goudsblom & Hermann Korte (eds) *Human Figurations: Essays for Norbert Elias*, Amsterdam: Sociologisch Tijdschrift.

—— (1986) 'Formalization and Informalization: Changing Tension Balances in Civilizing Processes', *Theory, Culture and Society* 3(2): 1–19.

—— (1987) 'Developments in Behavioural Codes between the Sexes: Formalization of Informalization in The Netherlands, 1930–85', *Theory, Culture and Society* 4(2–3): 405–27.

—— (1990) 'Social Stratification and Informalization in Global Perspective', *Theory, Culture and Society* 7(4), November: 69–90.

—— (1998) 'How Strange our Feelings of Superiority and Inferiority to Ourselves?', *Theory, Culture and Society* 15(1), February: 131–150.

Wright, Erik O. (1985) *Classes*, London: Verso.

Wrong, Dennis (1961) 'The Oversocialized Conception of Man in Modern Sociology', *American Sociological Review* 26(2), April: 183–93.

—— (1975) 'Postscript to The Oversocialized Conception of Man in Modern Sociology', in Wrong, Dennis, *Skeptical Sociology*, New York: Columbia University Press (1976).

Yalman, Nur (1967) ' "The Raw:the Cooked :: Nature:Culture" – Observations on *Le Cru et le cuit*', in Edmund Leach (ed.) *The Structural Study of Myth and Totemism*, London: Tavistock.

INDEX